D0668085

BY THE SAME AUTHOR

My Year Off
Globish
The Story of English
Wodehouse: A Life
In The Secret State
The Fabulous Englishman
Mainland
Suspicion
The World is a Banana

THE
100
BEST NOVELS
IN ENGLISH

THE
100
BEST NOVELS
IN ENGLISH

Robert McCrum

G

Galileo Publishers
Cambridge UK

Galileo Publishers
16 Woodlands Road
Great Shelford
Cambridge CB22 5LW
UK

www.galileopublishing.co.uk

ISBN 978-1-903385-47-0

First published in the UK 2015
First paperback edition 2016

© 2015, 2016 Robert McCrum

All rights reserved.

This book is sold subject to the
condition that it shall not, by way of trade or
otherwise, be lent, resold, hired out or otherwise
circulated in any form of binding or cover other
than that in which it is published and without a similar
condition including this condition being imposed
on the subsequent purchaser.

1 2 3 4 5 6 7 8 9

Cover Illustration by Rockwell Kent

Printed and bound by TJ International Ltd, Padstow, Cornwall.

INTRODUCTION

T he first classic of English literature I remember reading is *Animal Farm*. I must have been about eleven years old, lying on my bed with the rough tickle of a red school blanket on bare legs. I still have my Penguin edition, spine broken, and with loose yellowing pages. Somehow, the combination of Orwell and a scratchy institutional blanket seems appropriate.

For almost two years, compiling this *Observer* list from week to week became as much an autobiographical as a literary process, a common sensation, I think, among those who read and re-read. I kept meeting my juvenile self in forgotten guises: sitting in a cricket pavilion on a wet summer's afternoon with *Thank You, Jeeves,* or perhaps *The Code of the Woosters*; roaming Dorset on a bicycle, aged fifteen, with *Jude The Obscure*, or was it *The Mayor of Casterbridge*? Eking out the tedium of school with a copy of *Vanity Fair*, and so on.

I must also acknowledge how late I came to some of the greatest entries in this list: twenty-something before I even opened *The Great Gatsby*; and at least thirty before I completed my reading of Austen's classic six (from *Pride & Prejudice* to *Emma*). In advance, I sketched a draft list, but it never ceased changing with new discoveries. For me, it has been an extraordinary experience: a great novel is the place where you discover the deepest kind of empathy with humanity in all its variety, escaping into other worlds through the lives of others. To read a hundred classics must qualify as the all-time Great Escape.

The books that made it onto my list had to pass a fairly searching scrutiny. How great is it, actually? And why? How influential? There were other questions: where to end? (I chose the Millennium, 2000.) How to balance competing genres (childrens' books vs. detective fiction? Wait and see.) Where to start? Some would argue for the Elizabethans – Shakespeare's contemporaries Robert Greene, or Thomas Nashe – but I settled for John Bunyan and *Pilgrim's Progress*.

While the list was in process, friends and colleagues made many competing suggestions. But (since my selection was inflexibly chronological) once a date had been reached, there could be no second thoughts. The hardest decisions were to do with the giants of the past. With the really big hitters, which title do you choose? Dickens is a case in point. *Pickwick Papers* (his sensational debut)? The ever-popular

Great Expectations? The critically fashionable *Hard Times*? His perennial favourite, *A Christmas Carol*? You'll note that I settled on *David Copperfield*, and perhaps my arguments for it will be persuasive.

Finally, there were the wild cards. As the series passed the First World War, I was having lunch with a friend. The conversation turned to my list.

"What are you going to do about Pearl Buck?" she asked.

"Pearl Buck?"

"The best-selling author of *The Good Earth*, and winner of the Nobel Prize for Literature in 1938."

Struggling slightly, I replied that best-sellerism is no guide, but that one useful, first step might be actually to read *The Good Earth*. Did Pearl Buck make the cut? That's what this book should offer. Hours of harmless browsing. Meanwhile, here's one suggestion. Why not use the blank pages at the back of this book to compile your own list?

★★★

If lists are a guilty pleasure, then book lists are an almost sinful addiction. I can adduce empirical evidence for this. At the beginning of the new century, on 12 October 2003, in a headline-grabbing stunt, writing as Literary Editor of *The Observer*, I compiled a list (with help from colleagues), provocatively entitled "The 100 Greatest Novels of All Time", drawn from many sources.

Say what you want about lists, but this one rapidly developed a life of its own, like a sci-fi alien. Once the initial furore – why no Updike? how on earth could we exclude P.G. Wodehouse? etc. – had died down, the creature we had created continued to circulate in cyberspace, sponsoring a rare mixture of rage and delight, apparently without rhyme or reason. Every now and again some particular group would tangle with it, and it would drive them mad all over again. For reasons I have yet to fathom, that particular "100 Greatest Novels" excited special notice in Australia.

As well as puzzling over the strange appeal of that original 2003 list, I nurtured a sneaking worry that, chosen at random, from many different literatures, the selection had been too spontaneous. Was there not a case for a more considered compilation? What, for example, would a list of the 100 classic British and American novels look like? Here, within this book, I begin to provide the answer. And so, without any reference to the 2003 list, and for some 100 weeks, the *Observer* published a serial account of the classic English and American novel, from A to Z, and from the late 17th century to the present day.

I would argue that it could not occur at a more propitious time. Never have so many books been in play, for the ordinary reader. Never have the classics been more available. You can download all of Austen or Conrad for nothing, and take all of Dickens or Trollope on holiday. Call it the Joy of e.

★★★

The twenty-first century, with all its life-changing technological innovations, has ushered in a new age of reading and writing. Across the globe, on screens, laptops and mobile phones, more people than ever before are receiving the written word in any number of new formats, and transmitting it, too, in tweets and texts. What's more, this process shows no sign of slowing down. One unintended consequence of the e-revolution we've just been living through has been the new and enhanced attention paid by publishers to the traditional printed book of ink, paper and glue.

Whatever the nay-sayers and Jeremiahs might argue, the ordinary reader has been the beneficiary of the biggest transformation in the world of books since William Caxton set up shop in the precincts of Westminster. When cultural historians eventually come to describe the years 1990-2015, they will be hard put to resist phrases like "paradigm shift", "literary upheaval", and "IT revolution". No question: these past twenty-five years have seen a transformation in the world of books and letters unequalled since the days of Johannes Gutenberg.

In Britain, the figures tell one story. In 1997, the year of the New Labour landslide, the gross domestic consumption of books in the UK amounted to £1.914 billion. By 2000, it had grown to £2.242 billion. In 2007, the year Tony Blair left Downing Street, it peaked at £3.603 billion. The total number of new titles published per annum had risen from approximately 100,000 (1990) to almost 200,000 (2009). The credit crunch of 2009 (and subsequent recession) certainly pricked this bubble, but the underlying story is of a prolonged assault on the infrastructure of a time-hallowed trade, a sequence of seismic convulsions.

This boom in new titles, from far and wide, in many varieties of English, and in translation, combined with the collapse of a literary establishment formerly defined by a few literary critics, Sunday newspaper reviewers and some highbrow book programmes on Radio 4, has put the "Common Reader" in a spin. What to read? Whose word to trust? Where to look? Festivals and book groups provide some of the answers to those questions, but there's nothing like the settled certainty enjoyed by serious readers in the recent past.

Which is where lists, like the one you are holding now, come in. Lists provide an informal road-map, a point of departure and a grid reference for the confused literary traveller. Welcome to the classics of the English, American and Commonwealth world.

★★★

In the game called "Humiliation", introduced by David Lodge into *Changing Places*, his Seventies campus novel, the players score points by confessing the famous books they have never read. The comic climax to an entertaining sub-theme occurs when ambitious Howard Ringbaum, desperate to win, admits he has never read *Hamlet*, instantly wrecking his academic career.

Lodge's insight into the practice of literature is that everyone who steps into the world of books and letters risks humiliation. Rightly, for the well-being of culture and society, this is a competitive affair with high stakes. Beneath the eye of eternity, it's a matter of life and death: either some kind of literary afterlife or, (more likely) oblivion.

So: what is a classic? There are many definitions. T.S. Eliot, Ezra Pound, Italo Calvino and Sainte-Beuve have all written at length on the subject. Calvino's definition – "a classic is a book that has never finished what it wants to say" – is probably the sweetest, followed by Pound's identification of "a certain eternal and irresponsible freshness". One necessary, but not sufficient, characteristic of a classic is that it should remain in print.

After that, the issue quickly becomes subjective. Classics, for some, are books we know we should have read, but have not. For others, classics are simply the book we have read obsessively, many times over, and can quote from. The ordinary reader instinctively knows what he or she believes to be a classic. There is, as we know too well, no accounting for taste.

Speaking of taste, I chose, where possible, the title most central to the author's voice and vision. Jane Austen is a case in point. *Pride and Prejudice* is much-loved. *Northanger Abbey* is highly entertaining. Some readers revere *Sense and Sensibility*. But I settled on *Emma*.

Next, a word about the rules of eligibility governing this selection. My list of "top novels" is a) derived exclusively from fiction written in the English language; b) strictly chronological; and c) gives each writer equal space. That third criterion was especially restrictive. With a prolific writer, the selection of one "classic" text became impossibly demanding. To take one example – Dickens (*David Copperfield*) and Wilde (*The Picture of Dorian Gray*) appear in the list on the same footing, with one novel apiece. By the same rule, Jane Austen (*Emma*) gets no more advantage than Louisa May Alcott (*Little Women*).

Throughout, as you'll discover, my concern was with the English novel, meaning Scots, Irish, North American, Antipodean, Indian and African English, written across four centuries, and at least three empires, growing in variety, ambition and volubility until it has become an extraordinary mirror to the global phenomenon of English language culture worldwide. Indeed, as the series unfolded, the more its character as Mission Impossible began to take shape. For instance, the series spans about three centuries, roughly 1700 to 2000. Compiling a list for the first 100 years was relatively straightforward, from 1800 to 1900 progressively more difficult, and from 1900 to 2000 (my arbitrary cut-off) perilously close to impossible. Here's why.

★★★

Initially the novel's origins are quite humble, and confined to the British Isles. Like the English language itself, English fiction is "a snapper-up of unconsider'd trifles," (*Winter's Tale*), a magpie, and a thief. Appropriately for a vagabond, it starts in prison. My first choice, John Bunyan, was a puritan dissenter whose writing started with sermons and culminated with the allegory published as *Pilgrim's Progress*. That became the first of my criteria for classic fiction: that it should arise out of an urgent need for self-expression.

The other thing that all the pioneer English novelists – Defoe, Swift, Richardson, Fielding, Sterne – had in common was a deep sense of the market, and a passionate desire to entertain. For about two hundred years, until mid-Victorian times, the finest novels of the age were written at the cutting edge of life and art, and they set out to please the reader. Moreover, with some obvious exceptions like the Brontë sisters, they arise from, and speak to, a more or less homogenous domestic culture.

In the century that witnessed the making of the English novel, the genre was almost exclusively the work of upper- or middle-class English writers, predominantly male, and often with private means, living in the British Isles. Their novels were addressed to an elite minority, and expressed the concerns of a particular society. After Jane Austen, the Victorian novel roars into view, with America coming into the picture for the first time.

Looking back, various observations suggest themselves. First, there are some notable *longueurs*, whole decades when, with the benefit of hindsight, not much of consequence seems to have been published. For instance, between *Tristram Shandy* (1759) and *Emma* (1816) I could find nothing of significance to list. (In contemporary terms, this is like suggesting that between the publication of *Lolita* (1955) and *The Corrections* (2001), there's been nothing of note.) I was tempted by Ann Radcliffe's Gothic bestseller *The Mysteries of Udolpho* (1794), and perhaps even more by Oliver Goldsmith's *The Vicar of Wakefield* (1766), but in the end, I was not persuaded.

Another lesson is that, in contrast to some fallow years, we occasionally find sudden bursts of creativity. The most intense occurs in 1847 and 1848: the years of *Jane Eyre*, *Wuthering Heights*, followed by *Vanity Fair*. Charlotte Brontë, indeed, paid tribute to Thackeray in her preface to *Jane Eyre*.

At this mid-point of the Victorian novel, there was only one duty for the writer – to entertain the reader. Thackeray is explicit about this. The idea of "literary fiction", that fashionable tautology, did not exist. At this stage in the making of the list, I had paid virtually no attention to the demands of "genre", but as the Victorian literary scene evolved, especially after Forster's Education Act of 1870, it proved impossible to avoid the divergence of high and low culture – the theme of John Carey's *The Intellectuals and the Masses*. I found myself discriminating against writers like Rider Haggard ("low") and George Meredith ("high"), in favour of Stevenson, Hardy and Grossmith, who actually addressed the issue in *New Grub Street*. A once simple set of choices had become exceedingly awkward.

How to compare *The Way We Live Now* with *The Adventures of Huckleberry Finn* with *Kidnapped*? Was it right to exclude *Uncle Tom's Cabin* (massively popular, and influential), in favour of *Little Women* (also bestselling)? It was essential to acknowledge the emerging American literary tradition, but who trumps whom? Was there a transatlantic bias, an issue that still torments the judges of the Booker Prize? Wilkie Collins (*The Moonstone*) was in, but James Fenimore Cooper (*The Last of the Mohicans*) did not make the cut. Discuss.

Once I reached the 20th century and Modernism, Anglo-American literature was in full flood, symbolised by the towering figures of Henry James and Joseph Conrad. But then a new question, which had been lurking throughout much of the nineteenth century, starts to intrude. What should we do about global literature? Can the self-imposed limitations of Anglo-American literature be justified?

I say that it can.

First, because there is an inner, cultural coherence to a list expressed in just one language, and its variants. All the books on my list, with a few exceptions, are readily available to one and all. Not so long ago, a critic like F.R. Leavis could devote much of his scholarly career to what he described as "the Great Tradition". No critic today would find it useful, or even interesting, to attempt such a vision, but there is still a role for some cultural specificity. I would go further to argue that the global expression of the novel in English in the 20th and 21st centuries is so polyvalent, multifarious and downright impressive that it provides most readers with more than enough to be going on with. But first, there is Modernism and its consequences to consider.

★★★

With Modernism, a literary ecosystem gets torched. Before Conrad, Lawrence, and Joyce, the authors and publishers of the three-decker novel were in trouble. Some just gave up. Others found new kinds of employment. When, in the 1920s, after the cataclysm of the Great War, the smoke clears and a new literary landscape emerges, we can see that the novel will never be the same again. The idea of "the common reader", which had sustained a century of book publishing, was doomed.

This list reflects that transition. In hindsight, I still worry about some choices. I excluded Chesterton, Belloc and Erskine Childers, but included Max Beerbohm, Frederick Rolfe and Conan Doyle; ignored Galsworthy and Bennett, but included H.G. Wells. Why not be as ruthless with the Edwardians as I'd been with some Regency novelists?

As the series drew to a close I cursed the leniency I had exercised towards some of the novels published between 1880 and 1930. For instance, does Jack London (no. 35, *The Call of the Wild*) better deserve a place here than, say, James Salter (*Light Years* and *All That Is*), Thomas Pynchon (*Gravity's Rainbow*) or J.G. Ballard (*Crash*), three contemporary writers who got left out? I love *Hadrian The Seventh* (no. 36), and *Sister Carrie* (no. 33) has a dark energy that's crucial to the evolution of the American novel. But *A Confederacy of Dunces* by John Kennedy Toole should have been included, and so should *Slaughterhouse Five* (Kurt Vonnegut), plus *All The Pretty Horses* (or perhaps *Blood Meridian*) by Cormac McCarthy.

So: a few howlers, several regrets, and many sleepless nights. How on earth did I overlook Flannery O'Connor (*Wise Blood*) or Rose Macaulay (*The Towers of Trebizond*)? Or, more painful still, Nancy Mitford (*The Pursuit of Love*) and Shirley Hazzard (*The Transit of Venus*)? The chronological momentum also produced its casualties. The series was deep into the 1940s before I realised I'd missed the best of R.K. Narayan (*Swami and Friends*).

What else does this list teach? Somerset Maugham, characteristically sardonic, once observed that "There are just three rules for writing a novel. Unfortunately, no one knows what they are."

★★★

Actually, the only rule is that there are no rules. The novel can be about a little girl falling down a rabbit hole, or the obsessive hunt for a whale, or the quotidian wanderings of a middle-aged Jewish advertising canvasser in Dublin. The free range of our imagination is the only departure lounge for the flight of the mind. For that itinerary, mercifully, there's no GPS. The reader remains a free agent. In his or her freedom lies the joy of reading: it is un-policed, solitary and mostly private in a world without frontiers or governments.

Second, the novel that began *in extremis* (Bunyan in prison; Defoe dodging creditors), but learned to entertain, and make money (Sterne cashing in as a bestseller; Dickens selling like a box set), still has two basic modes. Between obsession and entertainment there is no middle ground. P.G. Wodehouse once said that there are two ways of writing, one is "a sort of musical comedy without music and ignoring real life altogether; the other is going right deep down into real life and not caring a damn." The creative fault-line of "musical comedy" vs. "real life" never goes away, and there are other continuities.

I would argue, thirdly, that not one of these 100 books or their authors is indifferent to the demands of Story. With our stone-age brains, we are still a storytelling species. The narrative gene is part of our DNA. As E.M. Forster put it, in *Aspects of the Novel*: "Yes—oh, dear, yes—the novel tells a story."

And yes—oh, dear, yes—I left out some great storytellers: H. Rider Haggard (*King Solomon's Mines*); Frank Baum (*The Wizard of Oz*); Margaret Mitchell (*Gone with the Wind*); Daphne du Maurier (*Rebecca*); Ian Fleming (*Casino Royale*); Charles Portis (*True Grit*); Erica Jong (*Fear of Flying*); John Le Carré (*Tinker, Tailor, Soldier, Spy*), and many other favourites no doubt.

There were some other deliberate omissions: Walter Scott (I've never finished even his best known novels); Elizabeth Gaskell (*North and South*), whose appeal I confess I don't understand; Rosamond Lehmann (*The Weather in the Streets*); Norman Mailer (*The Executioner's Song*), who was too much of an American celebrity in thrall to the media to be a truly great novelist; Kingsley Amis (*Lucky Jim*); John Fowles *(The French Lieutenant's Woman)*, whose work has not worn well; and Iris Murdoch (*The Black Prince*), whose fiction I've always found contrived and artificial.

The chronological imperative behind the selection occasionally became brutal. One casualty of this process that I deeply regret omitting is the Australian novelist Christina Stead's *The Man Who Loved Children* (1940), a profoundly moving study of family life so pitch-perfect that it's hard to believe her novel is not better known.

And so to the posterity question. The vagaries of literary history never cease to astonish. No one in 1890, a year before Herman Melville's death, would have put any money on the future supremacy, as America's greatest novel, of *Moby-Dick*. In Britain, the smart money on future renown would have been placed on George Meredith, author of *The Ordeal of Richard Feverel*.

George who? In this game of "Humiliation", reputations continue to fluctuate on an invisible stock exchange of taste. In my lifetime, I have seen trading in D.M. Thomas (acclaimed author of *The White Hotel*, 1981) or in Bruce Chatwin (ditto, *The Songlines*, 1987), go from boom to bust. It is an iron law that the living writers we most venerate are often the most vulnerable to long-term neglect.

There have also been some wonderful surprises. For years, creative writing at the University of East Anglia set the gold standard in the nurturing of new fiction. When, in 1992, the translated prose of a brilliant new writer, W.G. Sebald, burst on the scene with *The Emigrants*, it was an irony enjoyed by "Max" himself that he had been working in comparative obscurity in the Modern Languages department of UEA for some thirty years. Today, Sebald's reputation is more universally recognised than most, if not all, of the writers who've passed through UEA.

Meanwhile, although the novel in English retains deep roots in Britain and the United States – as this series has illustrated – its expression as a multi-cultural phenomenon, written in English, the world's second language, is now taking new fiction into new territory. My own prediction for the future of the novel is that, following every previous leap forward in the literary arts through the ages, it is inconceivable that the changes in IT technology, in communications, global capitalism, and above all in human consciousness, will not in the near future sponsor changes and innovations to rival the Modernist revolution of 1899 (*Heart of Darkness*) to 1925 (*Mrs Dalloway*).

★★★

Finally, we are left with the classics – yes, often by dead white males – those books to which English language readers worldwide return again and again. Say what you like (and thousands merrily did so on-line while I compiled this list), the Anglo-American literary tradition, a source of some sublime and imperishable masterpieces, deserves to be celebrated. Here, to provoke my readers just one last time, is my "All Time Top Ten" (chosen from this series, in chronological order):

Jane Austen: Emma
Emily Brontë: Wuthering Heights
Herman Melville: Moby Dick
George Eliot: Middlemarch
Mark Twain: The Adventures of Huckleberry Finn
Joseph Conrad: Heart of Darkness
DH Lawrence: The Rainbow
James Joyce: Ulysses
Virginia Woolf: Mrs Dalloway
F Scott Fitzgerald: The Great Gatsby

For readers who want a guide to more recent form, here is my verdict (again chronologically) on the "Ten Great Novels" of the past seventy-something years, roughly since World War Two.

Samuel Beckett: Murphy
Saul Bellow: The Adventures of Augie March
Graham Greene: The End of the Affair
Vladimir Nabokov: Lolita
Jack Kerouac: On The Road
Muriel Spark: The Prime of Miss Jean Brodie
Philip Roth: Portnoy's Complaint
V.S. Naipaul: A Bend in the River
Penelope Fitzgerald: The Beginning of Spring
Margaret Atwood: The Handmaid's Tale

For aficionados of contemporary classics, from a now global literary tradition, with the caveat that posterity will certainly prove me wrong, here's a more contemporary Top Ten:

Elizabeth Taylor: Mrs Palfrey at the Clairmont
Anthony Burgess: Earthly Powers
Toni Morrison: Song of Solomon
Salman Rushdie: Midnight's Children
Marilynne Robinson: Housekeeping
Kazuo Ishiguro: An Artist of the Floating World
Penelope Fitzgerald: The Beginning of Spring
John McGahern: Amongst Women
J.M. Coetzee: Disgrace
Peter Carey: True History of the Kelly Gang

In the words of the Victorian cartoon, "You pays your money and you makes your choice."

Robert McCrum,
London, August 2015

– 1 –
The Pilgrim's Progress
by John Bunyan (1678)

There are many scholarly arguments about the origins of the English novel, with claims made for Robert Greene, Thomas Lodge and Thomas Nashe, as well as William Baldwin's *Beware The Cat* (1553). But this list is for the common reader and for me, the English novel begins behind bars, in extremis. Its first author, John Bunyan, was a Puritan dissenter whose writing starts with sermons and ends with fiction. His famous allegory, the story of Christian, opens with a sentence of luminous simplicity that has the haunting compulsion of the hook in a great melody. "As I walk'd through the wilderness of this world, I lighted on a certain place, where was a Denn; And I laid me down in that place to sleep: And as I slept I dreamed a Dream."

A "Denn" is a prison, and Bunyan wrote most of the book in Bedford county gaol, having been arrested for his beliefs during the "Great Persecution" of 1660-1690. He shares the experience of prison with Cervantes, who had the idea for *Don Quixote* while incarcerated in La Mancha. Like so many novels that follow in this list, *The Pilgrim's Progress* blends fact and fiction. As well as being the record of Bunyan's dream, a well-known fictional device, it is also an archetypal tale – a quest, fraught with danger. Christian's pilgrimage takes him through the Slough of Despond, Vanity Fair and the Delectable Mountains in a succession of adventures that keep the reader turning the page. With his good companions, Faithful and Hopeful, he vanquishes many enemies before arriving at the Celestial City with the line that still reverberates through the English literary tradition: "So he passed over, and all the trumpets sounded for him on the other side."

In Hollywood terms, the novel has a perfect "arc". It also contains a cast of unforgettable characters, from Mr Worldly Wiseman to Lord Hategood, Mr Stand-fast and Mr Valiant-for-Truth. More profoundly, as an allegory of state repression, it has been described by the historian EP Thompson as one of the "foundation texts of the English working-class movement". Part of its uniquely English quality is a robust and engaging sense of humour that has cemented its appeal to generations of readers.

The Pilgrim's Progress is the ultimate English classic, a book that has been continuously in print, from its first publication to the present day, in an extraordinary number of editions. There's no book in English, apart from the Bible, to equal Bunyan's masterpiece for the range of its readership, or its influence on writers as diverse as William Thackeray, Charlotte Brontë, Mark Twain, CS Lewis, John Steinbeck and even Enid Blyton.

Huckleberry Finn speaks for many readers when, recalling his Mississippi education, he says: "There was some books too... One was 'Pilgrim's Progress', about a man that left his family it didn't say why. I read considerable in it now and then. The statements was interesting, but tough."

The story of a man in search of the truth is the plot of many kinds of fiction, from *Portnoy's Complaint* to *Tinker Tailor Soldier Spy*. Like many of the writers in the list that follows, Bunyan had a wonderful ear for the rhythms of colloquial speech and his allegorical characters come to life in dialogue that never fails to advance the narrative. Story is one thing. The simple clarity and beauty of Bunyan's prose is something else. Braided together, style and content unite to make a timeless English classic.

A Note on the Text:

The Pilgrim's Progress, From This World, to That Which Is to Come was first published in Holborn, London by Nathaniel Ponder, a non-conformist, at the beginning of 1678 in an edition of 191 pages. It was an immediate success. A second edition appeared before the end of 1678, with many new passages, a third in 1679, and several subsequent editions before Bunyan's death in August 1688. The Second Part of *The Pilgrim's Progress* was published in 1684, with a second edition in 1686. Eventually, the English text comprised some 108,260 words. It has never been out of print, and has been translated into more than 200 languages.

– 2 –
Robinson Crusoe
by Daniel Defoe (1719)

English fiction began with *The Pilgrim's Progress*, but nearly 50 turbulent years, including the Glorious Revolution, passed before it made its great leap forward. The author of this literary milestone is a strangely appealing literary hustler of nearly 60 years old originally named Daniel Foe (he added "De" to improve his social standing), a one-time journalist, pamphleteer, jack of all trades and spy. Like Bunyan, he had suffered at the hands of the state (the pillory, followed by prison in 1703). Unlike Bunyan, he was not religious.

His world-famous novel is a complex literary confection. It purports to be a history, written by Crusoe himself, and edited by Daniel Defoe who, in the preface, teasingly writes that he "believes the thing to be a just History of Fact; neither is there any Appearance of Fiction in it".

So what do we find in this "History"? Robinson Crusoe has three elements that make it irresistible. First, the narrative voice of the castaway is Defoe's stroke of genius. It's exciting, unhurried, conversational and capable of high and low sentiments. It's also often quasi-journalistic, which suits Defoe's style. This harmonious mix of tone puts the reader deep into the mind of the castaway and his predicament. His adventures become our adventures and we experience them inside out, viscerally, for ourselves. Readers often become especially entranced by Crusoe's great journal, the central passage of his enforced sequestration.

And here is Defoe's second great inspiration. He comes up with a tale, often said to be modelled on the story of the castaway Alexander Selkirk, that, like Bunyan's, follows an almost biblical pattern of transgression (youthful rebellion), retribution (successive shipwrecks), repentance (the painful lessons of isolation) and finally redemption (Crusoe's return home). In storytelling terms, this is pure gold.

And third, how can we forget Defoe's characters? The pioneer novelist understood the importance of attaching memorably concrete images to his narrative and its characters. Friday and his famous footstep in the sand, one of the four great moments in English fiction, according to Robert Louis Stevenson; Crusoe with his parrot and his umbrella: these have become part of English myth. Defoe, like Cervantes, also opts to give his protagonist a sidekick. Friday is to Crusoe what Sancho Panza is to Quixote. Doubles in English literature will regularly recur in this list: Jekyll and Hyde, Holmes and Watson, Jeeves and Wooster.

Which brings me to Defoe's final quality as a writer. He was the complete professional, dipped in ink. Throughout his life, he produced pamphlets, squibs, narrative verse and ghosted ephemera (he is said to have used almost 200 pen names). He was a man who liked to be paid for what he wrote, lived well and was almost always in debt. He was not a "literary novelist", and would not have understood the term, but his classic novel is English literature at its finest, and he hit the jackpot with Robinson Crusoe.

By the end of the 19th century, no book in English literary history had enjoyed more editions, spin-offs and translations than Robinson Crusoe, with more than 700 alternative versions, including illustrated children's versions. The now-forgotten term "Robinsonade" was coined to describe the Crusoe genre, which still flourishes and was recently revived by Hollywood in the Tom Hanks film, *Castaway* (2000).

A Note on the Text:
The text was first published in London by W Taylor on 25 April 1719. This first edition credited the work's fictional protagonist Robinson Crusoe as its author, and its title was *The Life and Strange Surprizing Adventures of Robinson Crusoe of York, Mariner: Written by Himself*. It sold well; four months later, it was followed by *The Further Adventures of Robinson Crusoe*. A year later, riding high on the market, came *Serious Reflections During the Life and Surprizing Adventures of Robinson Crusoe*. Most readers will only encounter the first edition.

– 3 –
Gulliver's Travels
by Jonathan Swift (1726)

Seven years after the publication of *Robinson Crusoe*, the great Tory essayist and poet Jonathan Swift – inspired by the Scriblerus club, whose members included John Gay and Alexander Pope – composed a satire on travel narratives that became an immediate bestseller. According to Gay, Gulliver was soon being read "from the cabinet council to the nursery".

In its afterlife as a classic, *Gulliver's Travels* works on many levels. First, it's a masterpiece of sustained and savage indignation, "furious, raging, obscene", according to Thackeray. Swift's satirical fury is directed against almost every aspect of early 18th century life: science, society, commerce and politics. Second, stripped of Swift's dark vision, it becomes a wonderful travel fantasy for children, a perennial favourite that continues to inspire countless versions, in books and films. Finally, as a polemical tour de force, full of wild imagination, it became a source for Voltaire, as well as the inspiration for a Telemann violin suite, Philip K Dick's science-fiction story *The Prize Ship*, and, perhaps most influential of all, George Orwell's *Animal Farm*.

Travels into Several Remote Nations of the World by Lemuel Gulliver (to give its original title) comes in four parts, and opens with Gulliver's shipwreck on the island of Lilliput, whose inhabitant are just six inches high. The most famous and familiar part of the book ("Lilliputian" soon became part of the language) is a satirical romp in which Swift takes some memorable shots at English political parties and their antics, especially the controversy on the matter of whether boiled eggs should be opened at the big or the little end.

Next, Gulliver's ship, the Adventure, gets blown off course and he is abandoned on Brobdingnag whose inhabitants are giants with a proportionately gigantic landscape. Here, having been dominant on Lilliput, Gulliver is exhibited as a curious midget, and has a number of local dramas such as fighting giant wasps. He also gets to discuss the condition of Europe with the King, who concludes with Swiftian venom that "the bulk of your natives [are] the most pernicious race of odious little vermin that Nature ever suffered to crawl upon the surface of the earth."

In the third part of his travels, Gulliver visits the flying island of Laputa (a place-name also referenced in Stanley Kubrick's film *Dr Strangelove*), and Swift mounts a dark and complicated assault on the speculations of contemporary science (notably spoofing the attempted extraction of sunbeams from cucumbers). Finally, in the section that influenced Orwell (*Gulliver's Travels* was one of his favourite books), Swift describes the country of the Houyhnhnms, horses with the qualities of rational men. These he contrasts with the loathsome Yahoos, brutes in human shape. Orwell would later echo Swift's misanthropy, looking ahead to a time "when the human race had finally been overthrown."

At the end of it all, Gulliver returns home from his travels in a state of alienated wisdom, purged and matured by his experiences. "I write," he concludes, "for the noblest end, to inform and instruct mankind… I write without any view to profit or praise. I never suffer a word to pass that may possibly give the least offence, even to those who are most ready to take it. So that I hope I may with justice pronounce myself an author perfectly blameless…"

When he died in 1745, Swift, remembered as "the gloomy Dean", was buried in Dublin with the famous epitaph "ubi saeva indignatio ulterius cor lacerare nequit" (where fierce indignation can no further tear apart his heart) inscribed on his tomb.

A Note on the Text:
Swift probably started writing *Gulliver's Travels* in 1720 (when Crusoe fever was at it height), and delivered the manuscript to the London publisher Benjamin Motte in March 1726. The book was published, anonymously, at top speed. Motte, who sensed a bestseller, used several presses to foil any attempt at piracy, and made many cuts to reduce the risk of prosecution. The first edition appeared, in two volumes, on 26 October 1726, priced 8s 6d, and sold out its first printing in less than a week. In 1735 the Irish publisher, George Faulkner, printed a collection of Swift's works. Volume III became *Gulliver's Travels*, based on a working copy of the original manuscript. The textual history of *Gulliver's Travels* now becomes incredibly complicated, and Swift later disowned most versions, including Motte's first edition, saying it was so much altered that "I do hardly know mine own work". Later scholarly editions of Swift have to choose between Motte and Faulkner, but whatever the version it has never been out of print since the day it first appeared.

– 4 –
Clarissa
by Samuel Richardson (1748)

After *The Pilgrim's Progress* and *Robinson Crusoe*, the next landmark in English fiction is a towering monument of approximately 970,000 words, *Clarissa*, the longest novel in the English canon. From time to time, its length is challenged by later upstarts – most recently by Vikram Seth's *A Suitable Boy* and *Infinite Jest* by David Foster Wallace – but Samuel Richardson's *The History of a Young Lady* remains an extraordinary achievement.

To Samuel Johnson, it was simply "the first book in the world for the knowledge it displays of the human heart". Most critics agree that it is one of the greatest European novels, whose influence casts a long shadow. I first read *Clarissa*, in France, in a gold-tooled library edition of many volumes. In the house where I was staying there was nothing else to read in English; I picked it up quite ignorant of its reputation and importance. Perhaps that's the best way to approach a classic – unawares. Soon, I was swept up in the headlong drama of Clarissa Harlowe's fate, a novel with the simplicity of myth.

Clarissa is a tragic heroine, pressured by her unscrupulous *nouveau-riche* family to marry a wealthy man she detests. When she is tricked into fleeing from her family's designs with the dashing and witty Robert Lovelace she inadvertently places herself in the power of an inveterate rake, perhaps the most charming villain in English literature. It's the magic of *Clarissa* that the lovers seduce the reader's imagination as much as any in our literature, including Romeo and Juliet. From this we have Dr Johnson's famous verdict, noted by Boswell: "Why, sir, if you were to read Richardson for the story… you would hang yourself… you must read him for the sentiment."

The genius of Richardson's narration is not simply the innovative use of epistolary fiction – the novel is told through a complex web of letters – but also the subtlety with which he unfolds the dark tragedy of Clarissa's fatal attraction to Lovelace. All too human in her capacity for self-deception in matters of sex, she finds his charm impossible to resist. It's the unique spell of the book that her fiercely protested virtue is tinged with intimations of unacknowledged desire.

Clarissa Harlowe also sets the gold standard for English fictional heroines. She is beautiful, intelligent, high-principled, resolute and proud, with deep humanity. A Marxist critic would also point out that she is profoundly middle-class. Her tragedy is to become the victim of a man who will imprison, drug and ultimately rape her. Lovelace is equally divided. His letters – "I love to write to the moment," he says – are brilliant. But his behaviour is villainous. Modern readers will find his treatment of Clarissa unbearably cruel. Still, softened and humanised, it's not too much of a stretch to see his inspiration standing behind a character like Mr Darcy in *Pride and Prejudice*.

The first parts of Richardson's masterpiece appeared in 1747-48 and rapidly became cult reading among the new class of English readers. By a neat conjunction, this "history of a young lady" was joined the following year by "the history of... a foundling", the novel (by Richardson's rival, Henry Fielding) better known as *Tom Jones*. English fiction had come of age. For a century and more, English writers would essentially explore imaginative terrain mapped out by Richardson and Fielding, the co-founders of the modern novel.

A Note on the Text:
Richardson was well-known in mid 8th century London as a leading master printer with a good business in Salisbury Square, just off Fleet Street. He began circulating his new manuscript among friends as early as 1744-45, and published the first edition in two volumes on 1 December 1747, printed on the presses of his own shop. The title page, according to current conventions, announced that *Clarissa* was "published by the editor of *Pamela*", and made no reference to Richardson. As an inveterate reviser, but "a poor pruner", he continued to tinker with the text. A second edition appeared in 1749, then a fully revised version in 1751, and finally a fourth edition in 1759, which is usually the basis for modern editions.

– 5 –
Tom Jones
by Henry Fielding (1749)

How many readers, if they are honest, discovered some of the greatest novels through film or television? *Gatsby*? *Pride and Prejudice*? *The English Patient*? *Dr Zhivago*? I first got interested in *Tom Jones* having seen John Osborne's famous adaptation, starring the young Albert Finney as the eponymous hero. That's an exceptional film. Classics often don't make good films, or only do so – such as *Oliver!* – through a process of reinterpretation.

Tom Jones, however, might have been made for the screen. Never mind its numerous chapters and teeming cast of misfits and scoundrels, the central character is an attractively unbridled young man of fierce temper and unrestrained sexuality who pursues true love through contemporary Britain in a sequence of scandalous and hilarious adventures. Published in the mid 18th century, *Tom Jones* is a classic English novel that captures the spirit of its age and whose famous characters – Squire Western, the chaplain Thwackum, the scheming Blifil, seductive Molly Seagrim and Sophia, Tom's true love – have come to represent Augustan society in all its loquacious, turbulent, comic variety.

The secret of *Tom Jones* was to be intimately connected to its contemporary audience. By the 1740s, the English novel was attracting new kinds of reader and, in turn, new kinds of writer. Not only was there an explosion of print media and a booming middle-class audience, there were innovative novelists for whom this popular new genre offered the prospect of a decent living. Many would continue to starve in Grub Street, but some had begun to make money. Samuel Johnson, famously, sold his over-earnest romance, *Rasselas*, to pay for his mother's funeral.

Henry Fielding was typical of this new generation. Born in 1707, he was a wholly 18th century man. With a classical education at Eton, family connections and a good career in the law, in which he is sometimes credited with laying the foundations of the Metropolitan police, he turned to fiction partly to fund an extravagant lifestyle and partly to engage with a stimulating contemporary audience.

Fielding was writing at a time of intense social and political change and took up his pen in response to the crises of the moment. Until the repressive Licensing Act of 1737, he had enjoyed a reputation as the author of satirical burlesques. When the Jacobite uprising (the '45) threatened the Hanoverian settlement, Fielding sprang to the defence of George II, and edited the *True Patriot*.

In hindsight, the English novel was an obvious new arena for his imagination, but it was literary rivalry that pushed him, in middle age, on to the path of fiction. In 1740, Samuel Richardson's *Pamela, or Virtue Rewarded*, the tale of a young woman who becomes a great lady and finds true happiness by defending her chastity, was the London sensation of the season, an early bestseller. Fielding's response to *Pamela* was complicated. He admired its success, scorned its sententious moralising, and attacked it in an anonymous parody, *Shamela* (1741). Thriving on the competition with Richardson, Fielding next completed his first novel, *Joseph Andrews* (1742), which began as a further parody of *Pamela* before finding its own narrative voice. After this debut, following the dramas of the '45, Fielding began work on his masterpiece, *The History of Tom Jones, a Foundling*.

For Coleridge, this long novel was, with *Oedipus Rex* and *The Alchemist*, one of "the three most perfect plots ever planned". It was also highly original and deeply comic. Fielding broke away from Richardson's epistolary technique of "writing to the moment" to compose his narrative in the third person. This engaging picaresque tale about the adventures of Tom, a high-spirited bastard, rollicking through England, was an instant hit, selling some 10,000 copies at a time when the population of London was only around 700,000.

One conservative critic denounced *Tom Jones* as "a motley history of bastardism, fornication, and adultery", which can't have done sales any harm. Samuel Johnson, more measured, thought that such novels were a dangerous distraction "to the young, the ignorant and the idle...", offering merely "the entertainment of minds unfurnished with ideas". However, for better or worse, this mass audience represented the future of the genre, and inspired Fielding's opening credo, which was to provide "an entertainment" for public consumption. "The author", he wrote in his first chapter, should provide "a mental entertainment", where "all persons are welcome for their money". Quite so.

A Note on the Text:

Fielding had read parts of *Tom Jones* to friends and circulated privately printed episodes from the novel in the autumn of 1748. The official publication date was 10 February 1749, though Fielding's bookseller, Andrew Millar, began distributing copies a week earlier, playing the role of publisher in an age when such a profession did not exist. The first edition was exhausted at once; second and third editions followed on 28 February and 12 April. The fourth edition came at the end of the same year and it's this text that remains the basis for modern editions.

– 6 –

The Life and Opinions of Tristram Shandy, Gentleman
by Laurence Sterne (1759)

 Tristram Shandy and its author, Laurence Sterne, are so intensely modern in mood and attitude, so profanely alert to the nuances of the human comedy, and so engaged with the narrative potentiality of the genre that it comes as something of a shock to discover that the novel was published during the Seven Years War. In other words, it appeared during the annus mirabilis of that prototype of international warfare that saw stunning British military victories in India, Canada and the Caribbean, and established the first British empire that would send the English language around the world. Some of the raw ebullience of the national mood is mirrored in the slightly mad pages of this uniquely entertaining novel.

"Shandy" is a word of obscure origin meaning "crack-brained, half-crazy". Tristram himself says he is writing a "civil, nonsensical, good-humoured Shandean book". As such, it became a huge bestseller in the 1760s. Sterne became a celebrity, and made a fortune, fulfilling a deep ambition. "I wrote, not to be fed but to be famous," he once said. Success had come late. Born in Ireland in 1713, Sterne spent much of his life as a country vicar near York. (In the novel, Parson Yorick is an ironical self-portrait.) His work had the difficulties often associated with original work. The first two volumes of *Tristram*

Shandy were rejected by the London publisher, Robert Dodsley, but, when privately printed, quickly sold out.

Like all subsequent bestsellers, Sterne and his book became the subject of fierce literary argument. The novel was obscene, preposterous and infuriating, the opposite of what a novel should be. The author was a "coxcomb", a vain and deplorable impostor, deficient in the good taste of a true artist. The notorious Black Page (between chapters 12 and 13 of volume I) was a silly stunt. And so on. Dr Johnson expressed the critical consensus when, in 1776, he boomed: "Nothing odd will do long. Tristram Shandy did not last."

But the good doctor was wrong. *Tristram Shandy* is odd; and it did last. Furthermore, it continues to exert a great influence on successive generations of writers. In the 1980s, magical realists such as Salman Rushdie rediscovered Sterne. Peter Carey, the Booker prizewinner, even acknowledged an influence in the title of his novel, *The Unusual Life of Tristan Smith*.

The secret of Sterne's hold on his readers is that *Tristram Shandy* is a comic tour de force whose humour, of observation and incident, explodes on to every page from the hilarious moment, in chapter 1, when Tristram Shandy is almost not conceived in a bizarre episode of coitus interruptus. An abrupt vitality is Sterne's great contribution to the art of the novel. Adopting Fielding's omniscient third-person narrative, he cheerfully set about subverting any authorial omniscience by humorously reflecting on how little he, the author, knew of his characters or their predicaments. The critic Christopher Ricks captures Sterne's playfulness when he describes *Tristram Shandy* as "the greatest shaggy dog story in the language".

So what is it about ? The short answer is that it is about 600 pages (in my Penguin Classics edition), and that, despite its title, it fails to give the reader much of the life or any of the opinions of its hero. Shandy himself only gets born in volume IV. Much of the narrative is taken up by Unce Toby, a veteran of the wars against Louis XIV, and his obsession with siegecraft. When, at the end, Tristram's long-suffering mother asks, "Lord! What is all this story about?" Parson Yorick replies, "A COCK and a BULL – and one of the best of its kind I ever heard."

A Note on the Text:

The first two volumes were published in 1759 in York by Ann Ward (at Sterne's expense) having been turned down by Robert Dodsley.

When the novel became a runaway success, Dodsley rushed out a second edition, with illustrations by Hogarth in April 1760, and then published volumes III and IV.

Sterne took a close interest in his publishers, and for the last volumes moved to Becket and De Hondt to get better terms. He enjoyed publishing his work serially, small octavo volumes of fewer than 200 pages. The full-length *Tristram Shandy* conveys none of the delight that the 18th century reader could expect, collecting the novel, volume by volume from year to year.

– 7 –
Emma
by Jane Austen (1816)

How on earth to choose just one Jane Austen novel? Austen, for some, is simply the supreme English novelist, on any list. Some will say: she is the greatest. Nominate all six, from *Pride and Prejudice* on. But the rules of our selection only allow one title per author: there has to be a choice. So, to represent her fiction here, I've chosen *Emma* for three particular reasons.

First, it's my personal favourite, a mature and brilliant comedy of manners (and much more besides) completed towards the end of her life. Second, published by John Murray, *Emma* takes us into a new literary landscape, the beginnings of a book world that lingers unto the 21st century. And third, most importantly of all, Austen's last novel has the sparkle of early books such as *Pride and Prejudice*, mixed with a sharper and deeper sensibility. There's no accounting for taste: I simply prefer it to the others.

Emma was written very fast – according to the scholars – between 21 January 1814 and 29 March 1815 (the year of Waterloo), and it comes as the climax to a remarkable period of intense creativity. *Pride and Prejudice* (whose first draft, "First Impressions", was written in 1796-7) had been published in 1813, *Mansfield Park* in 1814. Austen's work was becoming something of a cult, and she was aware of her audience. Indeed, the Prince Regent was a fan (*Emma* is dedicated to him). Austen must have been conscious that she was no longer writing just for herself. She was at the peak of her powers, yet had less than two years to live. All this, I think, gives *Emma* an added depth as the final flowering of a great artist and her work.

The novelist herself is highly conscious of her art. Emma, she wrote to a friend, is "a heroine whom no one but myself will much like". Perhaps. However, compared with her other heroines – Elizabeth Bennet, Fanny Price, Anne Elliot, and Catherine Morland – Emma is the most complex, subtle and complete. Yes, she is "handsome, clever and rich". But she's only 21 and will be sent on the familiar Austen cycle of wrong-headedness, remorse, repentance and ultimate self-realisation (with Mr Knightley) in a far deeper way than her predecessors.

Emma represents mature Austen in another way, too. She has perfected the art of free indirect speech to convey the inner life of her heroine while retaining her control of the narrative as the omniscient author. Light and shade are expertly and satisfyingly in harmony, and the novel's deceptively simple plot is spun into so much teasing variety, through games, letters and riddles – the book is exceedingly playful – that the reader is never less than fully engaged, even charmed. Then there's Austen's mature delight in her milieu. She herself famously wrote that "three or four families in a country village is the very thing to work on", and Emma's Highbury exemplifies this credo. Here, fully in command of her genre, Austen revels in her characters and their foibles. Mr Woodhouse, Mr and Mrs Elton, poor Miss Bates, Jane Fairfax and her fiancé, deceitful Frank Churchill and, of course, noble Mr Knightley – these are among the most vivid and universal characters in English fiction, as real to us as Pickwick or Jeeves.

Emma herself is endlessly fascinating, a woman to whom the reader returns again and again for the seductive intimacy of her thoughts, a secret communion that's braided with the lesson that self-knowledge is a mystery, vanity the source of the worst pain, and the subconscious a treacherous and imperfect instrument in the management of the psyche. You can object that Emma is a lady and a snob, but she also makes a timeless appeal to the reader's better nature.

Austen seems to have known that she was working on something special. *Mansfield Park* had been published by Thomas Egerton. This time, however, she wanted better terms and more literary prestige. There was only one address for that: 50 Albemarle Street, Mayfair. She approached John Murray, Byron's publisher, offering her new manuscript. Murray accepted at once and his edition appeared in December 1815, after a trouble-free editorial process in which her new publisher made a point of treating her with the greatest respect, though author and publisher never actually met.

Emma occupies a special place in this list because it is supremely English – in character, landscape, sensibility and wit. It's provincial, opaque, sparkling and wonderfully optimistic while being at the same time tinged with intimations of sorrow and mortality. In the end, it answers Jane Austen's own high-spirited prescription for the novel, expressed in *Northanger Abbey*: "in short, only some work in which the most thorough knowledge of human nature, the happiest delineation of its varieties, the liveliest effusions of wit and humour are conveyed to the world in the best chosen language".

A Note on the Text:
There was just one text prepared in Austen's lifetime, the John Murray edition, dated 1816, though it was actually published in three volumes in December 1815. No manuscript survives. Subsequent editions, notably by RW Chapman, have made silent corrections to typographical errors, but no substantial emendations. *Emma* has been continuously in print since its first publication: that's one definition of a classic.

– 8 –
Frankenstein
by Mary Shelley (1818)

The summer of 1816 was a washout. After the cataclysmic April 1815 eruption of Mount Tambora on the island of Sumbawa, part of what is now Indonesia, the world's weather turned cold, wet and miserable. In a holiday villa on the shores of Lake Geneva, a young English poet and his lover, the guests of another poet, discouraged from outdoor pursuits, sat discussing the hideousness of nature and speculating about the fashionable subject of "galvanism". Was it possible to reanimate a corpse?

The villa was Byron's. The other poet was Shelley. His future wife,

19-year-old Mary Shelley (née Godwin), who had recently lost a premature baby, was in distress. When Byron, inspired by some fireside readings of supernatural tales, suggested that each member of the party should write a ghost story to pass the time, there could scarcely have been a more propitious set of circumstances for the creation of the gothic and romantic classic called *Frankenstein*, the novel that some claim as the beginnings of science fiction and others as a masterpiece of horror and the macabre. Actually, it's both more and less than such labels might suggest. At a simple level, this is a novel about grief.

At first, Mary Shelley fretted about meeting Byron's challenge. Then, she said, she had a dream about a scientist who "galvanises" life from the bones he has collected in charnel houses: "I saw – with shut eyes, but acute mental vision – I saw the pale student of unhallowed arts kneeling beside the thing he had put together. I saw the hideous phantasm of a man stretched out, and then, on the working of some powerful engine, show signs of life, and stir with an uneasy, half vital motion."

The scientist Victor Frankenstein, then, is the author of the monster that has come in popular culture to bear his name. Frankenstein's story – immortalised in theatre and cinema – is framed by the correspondence of Captain Robert Walton, an Arctic explorer who, having rescued the unhappy scientist from the polar wastes, begins to record his extraordinary story. We hear how the young student Victor Frankenstein tries to create life: "By the glimmer of the half-extinguished light," he says, "I saw the dull yellow eye of the creature open; it breathed hard, and a convulsive motion agitated its limbs."

Unforgettably, Frankenstein has unleashed forces beyond his control, setting in motion a long and tragic chain of events that brings him to the brink of madness. Finally, Victor tries to destroy his creation, as it destroys everything he loves, and the tale becomes a story of friendship, hubris and horror. Frankenstein's narration, the core of Shelley's tale, culminates in the scientist's desperate pursuit of his monstrous creation to the North Pole. The novel ends with the destruction of both Frankenstein and his creature, "lost in darkness".

The subtitle of Frankenstein is "the modern Prometheus", a reference to the Titan of Greek mythology who was first instructed by Zeus to create mankind. This is the dominant source in a book that is also heavily influenced by *Paradise Lost* and *The Rime of the Ancient Mariner*. Mary Shelley, whose mother was the champion of women's rights, Mary Wollstonecraft, also makes frequent reference to ideas of motherhood and creation. The main theme of the book, however, is the ways in which man manipulates his power, through science, to pervert his own destiny.

Plainly, *Frankenstein* is rather different from, and much more complex than, its subsequent reinterpretations. The first reviews were mixed, attacking what one called a "disgusting absurdity". But the archetypal story of a monstrous, supernatural creation (cf Bram Stoker's *Dracula*, Wilde's *Dorian Gray* and Stevenson's *Jekyll & Hyde*) instantly caught readers' imaginations. The novel was adapted for the stage as early as 1822 and Walter Scott saluted "the author's original genius and happy power of expression". It has never been out of print; a new audiobook version, read by Dan Stevens, has been released by Audible Inc.

A Note on the Text:

The first edition of *Frankenstein; or, The Modern Prometheus* was published anonymously in three volumes by Lackington, Hughes, Harding, Mavor & Jones on 1 January 1818. A second edition appeared in 1822 to cash in on the success of a stage version, *Presumption*. A third edition, extensively revised, came out in 1831. Here, Mary Shelley pays touching tribute to her late husband, "my companion who, in this world, I shall never see more", and reveals that the first preface to the novel was actually written by Shelley himself. This is the text that is usually followed today.

– 9 –
Nightmare Abbey
by Thomas Love Peacock (1818)

Nightmare Abbey, like *Frankenstein*, appeared in 1818. Strangely, it was also inspired by Shelley, who was friends with Peacock. His satire, however, was lighthearted and whimsical and a kind of in-joke. There's no way of knowing if Peacock had actually read Mary Shelley's novel, but *Nightmare Abbey* makes a nice counterpoint, and speaks of the importance of a new audience.

The regency was a turning point for English fiction. It was not only that the prince regent was a man of culture who adored the works of Jane Austen, there was also a wholly new market for novels: middle-class readers with money, enthusiasm and taste.

After a long gestation, literary life had arrived. More than 100 years after Daniel Defoe had sat in the stocks and John Bunyan had composed *The Pilgrim's Progress* in Bedford jail, English novelists were now fully established at the centre of cultural life. Once upon a time, writers had published anonymously or under assumed names, fearing disgrace, or worse. Now they were known, talked about and sometimes even well-paid.

In the beginning, the review process had been patchy and vulnerable to actual violence. Now there were some influential magazines in play; literary criticism was recognisably the occupation we know today. Elsewhere on Grub Street, booksellers such as John Murray were becoming publishers. A rackety trade was acquiring respectability.

Simultaneously, the inhabitants of the literary world, especially in London, were beginning an informal dialogue, through their books, which knitted the community into an ongoing conversation about literature.

It's a process that survives to the present, a process we can follow through this catalogue of 100 novels. Jane Austen, for instance, would satirise Mrs Radcliffe's popular *Mysteries of Udolpho* in *Northanger Abbey*. The same engagement of artist and subject explains the career of this half-forgotten minor genius, Thomas Love Peacock.

Peacock was born to a naval family in Weymouth in 1785, inherited a small annuity, began to write poetry and went walking in Scotland like a true romantic, a young man of his time. He was clever and rather idle. To his friends, he must have seemed like a dilettante; all his life he behaved as though there were other things to do besides writing.

In 1812, however, he published a long and difficult poem, "The Philosophy of Melancholy". As a result, he met Shelley, fell under the spell of the great poet, became his friend and began to find his own voice as a writer, turning to prose satire. Peacock's claim on posterity derives from the very brief period 1813 to 1818, when he became part of Shelley's haphazard retinue and even accepted a kind of pension in lieu of household duties. In 1814, he published an attack on the Lake poets, "Sir Proteus: A Satirical Ballad". His first satirical novel, *Headlong Hall*, followed a year later.

Peacock is an original and has had few imitators. His fiction – *Nightmare Abbey* is the best of four country-house satires, including *Headlong Hall* and *Crotchet Castle* – occupies a special place in this list and deserves to be remembered as the enjoyable and undemanding beginnings of a strand in the canon that possibly includes the Aldous Huxley of *Antic Hay* and the Stella Gibbons of *Cold Comfort Farm*. I also think that there's something of Peacock's whimsical inventiveness in Lewis Carroll, but that's only a guess. I have no idea if the stuttering maths don had read any of Peacock's fiction.

Anyway, Peacock is not wholly unprecedented. His influences include Swift, Voltaire and Rabelais (who also influenced Sterne). *Nightmare Abbey* is amazingly allusive, with references to Shakespeare, Pope, Pliny and Goethe, among many others. Peacock's rather stagey, even theatrical effects find echoes in the later comic fiction of writers such as Jerome K Jerome, HH Munro ("Saki") and the young PG Wodehouse, among others. Wodehouse, indeed, appropriates Peacock's country-house milieu wholesale.

It would be interesting to know how many contemporary writers of light fiction are familiar with Peacock. He certainly deserves to be better known, hence his place here: he's a personal favourite.

The plot of *Nightmare Abbey* is cardboard-thin, and concerns the romantic ditherings of Scythrop Glowry between two love objects, Marionetta and Stella. This parodies the difficulties of Shelley's relations with Harriet Westbrook and Mary Godwin, but the real pleasure of the novel lies in Peacock's inimitable style, the exaggerated dialogue and the entertaining songs, and the delight he takes in poking fun at the romantic movement. Shelley himself was nothing but generous in his response. "I know not how to praise the lightness, chastity and strength of the language of the whole. It perhaps exceeds all your works in this."

Shelley, who is Scythrop, had been in on the game from the beginning. Peacock wrote to him on 30 May 1818 to say that "I have almost finished *Nightmare Abbey*" and to complain that "the fourth canto of *Childe Harold* is really too bad". Peacock cared passionately about the condition of English literature and was, in his mild-mannered way, a fierce champion of high standards. In another letter to Shelley, he says he wants "to let in a little daylight" on the "atrabilious complexion" of contemporary literature, a typical Peacock formulation. His concern, throughout, is for the wellbeing of the English literary tradition. The end of civilisation as we know it is another familiar starting point for lighthearted satire, from *Anything Goes* to *Chrome Yellow*.

A Note on the Text:

There was just one text of *Nightmare Abbey*, published by T Hookham Jr and Baldwin, Craddock & Joy of Paternoster Row in November 1818. With a few light revisions, it was republished in *Bentley's Standard Novels*, volume LVII in 1837. So Peacock became a set text for the Victorians and was later rediscovered by Edwardian and post-Edwardian critics.

– 10 –
The Narrative of Arthur Gordon Pym
of Nantucket
by Edgar Allan Poe (1838)

 The Yanks are coming. Thus far, as many readers will have noticed, ours has been an English list, with just one or two Irish diversions. All this, however, is about to change. Within a generation of the 1776 revolution, American writers were beginning to explore an identifiable American sensibility. Especially after the US victory over England in the war of 1812, there was a new literary self-confidence and a new sense of national identity that some have described as "literary nationalism". Writers such as Washington Irving (in his short stories "Rip Van Winkle" and "The Legend of Sleepy Hollow") and James Fenimore Cooper (in *The Last of the Mohicans*) had begun to pioneer American subjects in a distinctive American voice. Just as important, their work was beginning to find an audience in London and across the British Isles. Between 1830 and the end of the civil war (1865) there would be an American renaissance, mature and influential works by Ralph Waldo Emerson, Henry David Thoreau and (as we shall see) Nathaniel Hawthorne and Herman Melville, among many others.

But it was Edgar Allan Poe, born 1809, who signals the beginning of what would become a great Anglo-American literary dialogue. Poe was original in ways that Irving and Fenimore Cooper never were. As well as being the first American writer to attempt living exclusively by his pen, he is also the archetype of the romantic literary artist. Henry Miller, Jack Kerouac, William S Burroughs, and even Hunter S Thompson all owe something to Edgar Allan Poe. His nomadic, boho style and tortured, exigent career continue to exercise a powerful allure on any young American writers who see themselves as outsiders. In Britain, among later Victorian writers, Wilde, Stevenson, Swinburne and Yeats all responded to his unique imagination.

First and foremost, Poe was a fearless critic of the fledgling American literary scene, so fierce in his assaults on what he considered to be inferior writing that one fellow critic complained he used prussic acid not ink. Poe was a man of extremes, who knew the highs and lows of success and failure. His poem, "The Raven", was a popular sensation. Much of his other work was ignored or derided. Elsewhere, he was dismissed as a drunk, a drug addict and a derelict. When he died, in 1849, aged just 40, and unknown, on the streets of Baltimore, his fate was seen as all of a piece with his writing. Gradually, however, his genius came to be recognised. Today, his influence is crucial to the evolution of detective fiction, science fiction and almost any tale of the macabre. Poe's imagination has also become integral to the American literary aesthetic. Both he and Melville arrived late to their posterity.

Although Poe is most celebrated for stories such as "The Tell-Tale Heart" and "The Murders in the Rue Morgue", his only novel, *The Narrative of Arthur Gordon Pym of Nantucket*, stands as a classic adventure story with disturbing supernatural elements that has fascinated and influenced many subsequent writers. For example, the chapter entitled "The Whiteness of the Whale" in *Moby-Dick* would have been impossible without Poe; and Henry James's *The Golden Bowl* owes a clear debt to Poe.

The inspiration for *The Narrative of Arthur Gordon Pym* was both modern and American. Poe got the idea from a newspaper. In February 1836, the *Norfolk Beacon* published a vivid account of the sinking in a storm at sea of a ship named Ariel. Here was the perfect sea story for which Poe had been on the lookout. Like many ambitious young writers, he sought both popular success and literary acclaim. After he had written a number of successful short tales, his publisher, Wesley Harper, had advised him that "readers in this country have a decided and strong preference for works (especially fiction) in which a single and connected story occupies the whole volume." Plus ça change.

Seafaring adventure was hardly new for Poe. He had already won a prize for his tale of the Flying Dutchman, "MS Found in a Bottle". In the novel he began to plan, he despatched his protagonist (the rhythm of whose name suggests Edgar Allan Poe), in a whaler, the Grampus, on an extraordinary voyage to the southern seas, following (as it were) Coleridge's *Ancient Mariner*. But then he contrived a sequence of ever more dreadful jeopardy: mutiny, storm, shipwreck, sharks, the "exquisite horror" of cannibalism, a ghost ship, and frozen regions inhabited by savage natives. Poe had read and admired *Robinson Crusoe*, and had learned from Defoe's example. Indeed, the opening of *Arthur Gordon Pym* mirrors exactly the beginning of *Crusoe*, and borrows a similar authorial device. Like Defoe, Poe also ramped up "the potent magic of verisimilitude" (his own phrase) by borrowing freely from contemporary accounts of South Sea adventure.

But, because it's a novel by Poe, *The Narrative of Arthur Gordon Pym* is much more than just a yarn, and is replete with existential and psychoanalytical fascination. Freud, for one, made much of its darker side. Moreover, the later part of the 'narrative' explores one of Poe's recurring themes, man's unconscious desire for annihilation. Pym is not only on the brink of death, but in one chapter he actually appears as a dead man. This quasi-supernatural element infuriated many of Poe's readers on first publication, and will no doubt continue to trouble readers today.

And yet, despite or perhaps because of its strangeness, Pym's magic endures. In more popular writing, Arthur Conan Doyle, B Traven, and David Morrell all found a touchstone in Poe's only novel. Baudelaire translated it. Jules Verne wrote a sequel. When Paul Theroux, who reports the story in *The Old Patagonian Express* (1979), read aloud from it to Jorge Luis Borges, the older writer said: "It is Poe's greatest book."

A Note on the Text:
The beginning of *Arthur Gordon Pym* first appeared in serial form in some 1837 issues of the *Southern Literary Messenger*. For reasons that are unclear, but possibly to do with his drinking, Poe withdrew from this collaboration and continued to work on the manuscript while living in New York City. The novel was eventually published by Harper & Brothers on 30 July 1838. A British edition, from Wiley & Putnam, was published in October, the same year.

– 11 –
Sybil
by Benjamin Disraeli (1845)

For more than a decade after the death of Jane Austen in 1817, the English

novel was rather in the doldrums, a reflection of the times. English literary culture was making the transition from the high camp of the Regency to the hard grind of early Victorian society. A brilliant new generation would burst on the scene in the late 30s and early 40s. For the moment, the leading novelists of the age were Sir Walter Scott and his protégé, "the great Maria", Maria Edgeworth, the Irish-born author of *Castle Rackrent* and *Leonora*. Rightly or wrongly, I am choosing to pass over these names for the list on the grounds that I do not know enough about their work to make a good judgment.

Meanwhile, the British readership was avid. There was, more than ever, a booming market for new fiction. The novel had become the medium in which ambitious young writers could make a splash. Bulwer Lytton, author of *Pelham; or the Adventures of a Gentleman*, (and later, *The Last Days of Pompeii*) was one of these. Another was the young dandy and rising political star Benjamin Disraeli.

I've worried about Disraeli's place on this list. Would he have made the cut if he had not become prime minister? Or if he had not dazzled and enchanted Victorian society for so many years? His literary contemporaries such as Dickens, Thackeray, George Eliot, and even Anthony Trollope are much greater novelists. Disraeli's plots are far-fetched, and his characters balsa-wood. And yet… At the same time, he has flashes of brilliance that equal these greats at their best. There are, for instance, lines in his precocious early novels, notably *Vivian Gray*, that rival some of Oscar Wilde's. Is it fanciful to see *Dorian Gray* as a kind of homage from one outsider to another?

Disraeli is not just a fascinating literary sphinx who famously said, in answer to someone who asked him if he had read *Daniel Deronda*: "When I want to read a novel, I write one." With his polemical fiction of 1844-47 (*Coningsby*, *Sybil* and *Tancred*), he more or less invented the English political novel. From this trilogy, *Sybil, or the Two Nations* stands out as perhaps the most important Victorian condition-of-England novel of its time.

In its own day, *Sybil* precedes, and possibly influences, Mrs Gaskell's

Mary Barton (1848), Charles Kingsley's *Yeast* (1848) and Froude's *Nemesis of Faith* (1849). Occasionally, this genre was taken to ridiculous lengths, as in Mrs Frewin's *The Inheritance of Evil, or The Consequences of Marrying a Deceased Wife's Sister* (1849).

Disraeli, the novelist, is far more sparkling than all of these. The opening scene of *Sybil*, the eve of Derby day at Crockford's, is justly famous, a tour de force with some celebrated zingers. "I rather like bad wine," says Mr Mountchesney. "One gets so bored with good wine." Having begun in a London club, Disraeli moves swiftly to explore the two nations of the subtitle. His portrait of life in a grim, northern manufacturing town is vivid and memorable. Like Dickens, he made a point of researching those parts of the novel that fell outside his experience, and it shows.

As many critics have noted, the most important character in *Sybil* is Disraeli himself. As an author, he is irrepressibly at large in all his writing. His voice resonates from page to page, and his sympathy for the plight of the poor elevates even the dullest passages. The speech in which the young Chartist agitator, Morley (in love with Sybil) describes "the Two Nations… between whom there is no intercourse and no sympathy" is brilliant, passionate and unforgettable, reaching its climax in that celebrated upper-case line: "THE RICH AND THE POOR."

English political rhetoric still refers to one-nation ideals. Weirdly, Disraeli was occasionally appropriated by Ed Miliband's Labour party. In Taper and Tadpole, he created memorable archetypes who still crop up in the Westminster village. Without Disraeli, Charles Dickens might not have written *Hard Times*. We are approaching the summit of the mid-Victorian novel.

A Note on the Text:

Disraeli was unlike Dickens, Thackeray et al. He never published in serial form. His novels miss the advantages and problems of serialisation. Instead, he adopted the standard Victorian three-decker form – simultaneous publication in three volumes at a guinea and a half for the set. Disraeli was not a bestseller. *Coningsby* and *Sybil* sold about 3,000 copies, and gave him a profit of about £1,000 per title. *Sybil* was advertised for sale in the *Times*, on 8 May 1845. The publisher, Henry Colburn of Great Marlborough Street, owned one of the fashionable imprints of the day. Disraeli was a starry young MP. It was natural for publisher and author to do business.

– 12 –
Jane Eyre
Charlotte Brontë (1847)

"There was no possibility of taking a walk that day."

 From its haunting first line to its famous closer, "Reader, I married him", Charlotte Brontë takes her audience by the throat with a fierce narrative of great immediacy. Jane Eyre's voice on the page is almost hypnotic. The reader can hardly resist turning the next page, and the next…

In an extraordinary breakthrough for the English novel, borrowing the intimacy of the 18th century epistolary tradition, Charlotte had found a way to mesmerise the reader through an intensely private communion with her audience. We, the author, and Jane become one. For this, she can be claimed as the forerunner of the novel of interior consciousness. Add to this a prose style of unvarnished simplicity and you have the Victorian novel that cast a spell over its generation. Even today, many readers will never forget the moment they first entered the strange, bleak world of this remarkable book.

The magic of *Jane Eyre* begins with Charlotte Brontë herself. She began to write her second novel (*The Professor* had just been rejected) in August 1846. A year later it was done, much of it composed in a white heat. The reading public was spellbound. Thackeray's daughter says that the novel (which was dedicated to her father) "set all London talking, reading, speculating". She herself reports that she was "carried away by an undreamed-of and hitherto unimagined whirlwind".

There are three principal elements to Brontë's magic. First, the novel is cast, from the title page, as "an autobiography". This is a convention derived from Defoe's *Robinson Crusoe*. But the adventure offered by the author is an interior one. *Jane Eyre* portrays the urgent quest of its narrator for an identity. Jane, who cannot remember her parents, and as an orphan has no secure place in the world, is in search of her "self" as a young, downtrodden woman.

Related to this, *Jane Eyre* has a raw, occasionally erotic, immediacy. Not only does Jane reject Brocklehurst, St John Rivers and John Reed, she also craves submission to her "master", the Byronic Mr Rochester. The violence of men against women is implicit in many of Jane's transactions with both Rivers and Rochester. The thrill of this, to the Victorian reader, cannot be overestimated.

Finally, *Jane Eyre*, addressed insistently to "the reader", is so steeped in English literature that it becomes an echo chamber of earlier books. Within a very few pages of the opening, there are references to *Paradise Lost*, Walter Scott's *Marmion* and Jonathan Swift's *Gulliver's Travels*.

Brontë herself, the daughter of a tyrannical north country parson, was very familiar with John Bunyan's *Pilgrim's Progress*. Critics have described a five-fold Bunyanesque progression to *Jane Eyre*, beginning with "Gateshead", moving to the depths of "Lowood", then the trials of "Thornfield" and "Marsh End" before achieving the blessed release of "Ferndean". Jane's spiritual pilgrimage is also narrated with biblical simplicity, combined with considerable artifice.

Jane Eyre also displays the familiar tropes of the gothic novel. Thornfield is a gothic manor; Mr Rochester a gothic-romantic protagonist. The mad woman in the attic speaks for herself, as it were. In addition, Brontë herself knows the storytelling power of what she calls "the suspended revelation", a phrase coined in chapter 20, and never hesitates to tantalise and seduce the reader.

The year 1847 must be the annus mirabilis of English fiction. The manuscript of *Jane Eyre* reached the publisher, George Smith, in August. He began to read one Sunday morning. "The story quickly took me captive," he wrote. "Before twelve o'clock my horse came to the door but I could not put the book down... before I went to bed that night I had finished reading."

Publication in October 1847 became so sensational that publisher Smith, Elder & Co's rival, Thomas Newby, decided to bring forward the release of Emily Brontë's unpublished manuscript. In December, 1847, Victorian readers still digesting the thrill of *Jane Eyre* found themselves contemplating a new novel called *Wuthering Heights*.

A Note on the Text:

The publication history of *Jane Eyre* is intimately connected to Charlotte Brontë's return from Brussels in 1844. As soon as she read Emily's poetry, she persuaded Anne and Emily to submit a selection of their work under the names Currer, Ellis, and Acton Bell to London publishers, but without any immediate success. In the end, the poems were privately published. Then, in July 1847, Thomas Newby agreed to publish Emily's *Wuthering Heights*. Her elder sister Charlotte now sent her first novel, *The Professor*, to Smith, Elder & Co, who turned it down, but asked to see other work. Charlotte submitted *Jane Eyre*, which caught the eye of George Smith, and appeared at breakneck speed on 19 October 1847, in three volumes, "edited by Currer Bell". The first American edition, from Harper & Brothers, of New York, appeared in 1848. A second British edition, dedicated to William Thackeray, was published in 1850, with some local scandal. Charlotte Brontë did not apparently know that Thackeray had had his own wife declared insane.

– 13 –
Wuthering Heights
by Emily Brontë (1847)

One image of Emily Brontë – endlessly reproduced – is less a portrait, more an icon. Intense, fierce, inward, solitary, elusive and unknowable: the young author of *Wuthering Heights* in profile is of a piece with her first, and only, novel.

Her elder sister's work – *Jane Eyre* – hypnotises the reader through the calculated force of its tone, its "suspended revelations", and its hints of suppressed eroticism. It builds, slowly, to a poignant climax in which, finally, its protagonists are redeemed, though not in a way that's conventional. *Wuthering Heights*, by contrast, plunges impetuously into a wild and passionate exploration of love in all its destructive manifestations.

Brontë's narrative – fragmented, discordant and tortuous – revolves obsessively around a single, explosive transgression, and the theme of jealousy in the lives of Heathcliff and Catherine, before making a calmer return to the theme in the often neglected second half.

Where Charlotte comes from the puritan tradition of John Bunyan, Emily is the child of the Romantic movement, and both sisters are steeped in the gothic. However, it is Emily who takes the bigger creative risks. The first reviews of *Wuthering Heights* were mixed. Critics who had been swept away by *Jane Eyre* did not know what to make of it. For a long time it was judged to be inferior. Readers who love *Jane Eyre* are sometimes less enthusiastic about *Wuthering Heights*. And vice versa. I've included both in my list because their influence on the

English imagination, and on subsequent English-language fiction, has been incalculable.

Looking back, it's clear that where *Jane Eyre* comes out of a recognisable tradition, and is conscious of that affiliation, *Wuthering Heights* releases extraordinary new energies in the novel, renews its potential, and almost reinvents the genre. The scope and drift of its imagination, its passionate exploration of a fatal yet regenerative love affair, and its brilliant manipulation of time and space put it in a league of its own. This is great English literature, the fruit of a quite extraordinary childhood.

To look forward, I think we can say that the work as we know it of Thomas Hardy, DH Lawrence, and even Rosamond Lehmann would have been impossible without it. As a portrait of "star-cross'd lovers" it rivals *Romeo and Juliet*. There is also something operatic about its audacity and ambition. No wonder film-makers, song writers, actors and literary critics have been drawn to reinterpret its story.

And then there are its quieter pleasures. Like Hardy and Lawrence, Emily Brontë has an uncanny eye and ear for the natural world. When Lockwood visits Heathcliff's and Cathy's graves at the end of the novel, the poetry in the voice is Brontë's:

"I lingered round them, under that benign sky; watched the moths fluttering among the heath, and hare-bells; listened to the soft wind breathing through the grass; and wondered how any one could ever imagine unquiet slumbers, for the sleepers in that quiet earth."

Magic.

Wuthering Heights was published three months after *Jane Eyre* in December 1847. A year later, Emily was dead from consumption, aged just 30. Charlotte wrote later: "Stronger than a man, simpler than a child, her nature stood alone."

A Note on the Text:

Wuthering Heights, A Novel by Ellis Bell, was published by Thomas Newby in December 1847, three months after *Jane Eyre*. Several reviewers, impressed by the force of the book, believed it had been written by a man. After her sister's death, Charlotte Brontë edited a revised second edition, the text that is generally followed today.

A letter from Newby does survive which seems to suggest that Emily Brontë had begun to write a second novel, though the manuscript has never been found. If she had started a second novel, she was prevented by consumption from completing it. She died the same year in which *Wuthering Heights* was published, aged 30.

– 14 –
Vanity Fair
by William Thackeray (1848)

Vanity Fair jumps out of this list as a great Victorian novel, written and published deep in the middle of a great age of English fiction. Indeed, so commanding was Thackeray at the height of his powers (some say he never wrote as well, or as sharply, again) that Charlotte Brontë even dedicated *Jane Eyre* to the author of *Vanity Fair*.

One hundred years after the publication of *Clarissa* Thackeray not only revels in the possibilities of the genre, he even illustrated his own work with some decidedly inferior woodcuts. *Vanity Fair* was published in serial form (including some memorable cliff-hangers, for instance Becky Sharp's revelation of her marriage to Rawdon Crawley) from January 1847 to June 1848. Thackeray, on top form, cheerfully exploited an ebullient tradition, transcending all his previous efforts as a writer, novels such as *The Luck of Barry Lyndon* (1844).

Early drafts of the book, which had the working title "a novel without a hero" lacked the all-important figure of William Dobbin, a thoroughly good and likable character who owes much to Thackeray himself. "*Vanity Fair*", a title that came in a eureka moment to the author in bed one night, actually derives from *Pilgrim's Progress* and refers to the fair set up by the devils Beelzebub and Apollyon in the town of Vanity. Unlike Bunyan, Thackeray was hardly a die-hard Christian, but rather a man who relished a life of pleasure and luxury, and who, on the evidence of his letters, found much of the *Bible* either ludicrous or distasteful. As a title, however, "*Vanity Fair*" set the tone of the novel in its depiction of a society, rather as "*The Bonfire of the Vanities*" did for Tom Wolfe (who also illustrated his own work) in 1987.

Thackeray's intention was satirical and realistic. Writing mid-century, he set his masterpiece in Regency England during the Napoleonic wars, intending the lessons of his tale to be applied equally to his own times. In contemporary terms that would be like a modern literary novelist setting their scene during the Second World War, or the Blitz.

The climax of the novel comes with the battle of Waterloo. Unlike Tolstoy, whose *War and Peace* was influenced by *Vanity Fair*, Thackeray was squeamish about military matters, and chose to leave most of the fighting off-stage. This makes the irruptions of violence all the more shocking, as in the death of George Osborne, "lying on his face, dead, with a bullet through his heart" on the field of Waterloo, which occurs almost exactly halfway through the narrative.

Thackeray was highly conscious of his audience and repeatedly breaks off from his story to buttonhole and tease his readers ("the present chapter (8), is very mild. Others – but we will not anticipate those"). The tale, however, will not be denied for long. Upwardly mobile Becky Sharp, and her sweet, devoted friend, Amelia Sedley, are perfectly matched by the caddish rake, George Osborne, and clumsy, decent William Dobbin. The social trajectory of each pair gives the narrative an almost perfect symmetry.

The key to the novel's magic, in addition to the delight it takes in the Regency pageant, probably lies in the contrast between scheming Becky, one of fiction's great female protagonists and awkward, dutiful William whose unwavering love for Amelia mirrors Thackeray's own passion for another man's wife.

Finally, however, for all its realism, *Vanity Fair* is a bravura performance by a writer who has found his theme. As the serialisation of the novel that would transform its author's reputation draws to a close, Thackeray himself concluded his tale with a nod to the gaudy theatricality of the whole business: "Come children, let us shut up the box and the puppets, for our play is played out."

A Note on the Text:
Vanity Fair, subtitled "A Novel without a Hero", was first serialised in *Punch*, then published (from the same typesetting) by Bradbury & Evans of Bouverie Street in July 1848. A revised and more definitive text appeared in 1853, without illustrations. *Vanity Fair* was the first of Thackeray's books to appear under his own name. As a further sign of his self-confidence, in the introduction to the 1848 edition, dated 28 June, the author acknowledges "the kindness with which

it has been received in all the principal towns of England… where it has been most favourably noticed by the respected conductors of the public Press, and by the Nobility and Gentry. He is proud to think that his Puppets have given satisfaction to the very best company in this empire."

– 15 –
David Copperfield
by Charles Dickens (1850)

David Copperfield was the first book Sigmund Freud gave his fiancée, Martha Bernays, on their engagement in 1882. It was the gift of a lifelong Anglophile to his beloved, a book encrypted with peculiar meaning to a man with a special fascination for the complicated relation of autobiography to storytelling.

Freud's choice – and Dickens's own opinion that *David Copperfield* was "of all my books" the one he liked "the best" – helps clarify an impossible selection midway through the 19th century. At the outset, I'm going to anticipate your howls of rage. Some Dickens aficionados will be dismayed. Why not *Pickwick Papers*? Or, better still, *Great Expectations*? Or *Bleak House*? Or *Little Dorrit*? And why not that festive evergreen *A Christmas Carol*? Or the granite brilliance of *Hard Times*? Yes, in different ways, all masterpieces. Everyone has their favourite. This is mine.

I love *David Copperfield* because it is, in some ways, so un-Dickensian. The story – so appealing to Freud – is of a boy making his way in the world, and finding himself as a man and as a writer. In the first half, before Dickens's irrepressible storytelling kicks in and the motor of the novel starts to hum with incident, we find him almost meditating on his literary beginnings. Dickens is one of the first to acknowledge the inspiration of the emerging English canon: *Robinson Crusoe, The Adventures of Roderick Random* and *Tom Jones*, the books he finds in his father's library. His own early novels (*Oliver Twist, Nicholas Nickleby* and so on) are largely comic picaresques. But here, he focuses on the interior life of his hero, as if saving the plot for later.

The second half of *David Copperfield* displays Dickens at his magnificent, and often uneven, best. There are the characteristic prose arpeggios, the virtuoso similes and metaphors, and the parade of timeless characters: Mr Micawber, Mrs Gummidge, Betsey Trotwood, Barkis, Uriah Heep, Steerforth, Mr Spenlow (of Spenlow and Jorkins) and Miss Mowcher.

At the same time, Copperfield and Dickens, autobiographer and novelist, become so indistinguishable, the one from the other, that the novelist no longer has the necessary detachment from his material. When the lovely, tranquil reflections on boyhood of the opening pages become replaced by the urgent demands of plot-making, protagonist and author morph together in ways that are not completely success-ful, though always revealing. As the novel builds to a climax, in which Heep is imprisoned and Mr Micawber, free of his debts, finds redemp-tion as a colonial magistrate in Australia, Dickens succumbs to the pressure to please a hungry public with a satisfying fictional feast. Henceforth in his work, Dickens will become the supreme Victo-rian entertainer and moralist, the author of those mature, and darker, masterpieces, *Bleak House*, *Hard Times* and *Great Expectations*.

And so, as a key transitional text, *David Copperfield* becomes the antechamber to his subsequent mastery. But the door into the past is shut for ever; he can never go back. The young man daydreaming about literature among his father's old books has been replaced by the bestselling writer, "the Inimitable". Perhaps this was the poignant truth about creativity that so moved Freud.

Note on the Text:

The novel that Dickens described as his "favourite child" went through many titles, from "Only Once A Year" and "Mag's Diver-sions" to "The Copperfield Survey", "The Copperfield Confessions" and "The Last Will and Testament of David Copperfield". Eventually, with serial publication looming, he settled on *The Personal History, Adventures, Experience and Observation of David Copperfield the Younger of Blunderstone Rookery (Which He Never Meant to be Published On Any Account)*.

It is hard definitively to identify the true first edition. Following serial publication from May 1849 to November 1850 – in 19 monthly one-shilling instalments, each containing 32 pages of text and two illustrations by Hablot Knight Browne ("Phiz") – the novel, now simply inscribed *David Copperfield* on the title page, was published in a single volume of 624 pages on 14 November 1850 by Bradbury & Evans of Bouverie Street.

In any event, Dickens's MS, which is now in the V&A, had already undergone significant revision in the transition from magazine to book form. Three further editions (1858, 1859 and 1867) saw additional changes. The most scholarly edition to date is probably the text edited by Nina Burgis (Oxford: Clarendon Press, 1981).

– 16 –
The Scarlet Letter
by Nathaniel Hawthorne (1850)

Nathaniel Hawthorne, describing "a tale of human frailty and sorrow",
 insisted that *The Scarlet Letter* was "a Romance", not a novel. This distinction, in his mind, was important. Where a novel, as he put it, "aims at a very minute fidelity, not merely to the possible, but to the probable and ordinary course of man's experience", a romance expressed "the truth of the human heart". Here, in short, is the prototype of the psychological novel, a brilliant and groundbreaking example of a new genre within 19th century fiction.

Hawthorne's tale has a stark simplicity. In the 17th century town of Boston, a young woman, Hester Prynne, is publicly disgraced for committing adultery and giving birth to an illegitimate child, a girl named Pearl. Forced to wear a scarlet "A", Hester slowly redeems herself in the eyes of Puritan society. Over many years, she challenges the two men in her life – her husband and her lover – with the dark truth of their emotional responsibilities and failures, while at the same time wrestling with her own sinful nature. After seven long years of painful rehabilitation, she emerges as a strong, inspiring woman, while the pastor, Arthur Dimmesdale, who seduced her, dies of shame. Hester, too, eventually dies and is buried near Dimmesdale under a tombstone marked with a simple "A".

Such a bare summary does few favours to an extraordinary work of the imagination that burns from page to page with the fierce simplicity of scripture and an almost cinematic clarity of vision. *The Scarlet Letter* is an astounding book full of intense symbolism, as strange and haunting as anything by Edgar Allan Poe, a writer whom we know Hawthorne much admired.

The process of Hester Prynne's acquisition of self-knowledge, the recognition of her sin and her ultimate restoration in a sequence of enthralling scenes, punctuated by moments of confrontation with Dimmesdale, is utterly compelling and, at times, deeply moving. Nathaniel Hawthorne's understanding of the emotional transactions of the sexes is profound and modern, too. And very interesting about the price paid for the loss of love. Hester's reflections on her relationship with Dimmesdale ("How deeply had they known each other then! And was this the man? She hardly knew him now") could be found in many modern novels.

The most memorable and original aspect of *The Scarlet Letter* lies in Hawthorne's portrait of Hester Prynne, who has been described as "the first true heroine of American fiction", a woman whose experience evokes the biblical fate of Eve. Hawthorne's achievement is to make her passion noble, her defiance heartbreaking and her frailty inspiring. She becomes the archetype of the free-thinking American woman grappling with herself and her sexuality in a cold, patriarchal society.

There is also something emblematic of the newly settled American society about *The Scarlet Letter*, the belief that the public individual, subjected to a merciless democratic scrutiny, is owed the human right of ultimate restoration, if he or she deserves it. Hester Prynne is more than just a mother with a baby, she is an outcast woman who will ultimately be welcomed back into American life, purged and cleansed of her sin. Readers of *The Scarlet Letter* during, for instance, the Monica Lewinsky scandal of the 1990s, could not fail to miss the resonance of Hawthorne's "romance" with that bizarre political drama.

By chance, in his own time, Hawthorne was not alone in wanting to explore the mysteries of the American psyche through fiction. In summer 1850, after the successful publication of *The Scarlet Letter*, he met the young Herman Melville who had just begun, and was grappling with, his own dark meditation on America, *Moby-Dick*.

A Note on the Text:

The Scarlet Letter was published in Boston in the spring of 1850 by Ticknor, Reed and Fields. When he delivered the manuscript in February 1850, Hawthorne said "some portions of the book are powerfully written", but cautiously added that it would probably not prove popular. Secretly, he hoped for much more. After the night of 3 February 1850, when he read the final part of the novel to his wife, he told a friend that "it broke her heart … which I look upon as a triumphant success. Judging from its effect," he went on, "I may calculate on what bowlers call a 10-strike!" Hawthorne had struggled, with almost no recognition, for some 25 years. It's clear that he anticipated some success.

In fact, the book was an instant bestseller, a term not yet in use. *The Scarlet Letter* was one of the first mass-produced books in America and the mechanised first printing of 2,500 copies sold out in 10 days. However, after a promising start, it brought the author only $1,500 and, in the end, sold barely 7,800 copies in Hawthorne's lifetime. Thereafter, it continued to attract praise from perceptive writers. Henry James once wrote: "It is beautiful, admirable, extraordinary; it has in the highest degree that merit which I have spoken of as the mark of Hawthorne's best things – an indefinable purity and lightness of conception… it has the inexhaustible charm and mystery of great works of art."

– 17 –
Moby-Dick
by Herman Melville (1851)

On 5 August 1850 a party of writers and publishers climbed Monument

Mountain in Massachusetts, during the American equivalent of a hike in the Lakes. Among the literati on this excursion were Nathaniel Hawthorne, 46, author of *The Scarlet Letter* , a recently published bestseller, and the young novelist Herman Melville, who, after a very successful debut (*Typee*), was struggling to complete an unwieldy coming-of-age tale about a South Seas whaler.

Melville, who was just 31, had never met Hawthorne. But after a day in the open air, a quantity of champagne, and a sudden downpour, the younger man was enraptured with his new friend, who had "dropped germinous seeds into my soul". Rarely in Anglo-American literature has there been such a momentous meeting.

It was the attraction of opposites. Hawthorne, from an old New England family, was careful, cultivated and inward, a "dark angel", according to one. Melville was a ragged, voluble, romantic New Yorker from mercantile stock. Both writers had hovered on the edge of insolvency and each was a kind of outsider.

A fervent correspondence ensued. Melville, indeed, became so infatuated that he moved with his wife and family to become Hawthorne's neighbour. Thus liberated, fulfilled, and inspired to say "NO! in thunder, to Christianity", he completed *Moby-Dick; or, The Whale,* in the spring of 1851. After an early reading of the manuscript, Hawthorne acclaimed it in a letter that remains, tantalisingly, lost. All we have is Melville's ecstatic response ("Your heart beat in my ribs and mine in yours, and both in God's..."), and, subsequently, a dedicatory declaration of Melville's admiration for Hawthorne's "genius" at the front of *Moby-Dick* (the first edition hyphenated the whale's name).

So how homoerotic was this friendship? No one will ever know; it remains one of the mysteries of American letters. All we can say for certain is that, after climbing Monument Mountain, Melville adopted Hawthorne's idea of the "romance" as a mixed-genre, symbolic kind of fiction, and found his creative genius somehow released in the making of his new book.

And that is everything, because *Moby-Dick* is, for me, as for many, the supreme American novel, the source and the inspiration of everything that follows in the American literary canon. I first read it, inspired by my sixth-form English teacher, Lionel Bruce, aged about 15, and it's stayed with me ever since. *Moby-Dick* is a book you come back to, again and again, to find new treasures and delights, a storehouse of language, incident and strange wisdom.

Moby-Dick is – among some fierce contenders which will appear later in this series – the great American novel whose genius was only recognised long after its author was dead. From its celebrated opening line ("Call me Ishmael") it plunges the reader into the narrator's quest for meaning "in the damp, drizzly November of my soul".

Ishmael is an existential outsider. What follows is profoundly modern yet essentially Victorian, spanning 135 chapters. It is a literary performance that is exhilarating, extraordinary, sometimes exasperating and, towards its apocalyptic climax, unputdownable.

When Ishmael ships aboard the Pequod, his own quotidian search becomes inexorably joined to the darker quest, in which the captain of the doomed whaler, "monomaniacal Ahab", sets out to revenge himself on the great white whale that has bitten off his leg. This "grand, ungodly, godlike man", one of fiction's greatest characters – "crazy Ahab, the scheming, unappeasedly steadfast hunter of the white whale" – is not only pursuing his nemesis, a "hooded phantom", across the ocean's wastes, he is also fighting the God that lurks behind the "unreasoning mask" of the symbolic whale.

Eventually, a whaling expedition from Nantucket – something experienced by the young Melville himself – becomes the story of an obsession, an investigation into the meaning of life.

Next to Ahab and Ishmael, this massive novel is also rich in minor characters, from the tattooed harpooner Queequeg, the ship's mate Starbuck, Daggoo and Fedallah the Parsee – all told, a typically American crew. And so a "romance" (Hawthorne's term) inspired by the true story of the Essex, a whaler that sank when it was attacked by a sperm whale in the Pacific in November 1820, becomes like a terrifying (at times, intolerable) sea voyage, culminating in a thrilling three-day chase in which Moby-Dick destroys the Pequod. Ishmael survives to tell his tale by clinging to Queequeg's carved coffin.

Moby-Dick is usually described, as I've just done, as an elemental novel in which the outsider Ishmael is pitted against the fathomless infinity of the sea, grappling with the big questions of existence. That's not inaccurate, but there's also another *Moby-Dick*, full of rough humour, sharp comic moments, and witty asides. "Better sleep with a sober cannibal", says Ishmael, when forced to share a bed with the tattooed harpooner Queequeg, "than a drunken Christian." For those readers intimidated by the novel's bleak majesty, I think the humour offers a good way in.

A Note on the Text:
The pre-publication history of *Moby-Dick* has been the subject of endless scholarship, and provides a case study in Anglo-American co-publishing in the mid 19th century.

Melville, who was short of money, actually made his first contract for a new novel, then known as *The Whale*, with the British publisher

Richard Bentley. But he kept the printing in New York so he could oversee the proofs, and wrote to Hawthorne, from New York, that he must "work and slave on my 'Whale' while it is driving through the press". In fact, he was simultaneously working on revisions to his manuscript and proofreading what had been set.

Meanwhile, Melville had still not yet settled a contract with an American publisher. As a result, the British edition would differ from the American in hundreds of small ways. The most important was the change of title. Rather late in the day, he wrote to Bentley: "*Moby-Dick* is a legitimate title for the book, being the name given to a particular whale who, if I may so express myself, is the hero of the volume."

Bentley seems to have been slow to respond. On 18 October, the English edition, *The Whale*, was published, in an edition of only 500 copies. Then, on 14 November, the American edition, *Moby-Dick*, (with its hyphenated title), finally appeared from Harpers. Almost as significantly, the US edition contained an "Epilogue", which explains Ishmael's miraculous survival and, thus, how the story of the great white whale came to be told.

For some unknown reason, the epilogue is absent from the British edition. British reviewers were puzzled to read a book with a first-person narrator who apparently did not survive to tell the tale. Accordingly, the *Spectator* objected that "nothing should be introduced into a novel which it is physically impossible for the writer to have known: thus, he must not describe the conversation of miners in a pit if they all perish." Two other papers asked "How does it happen that the author is alive to tell the story?" The upshot was confusion, and poor English reviews. These, in turn, cast a shadow over the American reception of the novel. Melville's career never really recovered. He told Hawthorne in 1856, "I have pretty much made up my mind to be annihilated."

When he died, in 1891, Melville was virtually forgotten, with *Billy Budd* still in manuscript, unpublished. Today, *Moby-Dick* is, in the words of the *Oxford Companion to English Literature*, "the closest approach the United States has had to a national prose epic".

– 18 –
Alice's Adventures in Wonderland
by Lewis Carroll (1865)

On 4 July 1862, a shy young Oxford mathematics don with a taste for puzzles and whimsy named Charles Dodgson rowed the three daughters of Henry Liddell, dean of Christ Church, five miles up the Thames to Godstow. On the way, to entertain his passengers, who included a 10-year-old named Alice, with whom he was strangely infatuated, Dodgson began to improvise the "Adventures Under Ground" of a bored young girl, also named Alice. Wordplay, logical conundrums, parody and riddles: Dodgson surpassed himself, and the girls were enchanted by the nonsense dreamworld he conjured up. The weather for this trip was reportedly "overcast", but those on board would remember it as "a golden afternoon".

This well-known story marks the beginning of perhaps the greatest, possibly most influential, and certainly the most world-famous Victorian English fiction, a book that hovers between a nonsense tale and an elaborate in-joke. Just three years later, extended, revised, and retitled *Alice's Adventures in Wonderland*, now credited to a pseudonymous Lewis Carroll, *Alice in Wonderland* (its popular title) was about to become the publishing sensation of Christmas 1865. It is said that among the first avid readers of *Alice* were Queen Victoria and the young Oscar Wilde. A second volume about Alice (*Through the Looking-Glass*) followed in 1871. Together these two short books (*Wonderland* is barely 28,000 words long) became two of the most quoted and best-loved volumes in the English canon.

What is the secret of Carroll's spell? Everyone will have their own answer, but I want to identify three crucial elements to the magic of *Alice*. First, and most emphatically, this is a story about a quite bad-tempered child that is not really for children, while at the same time addressing childish preoccupations. (Who am I? is a question Alice repeatedly vexes herself with.) Next, it has a dreamlike unreality peopled with some of the most entertaining characters in English literature. The White Rabbit, the Mad Hatter, the Mock Turtle, the Cheshire Cat and the King and Queen of Hearts are simply the most memorable of a cast from which every reader will find his or her favourite. Third, Carroll possessed an unforced genius for the most brilliant nonsense and deliciously mad dialogue. With his best lines ("What is the use of a book without pictures or conversations?") he is never less than intensely quotable.

As well as the enchantment of Carroll's prose, both volumes of *Alice* contain numerous songs and poems, many of them parodies of popular Victorian originals, which have passed into folklore, like Alice herself: You Are Old, Father William; The Lobster Quadrille; Beautiful Soup; and (from *Through the Looking-Glass*) Jabberwocky; The Walrus and the Carpenter; and The White Knight's Song.

Finally, for 21st century readers, it is now almost obligatory to point out that these books are pre-Freudian, with a strange, bruised innocence whose self-interrogations also evoke the tormented banality of psychoanalysis.

A Note on the Text:

On 26 November 1865, the Reverend Charles Dodgson's tale was published by the house of Macmillan as *Alice's Adventures in Wonderland* by Lewis Carroll, illustrated by John Tenniel, with whom Dodgson had a most uneasy relationship. Indeed, the first printing, some 2,000 copies, was withdrawn after Tenniel objected to the print quality of his drawings. A new edition, released in December of the same year, but carrying a new date, 1866, was rushed out for the Christmas market.

Later, the discarded first edition was sold with Dodgson's approval to the New York publisher, Appleton. The title page of the American *Alice* became an insert cancelling the original Macmillan title page of 1865, and bearing the New York publisher's imprint with the date 1866. Here, too, the first print run sold quickly. First editions are now rare and highly prized. Both *Alice* books have never been out of print. *Alice's Adventures in Wonderland* has been translated into about 100 languages, including classical Latin.

– 19 –
The Moonstone
by Wilkie Collins (1868)

The Moonstone is often said to be the godfather of the classic English detective story, its founding text. TS Eliot, claiming that the genre was "invented by Collins and not by Poe", declared it to be "the first, the longest and the best of modern English detective novels". Dorothy L Sayers, a queen of crime in the 1930s and 40s, echoing Eliot, pronounced it "probably the finest detective story ever written". Its influence continues to animate the work of crime writers such as PD James.

Certainly, Collins adheres faithfully to the rules of detective fiction: a mysterious and compelling crime takes place in an English country house; a large cast of potential suspects is assembled, each with plenty of motive, means and opportunity; an incompetent constabulary is replaced by a celebrated sleuth/ investigator who, after a "recon-struction" of key elements in the crime, comes up with a satisfying explanation of the puzzle, based on a brilliant analysis of the clues. Finally, there's a denouement replete with surprise, excitement and a plausible solution. *The Moonstone* has this, and more, all of it brilliantly executed.

The original crime in *The Moonstone*, the theft of the Tippoo diamond after the fall of Seringapatam, is Collins's masterstroke. It connects every detail of the plot to the great imperial drama of India, the society over which Queen Victoria would eventually declare herself "Empress". The Indian factor imbues the tale with the sinister mystery of the east. Mid-century, this "moonstone" is given to a young Englishwoman, Rachel Verinder, on her 18th birthday and then myste-riously disappears. A quest ensues in which, after murder and marriage, the Moonstone is restored to its Indian source.

However, although this is classic detective fiction, its greatness really lies in its qualities as a novel. Collins signalled his ambitions for the book in the preface to the first edition, in which he wrote: "In some of my former novels, the object proposed has been to trace the influence of circumstances upon character. In the present story I have reversed the process." So it's the enthralling interplay of character (Rachel

Verinder, the hunchbacked servant girl Rosanna Spearman, Sergeant Cuff, the great detective, and compelling Franklin Blake, Rachel Verinder's cousin) that will hook the interest of most readers. Rosanna's tragic obsession with the adventurer Franklin Blake is among the most poignant renderings of thwarted love in Victorian literature. The fascinating and eccentric figure of Cuff (based on Scotland Yard's real life Inspector Whicher) introduces a figure central to the unravelling of the mystery on whom most readers come to dote.

A second, crucial element to the success and longevity of *The Moonstone* is less about detection than storytelling. This is Collins's virtuoso exploitation of the narrative viewpoint. In this series, we have already seen the power of epistolary fiction (*Clarissa* and *Frankenstein*). Collins first uses garrulous Gabriel Betteredge, then meddlesome Miss Clack, then the solicitor Matthew Bruff, and then the opium addict Ezra Jennings (drawing on his own opium habit). The narrative dividend for Collins is that he can use these different voices to vary the tone and tempo of a complicated (but not impossibly so) plot.

The upshot is his masterpiece, a brilliant marriage of the sensational and the realistic. In short, a classic.

A Note on the Text:
The Moonstone was originally serialised by Charles Dickens, a close friend of Wilkie Collins, in his magazine *All the Year Round* between 4 January and 8 August 1868. It was published in three hardback volumes on 16 July 1868 by Tinsley Brothers of Catherine Street, in Covent Garden. A second, revised edition was issued in 1871. In 1877, Collins adapted the novel for the stage, a production that ran for about two months.

Subsequently, there have been many film, radio and television adaptations. In 1934, *The Moonstone* was made into a critically acclaimed American film. In 1959, the BBC made the novel into a TV serial; in 1972, it was remade for Britain and the United States. In 1996, it was remade again, also in the United Kingdom, for television by the BBC, starring Greg Wise as Franklin Blake and Keeley Hawes as Rachel Verinder. It continues to earn its reputation as the founding text of English detective fiction.

Robert McCrum

– 20 –
Little Women
by Louisa May Alcott (1868-9)

 Little Women is probably unique in this series: it was conceived, and commissioned, by a publisher. An instant bestseller, and a coming-of-age classic, it continues to appear in polls of Anglo-American reading, and remains among the most widely read novels of all time.

Born in 1832, Louisa Alcott had grown up as the second of four daughters to a well-known Boston educationist with a penchant for reading aloud to his family from *The Pilgrim's Progress*. As a girl, Louisa was always "scribbling", selling her juvenile efforts to a range of publications aimed at the market for young women.

By her mid-30s, Alcott had published books for children, a first novel entitled *Moods*, and some journalism about her experiences as a nurse in the American civil war ("Hospital Sketches"). Pseudonymously, she had also written several romances and adventure stories for a variety of "penny-dreadful" publications.

At first, when, in 1867, the editor of the Boston publisher Roberts Brothers asked her to write "for girls", Alcott demurred. She wasn't interested, she said; but the idea stuck. Plus, she had some family debts to settle and, as a professional writer, Alcott would have been well aware of the booming market in contemporary fiction for young women.

As early as May 1868, she confided to her journal that although she was now at work on *Little Women* (the title also came from her publisher), she did not "enjoy this sort of thing" because she "never liked girls nor knew many, except my sisters; but our queer plays and experiences may prove interesting though I doubt it".

Rarely has an interim verdict on work-in-progress been so far from the mark. Alcott's use of her sisters' lives is crucial. The structure of *Little Women* was loosely inspired by *The Pilgrim's Progress*, but its material is mostly semi-autobiographical, drawn from Alcott's childhood memories. She, unequivocally, is Jo, the fearless girl (and aspiring writer) who longs "to do daring things", and who struggles to escape the Victorian prison of her gender. Jo March and her sisters would become vital role models for many subsequent generations of American woman.

Another key to the success of *Little Women* is Alcott's direct and easy style which is grounded in the reality of everyday life. The four girls – Jo, Margaret (Meg), Elizabeth (Beth), and Amy – speak and feel like regular young American women of their day. The device of the absent father (away serving as an army chaplain in the civil war), enhances their independence and places this lively quartet at the fulcrum of the narrative. In turn, this is conceived in a wholly original voice that's deeply realistic. For instance – spoiler alert – in the chapter ("The Valley of the Shadow") where Beth dies, Alcott draws, documentary-style, on her own journal of her sister Elizabeth's premature death.

Finally, Alcott's use of Bunyan's "quest", together with the romantic elements she weaves into her tale of "little women" (whom we might call "young adults"), ensured that her all-American girls became an immediate hit with the public. *Little Women* was published in October 1868. By 1 November, in the same year, Alcott was already at work on the sequel. Since then, neither book has ever been out of print.

A Note on the Text:

The Roberts Brothers edition of *Little Women* appeared on 1 October 1868 in a print run of some 2,000 copies. This success continued the following year with the publication of *Little Women, Part Two*, sometimes called *Good Wives*. Now the reprints of both titles were averaging about 1,000 copies a month. In 1881, both texts were revised, reillustrated and republished in a single volume.

Meanwhile, in England, although Sampson Low was the "official" publisher, he did not have a free market. In the absence of copyright agreements between the US and Britain, there were several competing editions from rival publishing houses (notably Routledge, Warne, and Blackie). Among UK readers, *Little Women* has never held quite the same iconic place it occupies in the United States.

– 21 –
Middlemarch
by George Eliot (1871-2)

Middlemarch is one of those books that can exert an almost hypnotic power over its readers. Few other titles in this series will inspire quite the same intensity of response. When, for instance, in 1873, the poet Emily Dickinson referred to the novel, she wrote in a letter: "What do I think of *Middlemarch*? What do I think of glory – except that in a few instances 'this mortal [George Eliot] has already put on immortality'."

As well as moving its admirers to rhapsody, *Middlemarch* is also supremely a work of serious literature. According to Virginia Woolf, it is "one of the few English novels written for grown-up people". Later in the 20th century the influential critic FR Leavis made *Middlemarch* a central feature of his "Great Tradition". Today it stands as perhaps the greatest of many great Victorian novels.

George Eliot's masterpiece, *Middlemarch*, appeared after the deaths of Thackeray (1863) and Dickens (1870). This is hardly an accident. Subtitled "a study of provincial life", the novel has a didactic realism that's a world away from *Vanity Fair* or *Great Expectations*. Indeed, *Middlemarch* looms above the mid-Victorian literary landscape like a cathedral of words in whose shadowy vastness its readers can find every kind of addictive discomfort, a sequence of raw truths: the loneliness of the disappointed failure, Dr Lydgate; the frustrations of his discontented wife; the humiliation of a good woman, Dorothea; the corrosive bitterness of Casaubon, and so on.

Few of Eliot's characters achieve what they really want, and all have to learn to compromise. Some learn the lessons and achieve a temporary happiness. Others refuse or are incapable of learning, and spend their lives resenting their situation, and blaming others. And others still realise their mistakes but are trapped by a wrong decision and never escape. Dr Lydgate is especially emblematic of *Middlemarch*: dying young, a bitter and disappointed man who knew he had married the wrong woman and could do nothing about it.

The action takes place some 40 years before the moment of composition. As well as making allusions to the death of George IV, outbreaks of cholera and the passing of the Great Reform Bill of 1832, its characters discuss the coming of the railway and the impact of industrialisation on a settled Midland English world. Here, the organising metaphor of *Middlemarch* becomes "the web", Eliot's representation of English society in all its airy complexity and resilience.

In the middle of this web we find the character whom all readers of *Middlemarch* will argue about and identify with, the fascinating figure of Dorothea, wife of the cold-hearted monster Rev Edward Casaubon. Dorothea becomes a true heroine because – despite all she suffers, her humiliations and heartache – she still tries to be a good person, and to do the right thing. Lydgate, in particular, sees this and understands to his great sorrow what sort of woman he should have married and how different his life could have been. In a larger sense, Dorothea's fate (and also the torments self-inflicted by Rosamond Vincy) dramatise another of the novel's major themes, the place of women in a changing but still patriarchal society.

There are no easy resolutions in a great novel. Some readers will be dismayed to find, in the final chapters, Dorothea discovering fulfilment in her work for Will Ladislaw as he becomes a reforming MP. But Eliot has the last word, a famous and deeply moving valedictory page celebrating Dorothea's "finely-touched spirit". Here, Eliot concludes that "the effect of [Dorothea's] being" was "incalculably diffusive: for the growing good of the world is partly dependent on unhistoric acts; and that things are not so ill with you and me as they might have been, is half owing to the number who lived faithfully a hidden life, and rest in unvisited tombs".

A Note on the Text:
At the beginning of 1869, George Eliot listed her tasks for the coming year in her journal, including "A Novel called Middlemarch". However, progress was slow, interrupted by the fatal illness of Thornie Lewes, the second son of her partner George Henry Lewes. By September, only three chapters of the story had been completed, and by the time Thornie finally died in November 1869, Eliot had stopped work on a novel that was at this stage just a study of Middlemarch society, with Lydgate, the doctor, and his ill-matched wife Rosamond Vincy, as the main characters.

However, more than a year later, in November 1870, she began work on a new story entitled "Miss Brooke", which introduced

Dorothea. Eventually Eliot combined Dorothea's story with the Lydgate-Vincy narrative, and began to unfold the full majesty of the *Middlemarch* we have today.

As it took wing the work became so unlike the traditional Victorian "three-decker" novel that Lewes, acting as his partner's agent, requested John Blackwood, the publisher, to launch the novel in eight parts, at two-monthly intervals from December 1871. Once Blackwood had agreed, the eight books appeared throughout 1872, culminating in the closing chapters of November and December 1872, although the title page of the first edition bears the date 1871. *Middlemarch* was immediately recognised as a work of genius, and secured Eliot's place high in the pantheon of English fiction. The first one-volume edition was published in 1874, and sold well to an enthusiastic reading public. In 2003 the novel was chosen as no 27 in the BBC survey "the Big Read".

– 22 –
The Way We Live Now
by Anthony Trollope (1875)

Anthony Trollope is the epitome of the 19th century English writer, indefatigable, popular and tightly wired-in to his society, a monument of productivity. In the course of his 67 years, Trollope published more than 40 novels including two series (*The Barchester Chronicles* and *The Pallisers*) that anchored him in the public mind as the model of the Victorian literary man.

His peers were less complimentary. To Henry James, he was "a novelist who hunted the fox". After the disastrous publication of his *An Autobiography*, his reputation became damaged by his ruthless attitude towards his art (so many words per day; his characters clinically subordinated to the needs of his narrative, and so on). Trollope's facility was held against him, and so was his popularity with a middle-class reading public. However, if there is one Trollope novel, written in a white heat during 1873, that rescues him from accusations of shallow commerciality, and puts him in the premier league, it must be *The Way We Live Now*.

The novel, fuelled by indignation, began as a satire. Trollope, who had been living in Australia for 18 months, had returned to London in 1872, to find a society (as he saw it) mired in corruption. He was appalled, he wrote later, by "a certain class of dishonesty, dishonesty magnificent in its proportions, and climbing into high places... so rampant and so splendid that there seems to be reason for fearing that men and women will be taught to feel that dishonesty, if it can become splendid, will cease to be abominable."

At first, what he called "the Carbury novel" was to be focused on Lady Carbury, a coquettish fortysomething operator "false from head to foot" on the brink of a shameful literary career. Here, Trollope's portrait owes something to his redoubtable mother, Frances Trollope, the bestselling author of *Domestic Manners of the Americans*. But once he introduced the character of Augustus Melmotte, one of English fiction's most memorable monsters, all literary equilibrium was lost. Perhaps because Trollope was now untethered from a lifetime of careful plotting, and scrupulous narration, he was able to plunge deeper into his subject unencumbered by the restraints of literary technique. *The Way We Live Now* has a raw and edgy vitality (fading towards the end) that's often missing in Trollope's more routine novels.

Melmotte, based on some scandalous financiers of the 1870s, is a figure we have come to know only too well: arrogant, ruthless, corrupt and so unfeasibly rich he believes he can buy anything, including political influence. In painting this character, Trollope's satirical fury is at full stretch. Melmotte is a "horrid, big, rich scoundrel... a bloated swindler... a vile city ruffian". How often, in the 1980s and 90s – Robert Maxwell comes to mind – have we not seen such characters in contemporary English life ?

Melmotte's story, which occupies the heart of *The Way We Live Now* is the tale of a railway fraud, mad speculation and, finally, the bursting of the bubble in a crash that utterly disgraces the deluded interloper. This is hardly the moment to reveal Melmotte's fate, which must be implicit in his corruption. Suffice to say that, once he has left the scene, a more familiar cast of bounders and rogues takes over: Lady Carbury and her feckless son Felix, whose contemptible ambition is "to marry an heiress"; Hamilton Fisker, Melmotte's crooked partner; "Dolly" Longstaffe, the pointless clubman; Mrs Hurtle, the social climbing American, plus an entertaining *galère* of literary types (Trollope has fun here) from Broune and Booker (yes!), Yeld, Barham and Alf, any one of whom could step into British literary prize management today, no questions asked.

One of my favourites in this series, *The Way We Live Now* is a wonderful, melodramatic tale-of-the-times, by a master of his craft. It begins in satire and finally resolves into entertaining social comedy. As a savage commentary on mid-Victorian England by a marvellously addictive writer steeped in every aspect of an extraordinary society, it could hardly be bettered. No wonder the first reviews were atrocious.

A Note on the Text:

Trollope, professional to his fingertips, often kept a calendar for the composition of his fiction. Before starting *The Way We Live Now* he made the following, slightly chilly, calculation: "Carbury novel. 20 numbers. 64 pages each number. 260 words each page. 40 pages a week. To be completed in 32 weeks."

But he was wrong. The "Carbury novel", begun in May 1873, took just 29 weeks, and ran to about 425,000 words. Incredibly, Trollope also polished off another work of fiction (*Harry Heathcote of Gangoil*) simultaneously. Meanwhile, the publishers Chapman & Hall had already made a contract with Trollope (an outright sale for £3,000) for *The Way We Live Now*, securing serialisation as well as volume rights. But the heyday of magazine publication was over. The novel did badly in serial form, from February 1874 to September 1875. A two-volume edition was published in July 1875, pre-empting the last stages of the serialisation. The reviews were poor. Trollope himself rather defensively wrote in *An Autobiography:* "I by no means look on the book as one of my failures; nor was it taken as a failure by the public." *The Way We Live Now* would not be recognised as the masterpiece it is until the 1940s. Now it is seen as his greatest achievement.

– 23 –
The Adventures of Huckleberry Finn
by Mark Twain (1884/5)

Mark Twain began his masterpiece, he said, as "a kind of companion to *Tom Sawyer*". Drafted in the 1870s, the first chapters of the new book continued the old mood with the sharp ironic humour of its famous opening line: "You don't know about me, without you have read a book… made by Mr Mark Twain, and he told the truth, mainly."

But when, after a troubled hiatus, he returned to complete the manuscript in 1883, what had begun as a reminiscent celebration became a darker elegy for a lost world. His alter ego, Sam Clemens, was appalled by the trend of American life in the fading century. For Mark Twain, the surest bulwark against the sterilising tide of progress became his pen.

With *Huck Finn*, he could recall life on America's great river as a permanent thing, a place of menacing sunsets, starlit nights and strange dawns, of the confessions of dying men, hints of buried treasure, murderous family feuds, overheard shoptalk, the crazy braggadocio of travelling showmen, the distant thunder of the civil war, and two American exiles, Huck the orphan and Jim the runaway slave, floating down the immensity of the great Mississippi. Huck's is a journey that will transform both characters, but in the end, Huck, like his creator, breaks free from bourgeois inhibition, from those who would "adopt" and "sivilise" him. "I can't stand it," he says. "I been there before."

Another American from the Midwest, TS Eliot, addressing Twain's genius, wrote that he was "one of those writers, of whom there are not a great many in any literature, who have discovered a new way of writing, valid not only for themselves but for others".

Hemingway put it more succinctly. "All modern literature comes from one book by Mark Twain called *Huckleberry Finn*… It's the best book we've had. All American writing comes from that. There was nothing before. There has been nothing as good since."

The voice of a new America resounds loud and clear from the first page to the last. *Huckleberry Finn*, inspired by a prequel (*The Adventures of Tom Sawyer*) that was for boys, is a book that celebrates the lost world of childhood, the space and mystery of the Midwest. Above all, it mythologises the issue – race – that had tormented the Union for so many decades. So Huck Finn floats down the great river that flows through the heart of America, and on this adventure he is accompanied by the magnificent figure of Jim, a runaway slave, who is also making his bid for freedom.

A Note on the Text:

The Adventures of Huckleberry Finn began as a manuscript originally entitled *Huckleberry Finn's Autobiography*. Twain eventually abandoned it following Huck Finn's development into adulthood. Twain wrote the bulk of the story in pen and ink between 1876 (the year of *Tom Sawyer*) and 1883. A later version became the first typewritten manuscript delivered to a printer. Ever since the publication of his story *The Celebrated Jumping Frog of Calaveras County* Twain was famous throughout the English-speaking world, and news of the book soon spread outside of the United States. *The Adventures of Huckleberry Finn* was eventually published by Chatto & Windus on 10 December 1884 in Canada and the United Kingdom, and then on 18 February 1885 in the United States by Charles L Webster and Co. (The American edition was delayed thanks to a last-minute change to an illustration plate.)

Even now, this great novel remains vulnerable to the censoring attentions of provincial reactionaries and classroom bigots, calling for the novel to be banned. In 2003 high school student Calista Phair and her grandmother, Beatrice Clark, in the state of Washington, proposed eliminating the book from the Renton school district, because of the frequent use of the word "nigger". In 2009 a Washington state high school teacher called for the removal of the novel from the school curriculum, stating that all "novels that use the 'N-word' repeatedly need to go". I'm happy to report that elsewhere in the world, *Huckleberry Finn* is still read, and taught, as an American classic.

– 24 –
Kidnapped
by Robert Louis Stevenson (1886)

In a society shaped by the profound transformations of the 1870 Education Act, Robert Louis Stevenson stands apart from his late-Victorian contemporaries as a strikingly romantic artist, and literary celebrity. He held a very modern attitude to his profession and yet, nevertheless, somehow seemed to sacrifice life to literature. He, of course, disclaimed his commitment, telling an American admirer that he was "a person who prefers life to art, and who knows it is a far finer thing to be in love…" The record of his creativity suggests the opposite, only adding to the aura of enigma that still surrounds him.

So Stevenson remains an elfin, paradoxical figure. In his day, he was read avidly as the author of adventure stories for boys and bestselling horror/fantasy for adults. *Treasure Island* and *The Strange Case of Dr Jekyll and Mr Hyde* were instant classics, each a brilliantly concise narrative of quasi-cinematic intensity. Both *Jekyll and Hyde* and *Treasure Island* were written incredibly fast, in a matter of days, or weeks. Perhaps this is why (more than many writers in this series), Stevenson was a master at capturing fictional moments with a single vivid image. This was his forte. It was RLS, for instance, who identified the footprint in the sand in *Robinson Crusoe*, as a narrative masterstroke.

Anyway, to me, *Kidnapped* is his masterpiece, an unforgettable novel of action that would inspire writers as varied as Joseph Conrad, John Buchan, Graham Greene and Muriel Spark. It is also a fascinating meditation on the complexity of the Scots character, half Celt, half Saxon. As in *Jekyll and Hyde*, it shows him obsessed with the divided self, and in the year of the independence vote, *Kidnapped* remains essential reading. I've chosen it for this series to represent Stevenson's profound Scottishness as well as his genius as a writer.

The novel is deceptively simple. Although it's presented as a boys' story, rooted in historical reality, it also demonstrates Stevenson's artistic sleight-of-hand. Indeed, *Kidnapped* achieves at least three things simultaneously. First, it's an astounding action adventure in which Stevenson's command of narrative, prose that's pared to the bone, is never less than enthralling. As a reader, he leaves one almost breathless with excitement and admiration. Henry James, no less, was a great fan of the "Flight in the Heather" sequence of chapters. For storytelling verve, turn to chapter 10, "The Siege of the Round House".

Second, *Kidnapped* takes an historical event, the Appin murder of May 1752, the killing of "the Red Fox", and renders it into a compelling popular tale for the mass audience who first encountered it in the magazine *Young Folks*. Stevenson did not disdain the genre in which he was operating. *Kidnapped*, like *Treasure Island*, comes with a map, to elucidate the drama; his chapter titles alone are designed to sell his tale: "I Run a Great Danger in the House of Shaws"; "The Man with the Belt of Gold"; and "The House of Fear".

Finally, *Kidnapped* stands out as an inspired and memorable study of the duality in the Scots character. David Balfour, the Whig, is a Lowland Scot of prudent Presbyterian stock whose shocking kidnap occurs as he sets out to claim his inheritance from his evil uncle, Ebenezer. Alan Breck (Stewart), described by Balfour as "a condemned rebel, and a deserter, and a man of the French king's", represents the proud spirit of the Highlands after the Jacobite rebellion of 1745, fiery, reckless, romantic and doomed, with a brilliant line in memorable dialogue. As a pair, they make an unforgettable, often contentious, double act, and both revel (with Stevenson) in the good Scots tongue. Like a rich country fruit cake, Kidnapped is seasoned throughout with handfuls of dialect words, "ain" (one), "bairn" (child), "blae" (cheerless), "chield" (fellow), "drammach" (raw oatmeal), "fash" (bother), "muckle" (big), "siller" (money), "unco" (extremely) , "wheesht!" (shush!), and dozens more.

The Scots dialect words somehow give *Kidnapped* an inexhaustible fire and brio, but its inner mood is sombre. Stevenson, in Balfour's voice, expresses this as he lives over again "the worst part of my adventures… Ransome carried below, Shaun dying on the round-house floor, or Colin Campbell (the Red Fox) grasping at the bosom of his coat…"

Balfour survives, of course, but for almost everyone else their fate is death. Stevenson himself died suddenly of a stroke on the island of Samoa on 3 December 1894, aged 44.

A Note on the Text:
Kidnapped was written as a "boys' novel" and first published in serial form in the magazine *Young Folks* from May to July 1886. The novel first appeared in book form from Cassell and Company in July

1886. In the *Collected Works of Stevenson*, it boasts one of the longest and most elaborate subtitles in English literature: "Being Memoirs of the Adventures of David Balfour in the Year 1751; How he was Cast Away; His Sufferings in a Desert Isle; His Journey in the Wild Highlands; His Acquaintance with Alan Breck Stewart and other Notorious Highland Jacobites; with All that He Suffered at the Hands of his Uncle, Ebenezer Balfour of Shaws, Falsely So-Called. Written by Himself and Now Set Forth by Robert Louis Stevenson with a Preface by Mrs Stevenson".

Kidnapped was well-received on publication and has since attracted the admiration of writers as diverse as Henry James, who praised its narrative brio, Jorge Luis Borges and Seamus Heaney, among many. An inferior sequel, *Catriona*, was published in 1893.

– 25 –
Three Men in a Boat
by Jerome K Jerome (1889)

An ancient river. The journey upstream of some impressionable young men into a mysterious, challenging interior. An inevitable reckoning at the source. Finally, the terrible return to reality. Here, surely, is pre-Edwardian English fiction at its classic finest.

But this is not *Heart of Darkness*, and the river is not the Congo. Actually, it's the Thames, and the narrator is not Marlow but J, or Jerome, K Jerome. Published in 1889, 10 years before Conrad's novel, *Three Men in a Boat (To Say Nothing of the Dog)*, is one of the comic gems in the English language. An accidental one, too. "I did not intend to write a funny book, at first," said its author.

Humour in literature is often not taken as seriously as it deserves. Nevertheless, there are a few seriously funny books that remain great for all time. *Three Men in a Boat* is one of these. Ostensibly the tale of three city clerks on a boating trip, an account that sometimes masquerades, against its will, as a travel guide, *Three Men in a Boat* hovers somewhere between a shaggy-dog story and episodes of late-Victorian farce.

What's it all about? Jerome K Jerome would probably say his

masterpiece was "about one hundred and fifty pages", but I would argue that *Three Men in a Boat* is about the camaraderie of youth, the absurdity of existence, camping holidays, playing truant, comic songs, and the sweet memories of lost time. You could also read it as an unconscious elegy for imperial Britain. Did I omit to say that it also features a dog named Montmorency? In short, like all the finest comic writing, it's about everything and nothing.

Jerome K Jerome is more or less forgotten now. He was a jobbing freelance literary journalist who had just got married and needed to provide for his wife and family. Encouraged by his new wife, Georgina, Jerome intended his account of a boating holiday to be a popular travel guide for a booming market. In late-Victorian England there was a vogue for recreational boating on the Thames between Kingston and Oxford. This was the golden age of the Henley regatta. Rowing boats, steam launches, even the occasional gondola: in the Season, up to 800 vessels a day passed through Boulter's Lock near Maidenhead. Here was an audience for a new river guide. In fact, Jerome's descriptions of Hampton Court, Marlow and Medmenham are all that survive from the original plan for a travel book.

But something funny happened on the way to publication, perhaps because it was first serialised in a magazine. Jerome's discursive comic voice took over. The river journey he makes with his friends George and Harris (and Montmorency) becomes the narrative line on which he hangs a sequence of comic anecdotes loosely associated with the journey upriver.

Jerome's themes are airily inconsequential and supremely English – boats, fishing, the weather, the atrocities of English food and the vicissitudes of suburban life – perfectly pitched in a light comic prose whose influence can be detected later in the work of, among many, PG Wodehouse, James Thurber, and Nick Hornby. My favourite Jerome set piece is the episode with the tinned pineapple.

The three mariners have had a long, hard day on the river. They reach their evening mooring, dog-tired and ravenously hungry. When George unearths a tin of pineapple chunks "we felt" writes Jerome, "that life was worth living after all". They were, he says, all of them exceedingly fond of pineapple. As the anticipation begins to build, he delivers the most perfect sentence in a book already buoyant with light comedy. "We looked at the picture on the tin," writes Jerome; "we thought of the juice."

Then they discover that they have no tin-opener. What follows is a passage of comic genius spun from nothing more – or less – than the banality of everyday life. Read it. This passage ("a fearful battle") comes as the brilliant climax to chapter 12.

Three Men in a Boat is one of those rare classics that seems to come, as it were, out of nowhere, and to defy the odds. Jerome K Jerome later wrote a hit West End play, *The Passing of the Third Floor Back*, but he never recaptured the mood of careless comic joy that aerates the pages of his immortal masterpiece.

A Note on the Text:
Three Men in a Boat began life as a travel commission for the magazine *Home Chimes*.

Its author later described what went wrong: "I did not know I was a humorist," he confessed. "The book was to have been 'The Story of the Thames', its scenery and history… I never got there. It seemed to be all 'humorous relief'. By grim determination I succeeded, before the end, in writing a dozen or so slabs of history and working them in, one to each chapter, and FW Robinson, who was publishing the book serially, promptly slung them out… From the beginning he had objected to the [since lost] title , and halfway through I hit upon *Three Men in a Boat*, because nothing else seemed right."

Jerome sold book publication rights to the Bristol publisher, JW Arrowsmith, who had been having a big success with a three-and-sixpenny single-volume series (including work by Arthur Conan Doyle and Anthony Hope), a new phenomenon which had begun to supplant the great Victorian "three-decker" novels. The Education Act of 1870 had created a new mass readership, and Jerome was eager to reach this new audience. On publication, however, it seemed as if his cunning marketing plans had gone awry. He had not allowed for the critics.

Jerome's fascination with bank clerks and "the lower orders" was denounced up and down. "One might have imagined," he later wrote in *My Life and Times*, "that the British Empire was in danger. The *Standard* spoke of me as a menace to English letters; and the *Morning Post* as an example of the sad results to be expected from the over-education of the lower orders…"

To be specific, the reviews ranged from the vitriolic to the merely hostile. The use of slang was condemned as "vulgar" and the book as a whole abused as a shameless appeal to "'Arrys and 'Arriets" – sneering critical terms for working-class Londoners. The magazine *Punch* dubbed Jerome K Jerome "'Arry K 'Arry".

Typically, the reading public paid absolutely no attention. *Three Men in a Boat* went on selling in vast numbers, defying gravity. It was also promptly pirated by unscrupulous American publishers. In Britain, Arrowsmith told a friend: "I pay Jerome so much in royalties, I cannot imagine what becomes of all the copies of that book I issue. I often think the public must eat them."

The first edition appeared in August 1889, and remained in print until March 1909, when, after the sale of some 200,000 copies, a second edition appeared. In his introduction to this printing, Jerome states that he had probably sold another million (pirated) copies in America.

The book was also translated into many languages. The Russian edition was particularly successful and became a standard school textbook, possibly as a documentary account of life in the heart of the capitalist empire. Since its publication, *Three Men in a Boat* has never been out of print. I'm unashamedly fond of it, and chose it as my "desert island" book on BBC Radio 4 in 2000.

– 26 –
The Sign of Four
by Arthur Conan Doyle (1890)

In the summer of 1889, the managing editor of the American magazine *Lippincott's* visited London to commission new fiction from some up-and-coming authors. On 30 August, he held a dinner at the Langham hotel attended by the young Oscar Wilde and Arthur Conan Doyle, among others. The upshot was an unprecedented and remarkable double: *Dorian Gray* and a new Sherlock Holmes novel, originally titled *The Sign of the Four*.

The influence of *The Moonstone* is unmistakable from the moment Holmes's client, Mary Morstan, presents herself in Baker Street. Her father, an Indian army captain, has gone missing. As a second puzzle, she reports that over the last several years, on 7 July, she has received six pearls in the mail from an unknown source. Mary Morstan can offer the great detective just one clue, a map of a fort found in her father's desk, with the names of three Sikhs, and a certain Jonathan Small. It is, of course, enough.

The story that Holmes swiftly unravels will involve some potent aspects of India in all its mystery and romance: the "mutiny" of 1857; stolen jewels from Agra; and a Sikh plot. On only his second outing in a full-length novel, Holmes is on top form throughout, stimulated by injections of cocaine and his celebrated deductive method ("How often have I said to you that when you have eliminated the impossible, whatever remains, however improbable, must be the truth?") Here, unmistakably, is the voice of the master.

Conan Doyle had stumbled on the idea of the brilliant detective and his stolid sidekick (a variation on a theme best known to literature in a double act like Don Quixote and Sancho Panza) in *A Study in Scarlet* (1888). In *The Sign of Four* he deepens the Holmes-Watson relationship and has the good doctor (also the narrator) fall in love with Mary Morstan ("A wondrous subtle thing is love," declares Watson). They will eventually get married.

As a novel about a crime, *The Sign of Four* is inferior to *The Moonstone*, though superbly constructed and compelling, complete with poison darts, a disputed legacy, and an exciting chase down the Thames. It also marks the reappearance of the "Baker Street Irregulars" and an important step in the evolution of Holmes and Watson, the most successful and popular literary duo in Victorian magazine fiction.

Doyle was a keen cricketer who used to play with other writers, including the young PG Wodehouse. They became friends and Wodehouse eventually paid homage to his mentor when he created English literature's supreme double act in his Jeeves and Wooster stories.

A Note on the Text:
In his memoirs, Conan Doyle describes how he was commissioned to write this story over a dinner at the Langham hotel with Joseph M Stoddart, managing editor of Lippincott's on 30 August 1889. Stoddart's first idea was to produce an English version of his magazine with local, British contributors. In the end, only Doyle, with typical professionalism and efficiency, delivered his copy on time for its

British publication in February 1890. On its first magazine appearance, the novel was titled *Sign of the Four*, following the description of the fatal symbol of murder in the text of the story. Thereafter, during several second serialisations in a variety of regional journals, the novel became known as *The Sign of Four*.

Eventually, Conan Doyle's second Sherlock Holmes novel would appear in volume form in October 1890 from the publisher Spencer Blackett, again with the title *The Sign of Four*. Later editions have varied between the two versions of the title, with most editions adopting the four-word form. The actual text in the novel nearly always uses "the Sign of the Four" (the five-word phrase) to describe the symbol in the story.

Like its prequel, *A Study in Scarlet*, published in 1888, *The Sign of the Four* was not an overnight success. It was Conan Doyle's Sherlock Holmes stories, published in the *Strand* magazine after 1890 that made Sherlock Holmes into a literary immortal.

– 27 –
The Picture of Dorian Gray
by Oscar Wilde (1891)

Of all the books in this series, Oscar Wilde's only novel enjoyed by far the worst reception on its publication. The reviews were dreadful, the sales poor, and it was not until many years after Wilde's death that this remarkable work of imagination was recognised as a classic.

Its gestation was troubled, too. First commissioned in the summer of 1889 by an American editor for *Lippincott's Monthly Magazine*, Wilde initially submitted a fairy tale "The Fisherman and his Soul", which was rejected. Eventually, his typescript for *The Picture of Dorian Gray* was delivered in April 1890, whereupon *Lippincott's* editor declared that "in its present condition there are a number of things an innocent woman would make an exception to".

In the light of several subsequent reviews, this was a comparatively mild critique. Wilde himself was steadfast in defending his author's vision. He always maintained that the Faustian idea of Dorian Gray, "the idea of a young man selling his soul in exchange for eternal youth", was "old in the history of literature". But when he gave an archetypal story a striking contemporary spin, with strong homoerotic undertones, he stirred up a furore of hostility.

Reread today, however, *The Picture of Dorian Gray* is a wonderfully entertaining parable of the aesthetic ideal (art for art's sake), and a sneak preview of the brilliance exhibited in plays such as *The Importance of Being Earnest* and *Lady Windermere's Fan*. What began as an outré, decadent novella, now seems more like an arresting, and slightly camp, exercise in late-Victorian gothic, than the depraved fiction alleged by his outraged critics.

Dorian Gray is the impossibly beautiful young man who becomes the subject of a portrait by the fashionable society painter, Basil Hallward. When the artist, who has become infatuated with his model, introduces the "young Adonis" to Lord Henry Wotton, he is rapidly seduced by the peer's witty and corrupting devotion to *fin-de-siècle* hedonism, some of it inspired by Wilde's own experience.

Among the influences that shaped the book, I would argue that Disraeli is a ghostly godfather to the novel. Wilde tips his hat not only to Disraeli's *Sybil*, but also to *Vivian Grey*, his first novel. Closer to his own time, Wilde also took inspiration from Robert Louis Stevenson and *The Strange Case of Dr Jekyll and Mr Hyde*. There was something about the literary alter ego that held a peculiar fascination for late Victorians.

Under the malign influence of Lord Henry – "the only way to get rid of temptation is to yield to it", is one of many Wildean epigrams scattered through the text – Dorian Gray plunges into a decadent and sinister milieu, becoming a slave to drugs and debauchery. His fatal love affair with the actress Sybil Vane alerts him to the secret of his eternal youth: he will remain untarnished while his portrait reflects the hideous corruption of his soul.

Eventually despairing, the young man blames the artist Hallward for his fate, and murders him. But Dorian Gray can never "be at peace". Finally, in a horrifying climax, he takes a knife to his own portrait. When his servants find him, the picture depicts their youthful master as they had once known him. The corpse next to it is as "withered, wrinkled and loathsome of visage" as the portrait had been. Art and life are back in harmony, as Wilde intended, and his brilliantly allusive moral tale is complete.

When the magazine version of *Dorian Gray* was published, there were howls of protest. Some reviewers declared that, far from exposing immorality, Wilde wanted to promote it. Elsewhere, the story was greeted with outrage by British reviewers, some of whom suggested that Wilde should be prosecuted on moral grounds, leading Wilde to defend his novel in letters to the press. One reviewer for a newspaper which declared that *Lippincott's* should be "ashamed to circulate" such filth, refused to describe the contents of the novel because he did not wish to "advertise the developments of an esoteric prurience".

As well as talk of prosecution, there was a strong hint of Francophobia against the decadent "yellow book" Lord Henry gives Dorian to recruit him to his belief in "Art". The *Daily Chronicle* found the novel to be "a tale spawned from the leprous literature of the French decadents". More dangerous were the attempts of some reviewers to link the novel to the Cleveland Street affair of 1889. This scandal, centred on a male brothel frequented by an upper-class clientele that included members of the British political elite, was an eerie forerunner, in its exposure of the demi-monde, of the Queensberry libel case that would eventually destroy Wilde in 1895.

A Note on the Text:
The Picture of Dorian Gray, was published on 20 June 1890 in the July edition of *Lippincott's*, as a novella of 13 chapters, and was the leading contribution to the magazine. Several British reviewers condemned the book for immorality. The novel became so controversial that WH Smith withdrew that month's edition of *Lippincott's* from its railway station bookstalls.

In fact, the magazine's editors, fearful of charges of "indecency" had already cut some 500 words, without Wilde's knowledge, before publication. Deletions to Wilde's typescript included the elimination of several passages alluding to homosexual desire, and the deletion of three references to Gray's female lovers Sibyl Vane and Hetty Merton as his "mistresses". Wilde, it must be said, conducted himself during this campaign, with impressive dignity and composure.

Later, Wilde himself further revised the story for book publication, making significant alterations, cutting the most controversial passages, adding new chapters, and including a preface that has since become famous in its own right as his defence of art for art's sake. The amended version, extended from 13 to 20 chapters, was published in a single volume by Ward Lock & Co, in April 1891. This is now the standard version of the text.

– 28 –
New Grub Street
by George Gissing (1891)

New Grub Street is the first novel in this series explicitly to address, in a realistic narrative, the contemporary working conditions of a new class, the professional author. George Gissing, born the son of a chemist in 1857, was breaking important new ground, as well as responding to significant cultural change in the literary generation after Dickens (*David Copperfield*) and Thackeray (*Pendennis*).

The eponymous hero of *David Copperfield* is a writer, of course, but Dickens's focus is chiefly on Copperfield's childhood, not his career as a novelist. He never delves as painfully as Gissing does into the threadbare texture of Victorian literary life.

Part of this is due to the social and cultural upheavals inspired by Forster's Education Act of 1870. Gissing's career as a man of letters was the product of this. For the rest of the century, the lives of writers and readers would undergo a profound transformation which would comprehensively reshape the British literary landscape. Henceforth, high and low literary culture would increasingly diverge. This is one of the main themes in John Carey's important critical study *The Intellectuals and the Masses*. It is also the animating idea of *New Grub Street*.

Gissing was hardly alone in finding the role and conduct of the modern writer an urgent topic in late Victorian literary London. A year before *New Grub Street*, Henry James also published a novel, *The Tragic Muse*, about "the conflict between art and 'the world'", though James focused on painting and the stage more than literature. In 2014, in the midst of another paradigm shift, Gissing's subject remains as topical as ever, and addresses timeless themes in the everyday life of the full-time, professional writer.

In *New Grub Street*, the narrative is set in the literary world with which Gissing himself was intimately familiar; the title refers to the London street that, in the age of Samuel Johnson and Laurence Sterne was synonymous with hack writing. By the 1890s, Grub Street no longer existed, though hack writing, of course, never goes away, with timeless imperatives. As one character puts it: "Our Grub Street of today is supplied with telegraphic communications, it knows what literary fare is in demand in every part of the world, its inhabitants are men of business, however seedy."

The novel's protagonists are a contrasted pair of writers: thoughtful Edwin Reardon, a shy "literary" novelist with few commercial prospects; and Jasper Milvain, a hard-driving young journalist who treats his writing as the means to an end in a ruthless literary marketplace. "I speak," he says, "only of good, marketable stuff for the world's vulgar." Reardon will die, unfulfilled, in poverty; Milvain will flourish in literary London ("I write for the upper-middle-class of intellect, the people who like to feel that what they are reading has some special cleverness"), navigate a complicated love life, and eventually marry Reardon's widow, Amy.

New Grub Street is Victorian in its realist depiction of a society in transition, but modern in the way it harks forward to the imminent new century with its portrait of the artist as an existential character making his solitary way in the world. The hero of *Jude the Obscure*, Jude Fawley, a working-class boy who dreams of becoming an Oxford scholar, is Reardon's West Country equivalent.

A Note on the Text:

New Grub Street, a regular "three-decker" novel, was first published in three volumes by Smith, Elder & Co in 1891. There was no serialisation. Gissing already had a modest reputation as a novelist of working-class conflict from books such as *Workers in the Dawn*, *Demos*, *Thyrza* and *The Nether World*, but had not achieved much financial security. In the 1890s, he began to write about middle-class life, with books such as *The Emancipated*, *Born in Exile*, *The Odd Women* and *The Paying Guest*.

In 1890, having completed, and sold the copyright for, *The Emancipated*, Gissing began work on a succession of new novels, none of which prospered in his mind. In April 1890, we find him beginning work on a new manuscript entitled "A Man of Letters", but then becoming distracted by other projects. Finally, in October 1890, he records "a fresh beginning" on a novel now entitled *New Grub Street*, which was swiftly completed in December. The proofs arrived from the publisher in February, and Gissing's masterpiece appeared on 7 April 1891.

Later, for George Orwell whose *Keep the Aspidistra Flying* is a comedy version on a similar theme, he was "perhaps the best novelist England has produced". Orwell argued that Gissing's "real masterpieces" were *The Odd Women*, *Demos* and *New Grub Street*. For Orwell, the central theme of these books is simple: "not enough money". Orwell's interest, as an indigent literary man, is understandable. From a longer perspective, it is *New Grub Street* that establishes Gissing as a writer of importance alongside George Meredith (not included in this series) and Thomas Hardy.

– 29 –
Jude the Obscure
by Thomas Hardy (1895)

The publication of *Jude the Obscure* is both an end and a beginning. In hindsight, it signals the transition to a modern literary sensibility while also painting a picture of a profoundly Victorian rural society. It was another kind of turning-point, too, because Thomas Hardy, shaken by the hostility aroused by the novel dubbed "Jude the Obscene", would never write fiction again. And it was a new beginning because henceforth he would become one of the greatest English poets of the 20th century.

When the novel opens, we seem to be in Hardy's Wessex, the world of *Far From the Madding Crowd* or *Tess of the d'Urbervilles*. But Jude Fawley, who talks to the crows he is supposed to be scaring away, is a modern English boy, with his eye on Christminster (Oxford). He wants an education. With brilliant economy, Hardy opens up three themes: the struggle of the poor and disadvantaged to make their way in a bourgeois world; the tyranny of marriage in the lives of women oppressed by a patriarchal society; and the stranglehold on English life inflicted by an established church, defensively circling its wagons in the aftermath of Darwin's *On the Origin of Species*.

These themes lie below the waterline, but they are perhaps the more menacing for being submerged. As the untutored folkteller of "Wessex", Hardy narrates Jude's tragedy inside-out through a sequence of failed relationships – with Arabella, his wife; with Sue Bridehead, his cousin and true love; and even with himself. The heart of the story will examine the humiliation of Jude's failure as a social animal, a profound and crippling obscurity ending in death.

The strangest and most moving moments in a novel many readers find harrowingly bleak, concern Jude's thwarted love for Sue, their two children perforce born out of wedlock, and the belated appearance in their midst of "Little Father Time", the son that Jude has had with Arabella. Hardy's brilliant portrait of a disturbed teenager tearing a family apart culminates in the famous scene in which, having murdered his half-siblings, the boy hangs himself with the note "Done because we are too menny".

Jude the Obscure is an angry book, and a deeply radical one. To write it, Hardy went further into himself than ever before, exposed his deepest feelings and was creatively wounded by the hostility of the response to what one critic called "the most indecent book ever written".

A Note on the Text:

The text of Hardy's last novel went through at least three stages of evolution, and became every bit as troubled as its subsequent publishing history.

The first version appeared as a serial in *Harper's New Monthly Magazine* from December 1894 to November 1895, under the title "The Simpletons", subsequently altered to "Hearts Insurgent". Many of the changes to a much-edited text were dictated by concerns about public taste, for instance Jude (originally Jack) and Sue Bridehead never become lovers, and Arabella Donn does not seduce Jude.

Next came the first edition in volume form in 1895 published by Osgood, McIlvaine & Co, as part of a complete set of Hardy's fiction, the Wessex novels. This version continued the bowdlerising of all references to sex and religion begun at the serial stage. This first edition would eventually become replaced in 1912 by the third, and now definitive, version of the novel, published by his principal publisher, Macmillan.

That was not the end of the matter. Hardy continued to tinker with the text for the rest of his life. There's a copy in the Dorset County museum which contains many of Hardy's second and third thoughts about the 1912 edition. Plainly the furore aroused by first publication, in which the bishop of Wakefield was said to have burned his copy of the book, affected him deeply.

– 30 –
The Red Badge of Courage
by Stephen Crane (1895)

Stephen Crane, born in Newark, New Jersey in 1871, completed the
 short novel that would become the godfather of all
American war novels, and an inspiration for writers as
diverse as Ernest Hemingway and JD Salinger, while still
in his early 20s. His subject, the war between the States,
had actually ended before he was born, and he never
experienced the horrors of battle. But the laconic realism
of his prose, the fierce investigation of the soldier's psyche, and his
impressionistic use of colour and detail convinced many readers that
Crane was a veteran turned novelist.

Some critics see *The Red Badge of Courage* as a founding text in the
modernist movement, a seminal novel whose influence haunts the
composition of *The Naked and the Dead*, *Catch-22*, *The Thin Red Line*
and *Matterhorn*, among others. Crane, a struggling freelance writer,
researched his subject partly through magazine accounts of the civil
war, a popular subject, and partly through conversations with veterans.
He later said that he "had been unconsciously working the detail of
the story out through most of his boyhood" and had imagined "war
stories ever since he was out of knickerbockers". The idea of a writer
immersing himself in the literary expression of his subject to make a
book for publication, so familiar today, was new in the 1890s, as was
his chosen genre, the war story. At this point he had published, unsuc-
cessfully, at his own expense, just one novel, *Maggie: A Girl of the Streets*
(1893), and was creatively out of sorts.

The Red Badge of Courage is not a conventional historical novel. Its
texture is cinematic; at the same time, breaking the rules, it eschews all
reference to time and place. As the "retiring fog" lifts on the opening
page, an army is revealed "stretched out on the hills, resting". This is
followed by a brilliant passage, surely an inspiration to subsequent
generations of screenwriters: "At night, when the stream had become
of a sorrowful blackness, one could see across it the red, eye-like gleam
of hostile camp fires set in the low brows of distant hills."

Having set the scene, and expanded it with swift economy in a
sequence of short chapters, Crane unfolds his creative purpose: to
get under the skin of a young soldier, the volunteer Henry Fleming,

who has enlisted as a challenge to himself. When fighting breaks out around him, Fleming's courage deserts him. He cannot face the possibility of suffering "a red badge", and flees, before later returning. More manoeuvres and skirmishes follow. Slowly, Fleming overcomes his fear, comes of age, learns to be a soldier and acquires an appetite for battle.

By the end, he has been "an animal blistered and sweating in the heat and pain of war", but he has come through, unscathed, and somehow made whole. "He turned now," Crane concludes, "with a lover's thirst to images of tranquil skies, fresh meadows, cool brooks – an existence of soft and eternal peace."

Possibly this was Crane's own wish-fulfilment. He was already fatally ill with tuberculosis. When this, his second novel, was published, he enjoyed a very brief moment of acclaim, while affecting to disdain his efforts. "I don't think *The Red Badge* to be any great shakes," he said. Crane died in Germany in 1900. After the first world war the novel was rediscovered, and has never been out of print since.

A Note on the Text:
Crane began writing the book that would become *The Red Badge of Courage* (at first it was titled "Private Fleming/His various battles") in June 1893, and submitted the completed manuscript of 55,000 words to the publisher SS McClure, who held it for six months without making a decision. Once Crane had retrieved his still unpublished work he gave it to another publisher, Irving Bacheller, who sold the serial rights to the *Philadelphia Press*. So *The Red Badge of Courage* made its first appearance as a serialisation of just 18,000 words, a version that was quickly reprinted in more than 200 city newspapers and nearly 600 weekly publications, where it was an immediate hit with readers.

The success of the serialisation led to publication in book form by D Appleton in October 1895. This version was 5,000 words shorter than Crane's original; many strange and disfiguring cuts were not restored until the definitive Norton & Co edition of 1982. Here in the UK, William Heinemann launched a British edition in 1896 as part of its Pioneer series. HG Wells, who was a friend of Crane's, noted enviously that *The Red Badge of Courage* was welcomed with "an orgy of praise" in England, which encouraged Crane to settle here in the years before his premature death in 1900. It was a brief moment of happiness for the young man. Crane wrote to a friend: "I have only one pride and that is that the English edition of *The Red Badge of Courage* has been received with great praise by the English reviewers. I am proud of this simply because the remoter people would seem more just and harder to win." Another critic, Harold Frederic, wrote that: "If there were in existence any books of a similar character, one could start confidently by saying that it was the best of its kind. But it has no fellows. It is a book outside of all classification. So unlike anything else is it that the temptation rises to deny that it is a book at all."

– 31 –
Dracula
by Bram Stoker (1897)

At the far end of the 19th century, in the age of Jack the Ripper, and

 80 years after *Frankenstein, Dracula* is a classic of Gothic horror by an Irish contemporary of Oscar Wilde who wrote popular fiction to boost his income. Like Mary Shelley's tale of the supernatural, the vampire tale of *Dracula* – partly derived from John Polidori's *The Vampyre* (1819) and Sheridan Le Fanu's *Carmilla* (1871), about a lesbian vampire – may also have begun with a bad dream. Just as Mary was partly motivated by Byron and her husband, the poet Shelley, so Bram Stoker, the business manager for the Lyceum theatre, was inspired by his devoted service to the great Shakespearean actor Henry Irving. The idea of the vampire as a silver-tongued aristocrat, like Count Dracula, is mirrored in Irving's thespian mannerisms, and his fascination with theatrical villains.

Stoker was very much of his time. He was writing in a sultry fin-de-siècle literary culture obsessed with crime, ghost, and horror stories, all steeped in exotic sensation and jeopardy, from Rider Haggard's *She* (1886) to Stevenson's *The Strange Case of Dr Jekyll and Mr Hyde* (also 1886) to Wilde's *The Picture of Dorian Gray* and *The Island of Dr Moreau* (1897) by H.G. Wells, and possibly including the *Yellow Book* of Aubrey Beardsley. Among the contemporary anxieties reflected in Stoker's tale was a fear about the future. While Victorians celebrated the empire on which the sun would never set with successive jubilees (golden, 1887, and diamond, 1897), many readers fretted over foreign (increasingly German) threats to the harmony of English life. A few years later, this would develop into the vogue for invasion-threat thrillers, notably HG Wells's *The War of the Worlds* (1897) and Erskine Childers's classic, *The Riddle of the Sands* (1903), both of which I have reluctantly had to exclude from a deeper consideration in this series.

Dracula marries many genre archetypes; Stoker followed the example of *Frankenstein* (and also the work of Wilkie Collins), to narrate his story through a collage of diary entries, letters, newspaper cuttings etc. He also placed the story of Jonathan Harker's visit to Transylvania in the present – 1893. The property transaction that Harker is supposed to be negotiating is quickly forgotten once the count has taken his lawyer prisoner. When Harker falls under the spell of the "sisters" (the Brides of Dracula) it seems impossible that he can escape with his life. What, the reader wonders, can happen now ?

In fact, this powerful opening is only the prelude to some increasingly bizarre twists: Dracula's arrival in Britain hidden in a coffin; his sinister pursuit of Harker's fiancee, Mina, and her friend Lucy; the intervention of the celebrated vampire-hunter Professor Abraham van Helsing, and his climactic battle with the count outside Dracula's castle, leading up to the moment when the noble vampire turns to dust. The plot is creaky and Stoker's prose is lurid – often homoerotic – but *Dracula* endures as a classic of popular culture.

Stoker certainly drew on earlier vampire literature, but he was also deeply original, relying on more than seven years' research to complete his story. Thereafter, Transylvania and the Balkans would become the go-to destination for English thriller writers from Ambler to Fleming. Meanwhile, partly thanks to cinema, *Dracula* still retains its hold, though many have scorned it. The critic Maurice Richardson described it as "a kind of incestuous, necrophilious, oral-anal-sadistic all-in wrestling match". What's not to like?

A Note on the Text:
The first edition of *Dracula* appeared in bookshops on 26 May 1897, price six shillings, in a print run (from the publishers Archibald Constable and Co) of some 3,000 copies bound in plain yellow cloth with the one-word title in simple red lettering. This, in fact, was a last-minute amendment. Stoker's working title for the novel in manuscript, until a very few weeks before publication, had been The Un-Dead.

The first reviews of *Dracula* were generally good, though with few hints of the novel's subsequent notoriety. The *Athenaeum*, indeed, declared that "It reads at times like a mere series of grotesquely incredible events." Elsewhere, in the *Daily Mail*, Bram Stoker was rated above both Mary Shelley and Edgar Allan Poe. Arthur Conan Doyle wrote to Stoker to tell him "how very much I have enjoyed reading *Dracula*. I think it is the very best story of diablerie which I have read for many years." *Dracula* now boasts a vast and wide-ranging bibliography which identifies it with many themes – vampire literature, gothic and horror fiction, Victorian sexuality, colonialism and the homoerotic. Bram Stoker's masterpiece has become a mirror in which later generations of readers can explore any number of secret fantasies.

Possibly the most gratifying comment reached the author from his mother in Ireland. Charlotte Stoker told her son that "No book since Mrs Shelley's *Frankenstein* or indeed any other at all has come near yours in originality, or terror…" It was not until much later, when this vampire novel became raw material for successive Hollywood versions (notably the 1931 movie starring Bela Lugosi) that it acquired its reputation as the supreme example of horror fiction.

– 32 –
Heart of Darkness
by Joseph Conrad (1899)

So far, on this list, with the possible exception of *Alice in Wonderland*, *Heart of Darkness* is probably the title that has aroused, and continues to arouse, most literary critical debate, not to say polemic. This is partly because the story it tells has the visceral simplicity of great myth, and also because the book takes its narrator (Charles Marlow, who had already made an appearance in *Lord Jim*), and the reader, on a journey into the heart of Africa.

Our encounter with Marlow's life-changing journey begins on the Thames in London, the great imperial capital, with his recollection of "the uttermost ends of the Earth". With brilliant economy, Conrad transports him to Congo on a quest that the writer himself undertook as a young man. There, working for the shadowy, but all-powerful "Company", Marlow hears of Mr Kurtz, who is described as a first-class Company servant. Once in the dark continent, Marlow is sent upriver to make contact with Kurtz, who is said to be very ill, and also to safeguard the security of the Inner Station. What he finds, after a gruelling journey to the interior, is a fellow European, who may or may not have gone mad, and who is worshipped as a god by the natives of the primitive interior. Kurtz, however, has paid a terrible price for his mastery. When Marlow finds him on his deathbed, he utters the famous and enigmatic last words: "The horror! The horror!"

This line is often said to refer to the atrocities Conrad himself witnessed in Congo as it suffered under the colonial administration of the Belgians. He himself is said to have remarked that his story was based on "experience, pushed a little (and only very little) beyond the actual facts of the case". The metaphorical force of the story and the indifferent contempt of the African who announces "Mistah Kurtz – He dead" (brilliantly expropriated by TS Eliot) gives *Heart of Darkness* the most modern air of all the books that make up the movement called Modernism. Welcome to the 20th century, possibly English and American fiction's golden age.

A Note on the Text:
Conrad's first and second languages were Polish and French, with his third language, English, not acquired until he was 20. English, however, was the medium he adopted to explore his youthful experience as a riverboat captain in Belgian Congo. Part of the work's strange hallucinatory atmosphere comes from the writer's struggle with a language that was not his mother tongue. He sometimes said he would have preferred to be a French novelist, and that English was a language without "clean edges". He once complained that "all English words are instruments for exciting blurred emotions". This, paradoxically, is perhaps what gives the book its famously enigmatic, and ambiguous, atmosphere.

Conrad finished writing *Heart of Darkness* on 9 February 1899. It was originally published as a three-part serialisation in *Blackwood's Magazine* from February to April 1899 (a commission for the 1,000th issue of the magazine), where it was promoted as a nautical tale by a writer whose work was at first (mistakenly) associated with the sea.

Heart of Darkness comes down to us in three other primary texts: a manuscript, a typescript and the final, revised version published in 1902. Not exactly a long story, and certainly not a novella, at barely 38,000 words long, it first appeared in volume form as part of a collection of stories that included "Youth: A Narrative" and "The End of the Tether". It has become Conrad's most famous, controversial and influential work. The English and American writers who fell under its spell include TS Eliot (*The Waste Land*), Graham Greene (*A Burnt-out Case*), George Orwell (*Nineteen-Eighty-Four*) and William Golding (*The Inheritors*). It also inspired the Francis Ford Coppola 1979 film *Apocalypse Now*, a work of homage that continues to renew the contemporary fascination with the text.

None of Conrad's other books have inspired such veneration, especially in America, though some (including me) might want to place *Nostromo* (1904) higher up the pantheon. Critics have endlessly debated it. Chinua Achebe denounced it, in a famous 1975 lecture, as the work of "a bloody racist". Among the novels in this series, few novels occupy such an unassailable place on the list. It is a haunting, hypnotic masterpiece by a great writer who towers over the literature of the 20th century.

– 33 –
Sister Carrie
by Theodore Dreiser (1900)

With no British equivalent, *Sister Carrie* is one of several novels in this series that address the American dream, and it does so in a radical spirit of naturalism that rejected the Victorian emphasis on morality. In some ways it's crude and heavy-handed, blazing with coarse indignation, but in its day it was, creatively speaking, a pioneer. Later, America's first Nobel laureate, Sinclair Lewis, said that Dreiser's powerful first novel "came to housebound and airless America like a great free Western wind, and to our stuffy domesticity gave us the first fresh air since Mark Twain and Whitman".

I will be the first to concede that Dreiser does not now look anything like their equal. He is no stylist, and yet the raw power of his narrative trumps the sometimes excruciating clunk of his prose. Saul Bellow, for instance, advised readers to take *Sister Carrie* at a gallop. There's no question Dreiser paints an intensely detailed, compelling and closely observed portrait of urban America at the turn of the 20th century – a century in which the US would play such a decisive part.

The novel opens with Caroline – Sister Carrie – Meeber moving from the country to the city, taking the train to Chicago to realise her hopes for a better, more glamorous future. En route, she meets a travelling salesman, Charles Drouet, who soon releases her from the drudgery of machine-work in the heartless city by making her his mistress. This is the first in a succession of Carrie's fruitless attempts to find happiness. Henceforth, she becomes the victim of increasingly desperate relationships which, combined with a starstruck fascination with the stage, take her to New York and the life of a Broadway chorus girl. The novel ends with Carrie changing her name to Carrie Madenda and becoming a star just as her estranged husband, George Hurstwood, gasses himself in rented lodgings. The closing chapters of the book, in which Hurstwood is ruined and then disgraced, are among the most powerful pages in a novel of merciless momentum, whose unsentimental depiction of big-city life sets it apart. Contemporary readers were baffled, however, and *Sister Carrie* did not sell well.

"The critics have not really understood what I was trying to do," Dreiser said later. "Here is a book that is close to life. It is intended not as a piece of literary craftsmanship, but as a picture of conditions done as simply and effectively as the English language will permit … It makes one feel that American criticism is the joke which English literary authorities maintain it to be. When [the novel] gets to the people, they will understand, because it is a story of real life, of their lives."

A Note on the Text:

Until the 1980s, the text of *Sister Carrie* was invariably based on the first Doubleday, Page edition of 1900 – a text that Dreiser himself amended only once, in 1907. But in 1981, the so-called "Pennsylvania edition" (Philadelphia: University of Pennsylvania Press) reverted to Dreiser's handwritten first draft, now held in the New York Public Library, and substituted his uncut holograph version as the scholarly text of the novel. This decision was challenged by a number of reviewers, introducing another level of controversy to a book whose publication history was dogged by trouble from the start. For this series, I have based my reading on the paperback Norton Critical edition (edited by Donald Pizer), which seems now to be accepted as the most reliable text – not least because it addresses in fascinating detail the furore surrounding the first printing of *Sister Carrie*, as well as illustrating the variations between Dreiser's first draft and the 1900 edition. This, for newcomers to Dreiser, is possibly the most interesting aspect of the novel's history, and runs (in summary) as follows:

Dreiser began *Sister Carrie* (occasionally titled "The Flesh and the Spirit" during its composition) at the suggestion of his friend Arthur Henry in 1899. Although he finished it on 29 March 1900, he was always dissatisfied with his work, and began to make revisions even as it was being submitted to New York publishers. At first, he offered it to Harper & Brothers (who "rejected it with a sharp slap"), and then to Doubleday, Page. This was a new imprint whose in-house reader, Frank Norris, was a published novelist whom Dreiser admired. Initially, it was Norris's enthusiasm that persuaded Doubleday to accept *Sister Carrie*. Then, possibly because Frank Doubleday's wife found the story repugnant and the text too sexually explicit, the firm turned it down. A row ensued in which Dreiser – who was always a combative character, at odds with the world – insisted on publication, standing on his legal rights, egged on by Arthur Henry. At one extraordinary moment, trying to get out of the contract, Frank Doubleday actually volunteered to offer the book to some of his rivals, including Macmillan and Lippincott. But Dreiser was adamant. He had a contract, and he would not be dissuaded.

Like any publisher bullied by one of their authors, Doubleday, Page did not launch *Sister Carrie* with much enthusiasm. It finally appeared on 8 November 1900 in an edition of 1,008 copies, of which 129 were sent out for review and 465 were actually sold. The balance of 423 copies was later turned over to a remainder house. Dreiser, mythologising his debut, subsequently claimed that Doubleday had effectively suppressed his first novel. The record shows, however, that it was well and widely reviewed, and appeared in Britain in 1901 from William Heinemann. In London, the *Daily Express* wrote of *Sister Carrie*: "It is a cruel, merciless story, intensely clever in its realism, and one that will remain impressed in the memory of the reader for many a long day." In America, the great critic HL Mencken referred to Dreiser as "a man of large originality, of profound feeling, and of unshakable courage".

– 34 –
Kim
by Rudyard Kipling (1901)

Kim, Kipling's extraordinarily topical masterpiece, has one of the most brilliant openings in this series: "He sat, in defiance of municipal orders, astride the gun Zam-Zammah on her brick platform opposite the old Ajaib-Ghar – the Wonder Horse, as the natives call the Lahore museum. Who hold Zam-Zammah, that 'fire-breathing dragon', hold the Punjab, for the great green-bronze piece is always first of the conqueror's loot."

"He" is Kimball O'Hara ("Kim"), an imperial orphan scavenging a hand-to-mouth existence in the India of the British Raj at the end of the 19th century. The "Great Game" (Anglo-Russian rivalry in central Asia, including the territory now known as AfPak), is afoot, with memories of the second Anglo-Afghan war (1878-81) still vivid. Some passages of the novel, indeed, could almost have been written last year. Kipling's Kim is so untamed and sunburned that very few see him as white, or even know that his father was a sergeant in the Mavericks and that his mother was a poor Irish girl carried off by cholera. So Kim represents the meeting of east and west, one of Kipling's obsessions, whose ethnic duality will be exploited in the covert war between Britain and Russia that provides the backdrop to this novel.

Kim, therefore, engages the reader at three contrasting levels. It fictionalises Kipling's own Indian childhood (his father, John Lockwood Kipling, was actually the curator of the Lahore museum, already described). Second, it tells an adventure story of the kind that became especially popular in the heyday of the British Empire (see also the popular works of GA Henty, not selected for this series). Finally, and most importantly, it unfolds a boy's own story in which, through the trials of the Great Game, Kim will be given greater insight into his divided east-west inheritance. The key to this strand of the novel, which shadows a thrillerish spy story, is Kim's friendship with an ancient Tibetan lama who is on a quest to find the sacred and fabled "River of the Arrow". Kim becomes his guru's "chela" or disciple, and joins him on his journey while at the same time pursuing a public-school education sponsored by the lama. In the end, Kim must make his choice. "I am not a Sahib," he tells his guru, "I am thy chela." He might play "King of the Castle" on a great British cannon, but he knows where his loyalties lie.

A Note on the Text:
Coming at the very end of Queen Victoria's reign, *Kim* marks the last gasp of a publishing tradition that was on the point of extinction. It appeared first in serial form in *McClure's Magazine* from December 1900 to October 1901, and also – because Kipling was so hugely popular and famous – in *Cassell's Magazine* from January to November 1901. Then it was published in single volume form by Macmillan & Co, with illustrations by HR Millar. Kim regularly appears on lists of classic fiction: in 1998, appearing as No 78 in the Modern Library list of the 100 best English-language novels of the 20th century; in 2003 it featured in the BBC's "Big Read" poll.

– 35 –
The Call of the Wild
by Jack London (1903)

The Call of the Wild, a short adventure novel about a sled dog named Buck (a cross between a St Bernard and a Scotch collie) will be one of the strangest, and most strangely potent, narratives in this series.

Its author was a one-off, too. Jack London was a maverick, macho young man, the son of an itinerant astrologer and a spiritualist mother. As a boy, he led a criminal life, specialising in the piracy of oysters in San Francisco Bay. As a writer, he blazed briefly, lived hard and dangerously, and died from drink and drugs aged just 40, having written more than 50 books in 20 years.

London is the archetype of the American writer as primeval hero, the forerunner of Hemingway, Dos Passos, Kerouac and possibly Hunter S Thompson. To George Orwell, he was "an adventurer and a man of action as few writers have ever been". A devotee of Kipling's *Jungle Book*, London found his literary voice writing about a dog that learns to live at the limit of civilisation. He was inspired to embark on his dog story as a means to explore what he saw as the essence of human nature in response to a wave of calls to American youth urging a new start for the turn-of-the-century generation. London's mythical creature became his answer to the complex challenges of modernity.

The reader discovers Buck, a domesticated prize dog, as the effete pet of a Californian judge. When he is stolen by his master's gardener to settle some gambling debts, Buck passes through a sequence of owners representing the highs and lows of humanity. Sold into a kind of canine slavery as an Alaskan sled dog, Buck ends up in the Yukon of the 1890s Klondike gold rush, a milieu familiar to the writer. Eventually, he becomes the property of a salt-of-the-earth outdoorsman named John Thornton who recognises Buck's qualities and with whom the dog enjoys a deep, and affecting rapport.

Among many adventures, in extremis, Buck saves Thornton from drowning, but when his master is killed by Yeehat Indians, he gives in to his true nature, answers the call of the wild and joins a wolf pack: "Man, and the claims of man, no longer bound him." Here, London is not just writing about dogs. He is expressing his belief, which owes something to Rousseau, that humanity is always in a state of conflict, and that the struggles of existence strengthen man's nature.

London's chapter titles – "Into the Primitive", "The Law of Club and Fang" and "The Dominant Primordial Beast" – might appear to set London's literary agenda. But what projects *The Call of the Wild* towards immortality is London's urgent and vivid style, and his astonishing identification with the world he's describing. His capacity to involve his readers in his story, regardless of literary subtlety, is what many generations of American writers became inspired by. For this alone, he deserves to be remembered.

A Note on the Text:
The Call of the Wild was first serialised in the *Saturday Evening Post* in the summer of 1903 and was an instant hit. Jack London had already sold the rights to the novel outright for $2,000 because he wanted to buy an old sloop for sailing. Accordingly, the story was first published as a volume in America by Macmillan and Company whose editor, George Brett, played a crucial role in London's success as a writer.

London achieved overnight acclaim. Inevitably, there was envy. A forgotten writer named Egerton Ryerson Young claimed that London had plagiarised his 1902 book, *My Dogs in the Northland*. London acknowledged the influence and deflected the charge, saying he had already corresponded with Young on the subject.

HL Mencken, a most perceptive critic, wrote: "No other popular writer of his time did any better writing than you will find in *The Call of the Wild*... Here, indeed, are all the elements of sound fiction: clear thinking, a sense of character, the dramatic instinct, and, above all, the adept putting together of words – words charming and slyly significant, words arranged, in a French phrase, for the respiration and the ear."

– 36 –
The Golden Bowl
by Henry James (1904)

There's an old joke (which only makes complete sense in Britain) that there are three, not one, manifestations of Henry James: James the First (*The Portrait of a Lady*); James the Second (*The Turn of the Screw*); and the Old Pretender (*The Wings of the Dove*; *The Golden Bowl*).

As we approach another giant in this series – for some, the only American writer of greater significance than Mark Twain or F Scott Fitzgerald – I've chosen to skip James I and II, and settle on late James, the Old Pretender, and his masterpiece, *The Golden Bowl*, a novel that takes its title from Ecclesiastes 12:6-7 ("Or ever the silver cord be loosed, or the golden bowl be broken, or the pitcher be broken at the fountain, or the wheel broken at the cistern... then shall the dust return to the earth as it was...").

I've made this choice for three reasons. First, because it addresses James's essential theme, the meeting of two great cultures, English and American, and mixes it with the sinister menace of his middle period. Second, because the novel is so intensely (maddeningly, some would say) Jamesian, often hovering between the difficult and the incomprehensible. And finally, because his last novel places him where he belongs, at the very beginning of the 20th century.

The Golden Bowl opens with Prince Amerigo, a charming Italian nobleman of reduced means, coming to London for his marriage to Maggie Verver, the only child of the wealthy widower Adam Verver, an American financier and art connoisseur.

The plot then reprises a Henry James short story of 1891 ("The Marriages"), in which a father and daughter become hopelessly caught up in "a mutual passion, an intrigue", a complex tale of treachery and betrayal made more complex by the fact that James, who suffered acutely from writer's cramp, dictated it to a typist every morning over a period of 13 months. Not since the blind John Milton dictated chunks of *Paradise Lost* to his daughters has a prominent writer expressed so much of his vision through the medium of the spoken word.

Each reader will take something different from this amazing, labyrinthine, terrifying and often claustrophobic narrative. For me, the dominant theme – very close to James's heart – is the story of Maggie Verver's education, both literal and emotional, and her subtle resolution of an impossible and perhaps dreadful situation. At the end, Maggie has saved her marriage, and her father prepares to return to America, leaving his daughter older, wiser and (apparently) reconciled to her husband. American literature contains nothing else quite like *The Golden Bowl.*

A Note on the Text:
The Golden Bowl is one of the first truly 20th century novels: it was never serialised, but first published in New York in December 1904 by Charles Scribner's Sons in two volumes, and then in London in February 1905 by Methuen in a one-volume edition. In 1909, a revised text appeared as volumes 23 and 24 of the New York edition, together with one of James's magisterial prefaces in which, with sometimes tortuous circumlocution, he reflected on the art of fiction as he understood it. Many years before, in *The Art of Fiction*, a brilliant, almost polemical declaration on behalf of the novel as an art form, he had written "A novel is a living thing, all one and continuous, like every other organism, and in proportion as it lives will it be found, I think, that in each of the parts there is something of each of the other parts." *The Golden Bowl* supremely exemplifies this claim, providing a literary texture of staggering complexity and richness.

– 37 –
Hadrian the Seventh
by Frederick Rolfe (1904)

Frederick Rolfe, who also styled himself "Baron Corvo" (and sometimes gave his full name as Frederick William Serafino Austin Lewis Mary Rolfe), is one of the strangest fish in the exotic aquarium of Edwardian literature. His masterpiece, *Hadrian the Seventh*, is both a book of its epoch – orchidaceous, eccentric and weirdly obsessive, some would say mad – as well as being, in DH Lawrence's summary, "the book of a man-demon".

Rolfe (pronounced "roaf") was born in London in 1860, the son of a piano manufacturer. He grew up, a homosexual with paedophile instincts, in the hot-house cultural climate that nurtured many late-Victorian literary men, notably Oscar Wilde and the Aubrey Beardsley of *The Yellow Book*, as well as Edwardians such as HH Munro ("Saki") and Max Beerbohm.

For 10 years, Rolfe was a provincial schoolmaster and would-be Roman Catholic priest. His conversion to Rome in 1886 proved abortive and frustrating. His awkward personality and angry tongue blighted his adult life and led to his dismissal from the priesthood not once but twice. Thereafter, he drifted into a hand-to-mouth career as journalist, painter and photographer.

At the age of 40 he began to write seriously, living in near-penury for years while sustaining an eccentric lifestyle, wearing silver spectacles and glycerine gloves (in bed), while writing with a "magic" glass egg on his desk, and chain-smoking like a devil. Quarrelling with almost everyone, Rolfe ended up, in extremis, living on an open gondola in Venice, as he put it, "homeless and often starving... only keeping alive from fear of crabs and rats".

Hadrian the Seventh, Rolfe's first novel (sometimes attributed to the pseudonym Baron Corvo), is a "romance" that reflects its author's life and work. It tells the story of George Arthur Rose, a hack writer and minor priest, who, through bizarre but semi-plausible ecclesiastical vicissitudes, becomes elected Pope. "The previous English pontiff," he declares, "was Hadrian the Fourth. The present English pontiff is Hadrian the Seventh. It pleases us; and so, by Our own impulse, We command."

The new pope embarks on a programme of reform, but Hadrian's one-year reign comes to an end when he is assassinated by a pope-hating Scot, prefiguring the 1981 attempt on the life of Pope John Paul II.

The air of contrivance that permeates this entertaining fantasy extends to Rolfe's highly artificial vocabulary, which reminds me of Will Self's vivid verbal extravagance, in its use of words such as "snarp", "diaphotick", "noluntary", "tolutiloquent", "purrothrixine", "xanthine", and on the opening page "prooimion".

Rolfe's pope is as cussed, rococo and autodidactic as his author, praying in Greek, dabbling in astrology and smoking in office. He's described, at his death, as "an incomprehensible creature", and Rolfe concludes with a line that might be his own epitaph: "Pray for the repose of His soul. He was so tired."

Frederick Rolfe died suddenly in Venice on 25 October 1913.

A Note on the Text:
Hadrian the Seventh was published in London by Chatto & Windus in 1904. (The first American edition appeared from Knopf in 1925.) The title page declared the book to be written by Fr. Rolfe, an abbreviation of the author's name that suggested he was a Roman Catholic priest.

This strange novel and even stranger author might have been forgotten but for the brilliant intervention of AJA Symons, whose "experiment in biography", *Quest For Corvo* (1934), helped to secure Rolfe's reputation. Corvo/Rolfe's severe creative paranoia was subsequently portrayed in *The Unspeakable Skipton* (1959), a novel by Pamela Hansford Johnson, and in 1968 in Peter Luke's hit stage play *Hadrian VII*, starring Alec McCowen. The theme of the starving writer finding authenticity in the forced asceticism of the garret is a sub-theme in this series. It also recurs in the work of George Orwell, notably in *Keep the Aspidistra Flying*, whose hero, Gordon Comstock, could have stepped from the pages of Rolfe's fiction, no questions asked.

– 38 –
The Wind in the Willows
by Kenneth Grahame (1908)

The Wind in the Willows, known to many readers through theatrical adaptations such as *Toad of Toad Hall*, belongs to a select group of English classics whose characters (Rat, Mole, Badger and Mr Toad) and their catchphrases ("messing about in boats"; "poop, poop!") require no introduction. Endlessly recycled, in print, cartoon and cinema, the ideas and images of Kenneth Grahame's masterpiece recur in the most unlikely places. Chapter seven, "The Piper at the Gates of Dawn", is also the name of Pink Floyd's first album in 1967.

A sentimental British favourite, *The Wind in the Willows* is a far more interesting book than its popular and often juvenile audience might suggest. First, it is the work of a writer who had known considerable success in the 1890s as a young contemporary of Oscar Wilde, and who was also an admired contributor to the literary quarterly *The Yellow Book*. At that point, Grahame was employed by the Bank of England but, still in his 20s, was publishing stories in literary magazines, work that became collected in *Dream Days* (1895) and an even more successful publication, *The Golden Age* (1898).

The text of *The Wind in the Willows* also encrypts a family tragedy. In 1899, Grahame married and had one child, a boy named Alastair who was troubled with health problems and a difficult personality, culminating in the boy's eventual suicide, the cause of much parental anguish. When Grahame retired from the Bank (as secretary) in 1908, he could concentrate on the stories he had been telling his son, the stories of the Thames riverbank on which Grahame himself had grown up. So *The Wind in the Willows* is a tale steeped in nostalgia, and inspired by a father's obsessive love for his only son.

Within the text, the reader discovers two tales, interwoven. There are, famously, the adventures of Mole, Ratty, Badger and Toad with the canary-coloured caravan, the succession of motor cars, and the climactic battle for Toad Hall. At the same time, there are Grahame's lyrical explorations of home life ("Dulce Domum"), river life ("Wayfarers All") and childhood itself ("The Piper at the Gates of Dawn"). In most theatrical adaptations of Grahame's book, these lyrical elements are ruthlessly subordinated to the demands of the plot.

Above all, *The Wind in the Willows* makes a powerful contribution to the mythology of Edwardian England not only through its evocation of the turning seasons of the English countryside, from the riverbank in summer to the rolling open road, but also through its hints of an imminent class struggle from the inhabitants (stoats and weasels) of the Wild Wood.

Like the other books for children selected for this series – notably *Alice's Adventures in Wonderland* and *Kim* – *The Wind in the Willows* deserves recognition as a novel in which adult readers will find wisdom, humour, entertainment and meaning, as well as many passages of great literary power, together with characters who live on in the English literary unconscious.

A Note on the Text:

The Wind in the Willows began as bedtime stories and letters addressed to Grahame's troubled son, a sickly boy known as "Mouse" who possibly inspired the wilful character of Mr Toad and who eventually committed suicide, aged 20, while at Oxford. Indeed, so personal were these stories that Grahame never intended to publish his material. The manuscript was first given to an American publisher, who rejected it. After the publication of *The Wind in the Willows* by Methuen in 1908, it found an unlikely transatlantic fan in US president Theodore Roosevelt who, in 1909, wrote to Grahame to tell him that he had "read it and reread it, and have come to accept the characters as old friends". Elsewhere, the critical response was more mixed, and it was not until AA Milne adapted parts of the book into a popular stage version, *Toad of Toad Hall*, in 1929, that it became established as the evergreen children's classic it is known as today.

– 39 –
The History of Mr Polly
by HG Wells (1910)

HG Wells is often catalogued as a pioneer of science fiction (which he was) with bestselling books like *The Invisible Man* and *The First Men in the Moon*. But he was also a great Edwardian writer of immense fame and influence who deserves to be remembered as a major literary figure, now somewhat eclipsed in the posterity stakes.

But which of his 50 novels to choose? *The Sleeper Awakes* (a far-sighted portrait of a world enslaved by money and machines)? *Love and Mr Lewisham* (the tale of a schoolteacher who becomes a socialist but subordinates politics to family life)? *Tono-Bungay* (a brilliant satire on advertising and the popular press)? *Kipps* (a Dickensian comedy about one ordinary man's struggle for self-improvement)?

Wells's fans will have their favourites. But I have chosen *The History of Mr Polly*, a novel from Wells's early middle age (he wrote it when he was 44), a delightful comedy of everyday Edwardian England that draws inspiration from its author's own life. Moreover, as Wells put it in the preface to "the Atlantic Edition" of 1924, "a small but influential group of critics maintain that *The History of Mr Polly* is the writer's best book". If he could not quite accept that, he said, he would still concede that "certainly it is his happiest book, and the one he cares for most".

I've always liked it (I've never been much of a sci-fi enthusiast) because it is, in many ways, so un-Wellsian. The story – still strikingly modern – is a comedy about a midlife crisis. Alfred Polly has a routine job as a gentlemen's outfitter in the small, provincial town of Fishbourne, a location widely agreed to be modelled on Sandgate in Kent, where Wells himself lived for several years. The tone is established at the outset: "He hated Fishbourne, he hated his shop and his wife and his neighbours. But most of all Mr Polly hated himself".

When he becomes threatened with bankruptcy, Mr Polly decides that the only way to liberate himself from his hateful predicament is to burn down his shop and commit suicide. But he makes a hash of his "bit of arson" and cannot find the courage to cut his throat with a razor. So then, acknowledging that "Fishbourne wasn't the world",

Mr Polly takes off "on the tramp" and walks himself into a better future through what he calls his "exploratious menanderings".

For me, there are three elements to *The History of Mr Polly* that unite to give the book an enduring appeal, and to place it at the top of Wells's extraordinary output. First, Wells's picture of Mr Polly – an ironic self-portrait – is deliciously appealing. In the literary tradition of Mrs Malaprop, and many minor Dickens characters, Mr Polly has an "innate sense of epithet" that inspires a teeming vocabulary: "intrudacious", "jawbacious" and "retrospectatiousness".

Second, Mr Polly (who could have stepped from the pages of Dickens) is a "little man" of a kind typical of late Victorian and Edwardian England, a man painfully, even doggedly, liberating himself from an oppressive class-ridden society. The debt to Dickens is unequivocal. Alfred Polly is descended from Joe Gargery, Bob Cratchit and Mr Wemmick. He's also related, as it were, to Mr Pooter, is contemporary with EM Forster's Leonard Bast, and will subsequently inspire many Kingsley Amis protagonists, as well as Billy Liar.

Finally, *The History of Mr Polly* is a comedy of ordinary, provincial life, rooted in the everyday, with countless brilliantly observed details. In part of the long flashback that composes the middle part of Mr Polly's "history", there's a hilarious wedding which commits him to Miriam, an event that inspires one of Wells's best lines: "He had a curious feeling that it would be very satisfying to marry and have a wife – only somehow he wished it wasn't Miriam."

In later life, Wells became one of Britain's most famous writers, courted by US presidents, and rarely out of one political scrape or another. His meeting with Lenin (1920) and his interview with Stalin (1934) made world news. By the end of his long life, Wells had published 150 books and pamphlets, including 50 works of fiction. In this bibliography *The History of Mr Polly* has a special charm as a novel in which, for once, Wells became carefree and relaxed, and described the thing he could never find for himself – peace of mind.

A Note on the Text:
HG Wells wrote *The History of Mr Polly* in 1909, simultaneously with the completion and publication of his novel *Ann Veronica*, and published it, with Thomas Nelson, in 1910, while an American edition was published by Duffield & Co. In both these first editions there were some small, but significant, errors which were subsequently corrected.

Mr Polly's age, on first mention, is given as 35 but later as 37. In the US edition chapter 5, "Mr Polly takes a Vacation", replaces the original "Romance". And so on. Today, the MS for *The History of Mr Polly* is held in the HG Wells archive at the University of Illinois at Urbana-Champaign.

– 40 –
Zuleika Dobson
by Max Beerbohm (1911)

Zuleika Dobson is a brilliant Edwardian satire on Oxford life by one of English literature's most glittering wits that now reads as something much darker and more compelling. Readers new to Max Beerbohm's masterpiece, which is subtitled *An Oxford Love Story*, will find a diaphanous novel possessed of a delayed explosive charge that detonates today with surprising power.

Zuleika, the granddaughter of the warden of Judas College, is a female sleight-of-hand magician, a "prestidigitator", renowned from New York to St Petersburg. She is also a femme fatale, a turn-of-the-century It girl and a minor celebrity. This fascinating young woman of extraordinary beauty arrives in Oxford, a privileged all-male academic society, and immediately devastates the student body, becoming first its icon and then its nemesis. Having fallen in love with Zuleika, the undergraduates, happy to die for what can never be theirs, plunge en masse into the Isis shouting "Zuleika" (this, instructs Beerbohm, is "pronounced Zu-lee-ka not Zu-like-a").

But that is not the whole story. The Duke of Dorset, an absurdly accomplished peer – "He was fluent in all modern languages, had a very real talent in watercolour, and was accounted, by those who had had the privilege of hearing him, the best amateur pianist on this side of the Tweed" – and emotionally backward golden youth, has fallen in love with her, and she with him. But since Zuleika cannot commit to anyone remotely responsive to her charms, she rejects him, whereupon he too commits suicide, in full Garter regalia.

This middle part of the novel, narrated as the fantasy of Clio, muse of history, gives the book an experimental flavour that it soon abandons in favour of high comedy. Once Oxford's undergraduates are extinct, Zuleika has few options. The novel ends with her ordering a special train – bound for Cambridge.

Beerbohm was a friend and admirer of Oscar Wilde. The scintillating heartlessness of this novel is deeply Wildean in its instincts. His celebrated line "Death cancels all engagements" is pure Wilde, and Zuleika herself – selfish, vain and capricious – is a fictional cousin to *Dorian Gray*. Beerbohm's text, indeed, provides a satirical commentary on the aesthetic movement of the 1880s and 1890s, and continued to reverberate throughout the dark decade following publication. Its influence on the early novels of Evelyn Waugh, and possibly the *Mayfair* stories of PG Wodehouse, is unmistakable. Possibly, too, "the Incomparable Max", as George Bernard Shaw called him, was also looking back to *Vanity Fair* and to Becky Sharp, another self-willed minx-cum-monster.

Several critics have noticed that Beerbohm's hilarious fantasy about the untimely slaughter of a generation of young men spookily prefigures the carnage that would soon break out on the fields of France. That is, I think, to mistake the essence of Beerbohm's wit. He was a *farceur*, not a seer. His novel was intended to divert, not educate. *Zuleika Dobson* is the finest, and darkest, kind of satire: as intoxicating as champagne, as addictive as morphine, and as lethal as prussic acid. Rarely has a minor book by a minor writer made such a claim on posterity.

A Note on the Text:
Zuleika Dobson was published in 1911 by William Heinemann, and quickly acquired some influential admirers. Virginia Woolf wrote: "Mr Beerbohm in his way is perfect… He is without doubt the prince of his profession." Another Edwardian, EM Forster, declared: "*Zuleika Dobson* is a highly accomplished and superbly written book whose spirit is farcical. It is a great work – the most consistent achievement of fantasy in our time… So funny and charming, so iridescent and yet so profound." Later, Evelyn Waugh echoed these verdicts, writing: "Beerbohm was a genius of the purest kind. He stands at the summit of his art."

As a footnote, I must mention *Zuleika in Cambridge* by SC Roberts, a parody. Fittingly, the students at the more cerebral, hearty and less romantic university pay her no attention, never give suicide a second thought, and send her on her way – rejected, and possibly even humiliated.

– 41 –
The Good Soldier
by Ford Madox Ford (1915)

The Good Soldier was conceived by Ford Madox Ford as the summation of his career as an admired and influential Edwardian novelist, his "last book", and a middle-aged writer's traditional riposte to the literary Cubists, Vorticists and Imagists of the day. In fact, it far outlives those heady innovators and stands at the entrance to 20th century fiction as a dark, spellbinding puzzle, a novel of perennially enthralling and mysterious depths whose influence lingers like gun-smoke after a shooting.

The "good soldier" of the title is the retired Indian army veteran Captain Edward Ashburnham, who, with his wife Leonora, forms an apparently normal friendship with two Americans, John and Florence Dowell, at the German spa town of Nauheim, where, in August 1913, all four have gone for a cure.

The apparent perfection of these two marriages quickly unravels. Dowell's steady unfolding of this "saddest story", in a series of flashbacks, exposes not only his wife's infidelity with "the good soldier" but also his own blind folly in not recognising the truth about his empty and loveless marriage.

The first part of Dowell's narration reaches its terrible climax with his wife Florence's suicide over her lover's betrayal. But here, where a more conventional novelist might have explored some of the nuances in the triangular relationship of the survivors – the Captain, Leonora and Dowell, their friend – Ford plunges into the terrible abyss of "the good soldier's" relations with his wife, his many affairs, and his shameful infatuation with his young ward, Nancy, a tormented affair that culminates in Ashburnham's suicide.

At the end, two marriages are in ruins, Nancy has gone mad, and Dowell, looking back in desolation, is alone with the dreadful memory of that perfect English gentleman, Edward Ashburnham, whose fatal flaw was his desperate and ruthless pursuit of love. Subtitled "A Tale of Passion", *The Good Soldier* is also an extraordinary story of broken hearts and betrayal.

A Note on the Text:

Ford's masterpiece, published as a single volume in March 1915 by John Lane of The Bodley Head, was originally entitled *The Saddest Story*, inspired by its famous first line: "This is the saddest story I have ever heard." This was Ford's dominant motif. An earlier version of the novel's opening section had already appeared in *Blast*, on 20 June 1914, as "The Saddest Story". However, in the depths of the Great War, Ford's publisher was concerned that such a title would render the book unsaleable, and begged him to change it. The author, having enlisted in the army, was otherwise engaged, and inattentive to these concerns. "One day, when I was on parade," Ford later wrote, "I received a final wire of appeal from Mr Lane, and the telegraph being reply-paid I seized the reply form and wrote in hasty irony: 'Dear Lane, Why not *The Good Soldier*?'"

Six months later the book appeared under that title, subtitled "A Tale of Passion". Ford says he was horrified, but it was too late.

Ford's insouciance about the title is odd, because not only did he regard it as "my best book", he had also invested so much of himself in its composition. Previously, he wrote, "I had never really tried to put into any novel of mine all that I knew about writing." This one would be different. "On the day I was 40," he writes, "I sat down to show what I could do – and *The Good Soldier* resulted."

Actually, he did not sit down: he walked up and down the offices of his magazine, *The English Review*, dictating what he imagined would be his swansong. "I fully intended it to be my last book," he said. There was a new generation – Ezra Pound, TS Eliot, Wyndham Lewis and many others – coming to prominence. Ford felt *The Good Soldier* to be like a member of "a race that will have no successors".

He was wrong, of course. A succession of writers, from Graham Greene to Kazuo Ishiguro, have found things to admire here, and to venerate. A masterclass in the tale of the "unreliable narrator", it remains an evergreen English classic about an "English gentleman" and the "black and merciless things" concealed behind that label. *The Good Soldier* is a novel with an extraordinary afterlife, a text that repays every re-reading with significant new insights.

– 42 –
The Thirty-Nine Steps
by John Buchan (1915)

When 39-year-old John Buchan, recuperating from a duodenal ulcer, turned to writing (in a matter of weeks) a "shocker" or "dime novel" in the first months of the first world war, he was already the admired author of more than 10 works of fiction and spoken of in literary circles as a name to watch. Indeed, Buchan might quite plausibly have become a great Scots novelist following in the footsteps of Walter Scott and RL Stevenson. Instead, with ideal timing, he wrote another kind of classic, *The Thirty-Nine Steps*, an archetypal English spy thriller.

Long before the outbreak of war, the English reading public had become gripped by invasion fever. This was a volatile cocktail of jingoism and xenophobia inspired by the Anglo-German naval arms race and stoked by bestsellers such as *The Great War in England in 1897* by William Le Queux and the infinitely greater 1903 classic *The Riddle of the Sands* by Erskine Childers.

Buchan, who worked for the British War Propaganda Bureau, was well-versed in this Edwardian genre and the outbreak of war across the Channel became the perfect inspiration for a topical and thrilling tale of acute jeopardy involving British secrets, German spies and the sinister plotting of the Black Stone gang, a conspiracy hellbent on fomenting a vicious global conflict.

So far, so (fairly) conventional. Buchan's contribution to this "dime novel" scenario was to create in his protagonist, Richard Hannay, an appealing antihero, both cool and brave, but also "pretty well disgusted with life" who, caught up in a high-octane international drama, has the resource, intelligence and daring to thwart a naked foreign attempt to drag Britain into war.

Hannay, who would feature in four more subsequent Buchan thrillers, is a mix of sleuth and action man, a cross between Sherlock Holmes and James Bond. His creator was obviously influenced by Conan Doyle and would, in turn, later influence Graham Greene and Ian Fleming.

Buchan's other great contribution to this genre, which also owes something to *Kidnapped* was to refine the "man on the run" yarn into a page-turning adventure. He knew exactly what he was doing, describing a "romance where the incidents defy the probabilities, and march just inside the border of the possible". None of this would have amounted to a hill of beans without Buchan's brisk characterisation, loving evocation of Scottish landscape and his switchblade prose. This is lethal, spare, clean and contemporary. When Hannay returns to his London flat after dinner in clubland, the reader can hardly escape the grip of Buchan's brilliant narration: "I snapped the switch, but there was nobody there. Then I saw something in the far corner which made me drop my cigar and fall into a cold sweat." Now read on.

A Note on the Text:
The Thirty-Nine Steps, a brilliantly teasing and memorable title, was first published as a serial adventure story in *Blackwood's Magazine* from August to September 1915, appearing in book form that same October from the Scots publisher, William Blackwood & Sons, Edinburgh.

The book has never been out of print and has inspired many film and television adaptations: Alfred Hitchcock's liberty-taking 1935 version, starring Robert Donat and Madeleine Carroll, a female character absent from the novel; a 1959 colour remake; a 1978 version, with Robert Powell as Hannay, that sticks rather more faithfully to Buchan's text than Hitchcock; and finally a 2008 British television version, starring Rupert Penry-Jones. There's also a long-running West End spoof abridgement, indicating the novel's enduring appeal.

– 43 –
The Rainbow
by DH Lawrence (1915)

Which Lawrence to choose? *Lady Chatterley's Lover* is arguably the most influential, and certainly the most famous, or notorious. But much of it now seems embarrassing. *Sons and Lovers*, his unforgettable third novel, is many readers' favourite, but I've chosen *The Rainbow*, the more perfect twin of the diptych that also contains *Women in Love*.

No question: Lawrence is uneven, and troubling. In the last century he was fiercely attacked, and wildly overpraised, not least by the critic FR Leavis who clobbered generations of students with his verdict that Lawrence was "the great genius of our time". At the same time, my generation ingested Lawrence – his novels, poems, and stories – like junkies. Here, at last, was a writer who was unequivocally all about the human soul, and who loved nothing better than to explore every nuance of family and marital, and sexual, relations.

For readers who had grown up with JM Barrie, CS Lewis, Arthur Ransome, E Nesbit and all the repressed masters of post-Victorian children's literature, Lawrence seemed to offer the most exhilarating liberation. We, by contrast, would feel the blood thunder in our veins, become spontaneous and vital and instinctual. We would, as Lawrence put it, "break down those artificial conduits and canals through which we do so love to form our utterance". We would celebrate Dionysus, and we would be free. Adolescents had worn khaki in the 1940s, and flannel in the 50s, but we would dress like clowns.

It's an undifferentiated blur now, but if I stop to focus on my DH Lawrence, the Lawrence of the 60s, I can begin to discern the fuzzy but recognisable outline of a literary aesthetic that was both persuasive and, for Lawrence at least, coherent. Anyway, don't we expect our greatest writers to be a little bit mad? As compelling as the fantasy of the creative crucible, we had the puritanical cold steel of FR Leavis to remind us, in *The Great Tradition*, about Lawrence's artistic integrity and moral grandeur, his profound artistic seriousness. As he once wrote to Aldous Huxley: "I always say, my motto is 'Art for my sake'." This Lawrence was also the magnificent standard-bearer for English modernism. By the 60s, we didn't need to box him into a pigeonhole: he was protean, inspiring, and with the kind of grandeur that is unknown today. As the novelist and critic Howard Jacobson has written, "*Women in Love* is the nearest any English novel has so far approximated to the fearful grandeur of *Medea* or the *Oresteia*."

In addition to the attractions of his literary genius, there was the thrill of Lawrence's personal philosophy. This had begun in heterodox meditations on Christianity, and had then swerved towards mysticism, Buddhism and – most arousing of all – earthy, pagan theologies. Seductively, for English adolescents in, say, 1967, Lawrence seemed to celebrate the liberation of the individual in the mass, through the celebration of primal instincts.

The DH Lawrence with whom we fell in love with was a protean figure, for sure. The barest sketch of his biography – the humble origins in mining Nottinghamshire; the escape to metropolitan London; his elopement with Frieda, a married woman; the long exile; his "savage pilgrimage" to self-knowledge; and finally his early death from tuberculosis in 1930, aged just 44 – put him effortlessly in the company of the great Romantics, Byron and Keats.

But he was more than a Romantic, apparently in a deep colloquy with some darker forces. He was also intimately in touch with nature, which plays a vital role in all Lawrence's best work. Thomas Hardy had written about rural Dorset with a poet's eye, but Hardy was a Victorian who treated the landscape as an attractive backdrop to the human drama. Lawrence is a 20th century writer and his vision is fresh, dynamic and modern – as if nature is there to galvanise the human soul, not merely to decorate his or her environment.

Listen to Lawrence describe the scene beyond the grime of the colliery in *Women in Love*: "Still the faint glamour of blackness persisted over the fields and the wooded hills, and seemed darkly to gleam in the air. It was a spring day, chill, with snatches of sunshine. Yellow celandines showed out from the hedge-bottoms… currant bushes were breaking into leaf, and little flowers were coming white on the grey alyssum that hung over stone walls."

And then, beyond the confines of *The Great Tradition*, there was that notorious novel with those forbidden words, and those ecstatic descriptions of sexual intercourse. *Lady Chatterley* was an essential handbook to the 60s. Lawrence's fascination with sex made a wonderful contrast with the terribly grey dullness of the postwar world.

Similarly, in *The Rainbow* and *Women in Love*, the sexuality of his characters throbs through the narrative like a feverish pulse. No one writes better than Lawrence about the complexity of desire, especially homosexual desire. "I should like to know," he wrote in one letter, "why nearly every man that approaches greatness tends to homosexuality, whether he admits it or not."

Looking back, *Lady Chatterley's Lover* was both the making of DH Lawrence in the postwar English imagination, and ultimately, the ruining of his reputation. Most damaging of all – from one book that's a long way below his best – DH Lawrence became fatally attached to the zeitgeist, and fatally identified with just one novel. In time, inevitably, there was a reaction against the bells and the beards, the drugs, the pan pipes and the liberation. So Lawrence got thrown out with the flared trousers, the Beatles and, in America, the Vietnam war. By the dawn of the 80s there was no place for clowns, and four-letter words were two a penny.

And so, from the occasionally ridiculous to the sublime. Lawrence first attracted the attention of literary London with a short story entitled "Odour of Chrysanthemums", and it's as the master of the short story that I began to read him. Where to start? There are many options, including "The Rocking-Horse Winner", but one of his finest collections is *The Prussian Officer and Other Stories*, published in 1914. This places it after his acclaimed third novel, *Sons and Lovers* (1913), but before *The Rainbow* (1915), the novel that secures his claim on posterity.

The Rainbow, for me, is as close to perfection as any of his mature fiction. The novel opens with Marsh Farm, the home of the Brangwen family whose men and women, Lawrentian archetypes, inhabit the landscape that Lawrence loved. One of the many joys of *The Rainbow* is his evocation of the natural world, physical, timeless and symbolic. The novel is also conceived on a majestic scale, spanning a period from the 1840s to 1905, and showing how the Brangwen farming family is changed by Britain's industrial revolution, evolving from pastoral idyll to the chaos of modernity.

Once Tom Brangwen has married his "Polish lady" (chapter 1) and adopts her daughter Anna as his own, the narrative kicks into a high gear, the close-knit exploration of feelings. Anna meets Tom's nephew, Will. They marry; she becomes pregnant with Ursula; and the novel slowly builds to its celebrated concluding section: Ursula's quest for fulfilment in a heartless, repressive society. After her doomed passion for Skrebensky, a British soldier of Polish ancestry, Ursula is left with a more personal epiphany, one doubtless shared by its author, a vision of a rainbow: "She saw in the rainbow the earth's new architecture, the old brittle corruption of houses and factories swept away, the world built up in a living fabric of truth, fitting to the overarching heaven." With this spiritual regeneration, the novel ends, to be taken up again with *Women in Love*, the story of Ursula and Gudrun Brangwen, the sisters of Lawrence's first draft.

The more we look at DH Lawrence, the harder it is to understand why – apart from a shift in the cultural mood – he should have become so neglected. Certainly, he held some perverse, and often baffling, views on sexual politics, especially feminism; also on democracy and organised labour; and on modernity. Like all radicals, he made some ridiculous utterances from time to time. He is a writer that adolescents devour omnivorously, but then cannot return to. Perhaps if we read him in a less compulsive way, we could learn to benefit from the nurture of the diet he offers, and stay with him at all ages, young and old.

A Note on the Text:

Lawrence began to write a novel entitled *The Sisters* in the spring of 1913, while staying in Italy. "It is a queer novel," he wrote to his editor Edward Garnett, "which seems to have come by itself." After many drafts and revisions, this urtext would become the source of his two great novels, *The Rainbow* and *Women in Love*. Meanwhile, another version, written in the spring of 1914, entitled *The Wedding Ring*, was accepted for publication by Methuen & Co but then returned to Lawrence on the outbreak of war in August 1914. The publishers blamed the hostilities, but a deeper reason was probably their anxiety about obscenity, a fear that would soon be fulfilled.

After this troubled start, Lawrence rewrote the book completely in the winter of 1914-15, removing material he would later use for *Women in Love*, and completed the novel now known as *The Rainbow* on 2 March 1915. "I know it is quite a lovely novel, really," he wrote to a friend in February 1914. "The perfect statue is in the marble, the kernel of it. But the thing is the getting it out clean." Methuen, meanwhile, continued to worry about the novel's sexual content, urging Lawrence to make additional changes, while also making unauthorised changes to the proofs themselves.

The Rainbow was finally published in Britain on 30 September 1915, whereupon Methuen were almost immediately prosecuted, in November, for Lawrence's frank treatment of sexual love. After the trial, all copies of the novel were seized and burnt, and *The Rainbow* remained banned in Britain for 11 years under the Obscene Publications Act 1857. However, it escaped repression in America where BW Huebsch published the first US edition in November 1915. After many vicissitudes, the text that is now canonical is the Cambridge University Press edition (1989) edited by Mark Kinkead-Weekes.

Of Human Bondage
by W Somerset Maugham (1915)

In *Aspects of the Novel*, EM Forster wrote: "The final test of a novel will be our affection for it, as it is the test of our friends, of anything else that we cannot define." He might have been writing about W Somerset Maugham's masterpiece, *Of Human Bondage*. For English readers, this is a *Bildungsroman* we mostly first encounter as adolescents. It earns its place in this list for the edgy economy of its dark, often cruel narrative more than its style (prosaic) or its humanity (tormented). Maugham's unforgettable portrait of Philip Carey is one that teenagers, typically, will ingest like junkies, not least because Maugham poured so much of himself into the plot of the novel and its strangely sympathetic protagonist. Perhaps not since *David Copperfield*, an obvious inspiration had an English writer mined his own life so explicitly or so ruthlessly.

Philip Carey is an orphan hungry for love and experience. Like Maugham, who was a homosexual with a bad stammer, he is afflicted with a disabling deformity, a club foot. Raised by his clergyman uncle, the boy is imprisoned in late-Victorian vicarage life dreaming of his release from bondage, and praying to an indifferent God to have his disability healed. After a closely observed passage through boarding school, Philip escapes to study in Heidelberg, enjoys a brief spell as a struggling but failing artist in Paris, and then returns home. Now begins the most poignant and memorable passage of the novel, Carey's hopeless affair with Mildred, a waitress.

Maugham was a self-hating homosexual, and his picture of Mildred as Philip's love-object reflects the trials of a young gay man in the aftermath of the Oscar Wilde case. Mildred is "boy-like", vulgar and contemptuous of her crippled lover. She often betrays him, going off with his other men friends, steals from him, and scorns his sexuality. Theirs is a sad, on-off affair, during which she gets pregnant by another man, while Philip remains obsessively in love. Finally, after a hideous crisis in which Mildred wrecks his flat and shreds his wardrobe, she leaves to become a Shaftesbury Avenue prostitute. Only then does Philip realise he no longer loves her. He escapes her spell just in time to redeem himself, and marry a girl called Sally, a sentimental conclusion that does no justice to the savage honesty that permeates the heart of the novel.

A Note on the Text:

Of Human Bondage was initially called "The Artistic Temperament of Stephen Carey", then "Beauty from the Ashes", a quotation from Isaiah. When Maugham discovered that this title had been used already, he borrowed his final title from one of the books in Spinoza's *Ethics*. It was published in Britain by William Heinemann on 13 August 1915, during an annus mirabilis for British fiction. This series has already listed entries for *The Good Soldier*, *The Thirty-Nine Steps* and *The Rainbow*. From a long list of titles published that year, I've also excluded some other big names: Woolf's *The Voyage Out*, Wodehouse's *Psmith Journalist*, and Conrad's *Victory*.

The novel's history is interesting. Maugham first wrote the manuscript that would become *Of Human Bondage* when he was 23, having just taken his medical degree after five years at St Thomas's. He sent it to Fisher Unwin which, while he was still a medical student, had published his first novel *Liza of Lambeth* to some acclaim. Maugham asked for an advance of £100, but was refused. "Rebuffed," he wrote later, "I put the manuscript away." He turned to writing for the theatre, where he enjoyed considerable success. "I was no sooner firmly established as the most popular dramatist of the day," he writes, "than I began once more to be obsessed by the teeming memories of my past life."

Maugham was at pains, however, to insist that this was "not an autobiography, but an autobiographical novel". It was, in short, a mash-up of fact and fiction, seasoned with his own emotions, even when some incidents were borrowed from elsewhere. Whatever the process of composition, it satisfied its author. "I found myself free from the pains and unhappy recollections that had tormented me," he wrote later.

Maugham was always fiercely self-critical. "I knew I had no lyrical quality," he once wrote. "I had a small vocabulary and no efforts that I could make to enlarge it much availed me. I had little gift of metaphor; the original and striking simile seldom occurred to me." But he did have an instinctive gift for storytelling. Many would say that his short stories embody his best work, and he remains a substantial figure in the early 20th century literary landscape. Although Maugham's former reputation has become somewhat eclipsed, *Of Human Bondage* can still be cited as his masterpiece, a 20th century English classic with a devoted following.

– 45 –
The Age of Innocence
by Edith Wharton (1920)

Edith Wharton (nee Newbold Jones), who was born into a rich and distinguished New York family in 1862, is perhaps a great city's greatest novelist. From *The House of Mirth* (1905) to *The Custom of the Country* (1913) to her masterpiece *The Age of Innocence*, Wharton's subject was the changing scene of New York City, the foibles of its fashionable elites and the ambitions of the "new people" who, she felt, threatened its traditional culture. Wharton was also close to Henry James whom she described as "perhaps the most intimate friend I ever had, though in many ways we were so different". Together, from 1900 to the end of the Great War, the work of James and Wharton dominates American literature.

The Age of Innocence tells the story of a forthcoming society wedding, and the threat to the happy couple from the appearance in their midst of an exotic and beautiful femme fatale, a cousin of the bride. Newland Archer (the name makes a nod to James's heroine Isabel Archer) is a distinguished lawyer looking forward to his marriage to shy, lovely, sheltered May Welland. But when he meets Countess Ellen Olenska, scandalously separated from her European husband, a Polish count, he falls hopelessly in love and blights his marriage to May by failing to break off his relationship with the countess. Meanwhile, in a typical Wharton twist, Newland Archer's bride may be timid, but she is determined to marry her fiance and uses all the power of New York society to bring him to heel.

The social tragedy of Newland Archer's unhappy union was informed by Wharton's own marital breakdown, a crisis brought on by her husband's acute nervous collapse. By 1913, however, Wharton was divorced and free to explore her gifts as a writer of fiction.

As with all her New York novels, *The Age of Innocence* makes an ironic commentary on the cruelties and hypocrisies of Manhattan society in the years before, during and after the Great War. Strangely, when it won the 1921 Pulitzer prize, the judges praised it for revealing "the wholesome atmosphere of American life and the highest standard of American manners and manhood". Today, while not as merciless in its analysis as *The House of Mirth*, Wharton's late masterpiece stands as a fierce indictment of a society estranged from culture and in desperate need of a European sensibility. This had been an issue for American writers since Washington Irving, Melville and Hawthorne. Some critics would say it remains unresolved to this day.

A Note on the Text:
The Age of Innocence, Edith Wharton's 12th novel, which takes its title from a 1785 painting of *A Little Girl* by Joshua Reynolds, was first serialised in four parts during 1920 in the *Pictorial Review*. It subsequently appeared in book form from the American publisher D Appleton & Company of New York. In 1921, *The Age of Innocence* became the first novel written by a woman to win a Pulitzer.

The book has inspired many film, television and theatrical adaptations: most recently, in 1993, Martin Scorsese directed a film version starring Michelle Pfeiffer as Countess Ellen Olenska, Daniel Day-Lewis as Newland Archer and Winona Ryder as May Welland Archer.

– 46 –
Ulysses
by James Joyce (1922)

1922 is one of those extraordinary years in the history of English literature – the moment when Modernism came of age – after which nothing would ever be the same again. TS Eliot's *The Waste Land* appeared, first in magazine and then in volume form towards the end of the year. By then, James Joyce had already seen *Ulysses*, a text of approximately 265,000 words, privately published in Paris by Sylvia Beach, the philanthropic proprietor of the bookshop Shakespeare & Company, after a tortuous gestation in which his novel had been prosecuted for obscenity, and almost hounded into oblivion.

Joyce, however, was creatively obdurate. Earlier, in his autobiographical novel, *A Portrait of the Artist as a Young Man*, he had made an unforgettable declaration of artistic intent. His answer to the challenge of the 20th century was to declare independence. He wrote: "I will not serve that in which I no longer believe, whether it call itself my home, my fatherland, or my church: and I will try to express myself in some mode of life or art as freely as I can and as wholly as I can, using for my defence the only arms I allow myself to use – silence, exile and cunning."

Today, novelists writing a hundred years after the composition of *Ulysses* still write in the shadow of this extraordinary achievement. Occasionally, it is said that English-language fiction since 1922 has been a series of footnotes to Joyce's masterpiece.

Ulysses began as a discarded chapter from Joyce's first collection, *Dubliners* (1914) and for all its length it retains the fierce intimacy of a great short story. The action of the novel, famously, occurs on a single day, 16 June 1904, coincidentally the date of Joyce's first outing with Nora Barnacle, later his beloved wife. On "Bloomsday", the reader follows Stephen Dedalus (the protagonist of *A Portrait of the Artist as a Young Man*), Leopold Bloom, a part-Jewish advertising canvasser, and his wife Molly.

The connection to *The Odyssey* is informal (Bloom is Odysseus, Stephen matches Telemachus and Molly is Penelope) and the chapters roughly correspond to episodes in Homer ("Calypso", "Nausicaa", "Oxen of the Sun", etc.). Joyce himself revered the book that had inspired his masterpiece. The theme of *The Odyssey*, he said in 1917, while working on his novel, was "the most beautiful, all-embracing theme… greater, more human than that of *Hamlet*, *Don Quixote*, Dante, Faust".

Ulysses is often said to be "difficult", but really it is not. Joyce's wordplay, rivalling Shakespeare, whose teeming vocabulary he surpasses, is intoxicating, and deeply Irish. One of the best ways to encounter the novel is through any good audiobook recording. As Stephen Dedalus remarks: "Every life is many days, day after day. We walk through ourselves, meeting robbers, ghosts, giants, old men, young men, wives, widows, brothers-in-love. But always meeting ourselves."

A Note on the Text:

The textual history of *Ulysses*, first published on 2 February 1922, is every bit as complex as the novel itself, and what follows is a necessary over-simplification of an editorial cat's cradle. For instance, I have referred to the 1922 edition published by Sylvia Beach, an edition I have owned for years. To a Joyce scholar, however, that is like working on Shakespeare exclusively from the First Folio. By some calculations, there are no fewer than 18 separate editions of this book.

Yet it had all begun so modestly, in about 1907. "When I was writing *Dubliners*," Joyce told Georges Borach, one of his language students, "I first wished to choose the title *Ulysses in Dublin*, but I gave up the idea. In Rome, when I had finished about half of the *Portrait*, I realised that the Odyssey had to be the sequel, and I began to write *Ulysses*."

The first appearance of pages from this astonishing new novel occurred in 1918, in *The Little Review*, whose foreign editor was Ezra Pound. From the first, the text ran into difficulties with the authorities on the grounds of alleged obscenity. By 1920, this first serialisation was over, and *The Little Review* was no longer publishing monthly instalments. Joyce, who was now living in Paris, had met Sylvia Beach, the proprietor of Shakespeare & Company, a celebrated left bank bookshop. Beach offered to publish the novel privately, avoiding censorship.

Now began the second, chaotic stage of *Ulysses*' progress towards full and final publication. For Joyce, his novel was always evolving; he could never quite leave his text alone. Every proof that was pulled became another invitation to yet further revision. The current draft of the novel was always a palimpsest of the author's second and third thoughts. In addition, there were numerous misprints, many of them attributable to the French typesetters' ignorance of basic English, let alone the allusive, polysyllabic stew we know as Joycean English.

After the Shakespeare & Company edition, Harriet Weaver of the Egoist Press also published an "English edition" in 1922. This, for some, is the first canonical text (the current OUP paperback version, for instance, adopts this edition, warts and all). But then the 1922 text was banned and the novel forced underground. In 1933, Random House successfully applied to the US courts to overturn the ban, and published its first, American edition in January 1934. This was followed, a generation later, in the 1960s, with new editions from

Penguin Books, The Bodley Head and Random House in the US. To scholars and some critics, the text of *Ulysses* was still "corrupt" from the tortuous process of the novel's gestation. This, it was argued, should be put right with a full-blown edition representing Joyce's intentions. But how to achieve that? The answer was not obvious, which may have been Joyce's unconscious wish from the first.

Finally, in the late 1970s a German critic and scholar named Hans Walter Gabler began the task of preparing a "corrected text". This was finally published in 1984, and greeted with, first, acclaim, then doubts, and finally outrage. From a deep split in English and German textual theory, the status of the all-important "copy-text" (either the 1922 edition or Joyce's chaotic and imperfect manuscript) became the subject of a fierce scholarly debate between Gabler and his nemesis, John Kidd. The climax of this crisis occurred in June 1988 with Kidd's article in the *New York Review of Books*, entitled "The Scandal of Ulysses".

Since then, the row has gradually subsided, with a loose consensus forming in support of Gabler's "synoptic" text, while nevertheless acknowledging that it, too, contains some rank inconsistencies. Today, the first 1922 edition, a text of huge historical consequence, stands as the shortest route to the author's intentions, despite numerous Joycean "misses in print".

– 47 –
Babbitt
by Sinclair Lewis (1922)

Babbitt, dedicated to Edith Wharton, was published in the same year as *Ulysses* and likewise explores the passage through life of a middle-aged man. Coincidentally, the opening chapters follow the eponymous house agent's life during a single day. However, George F Babbitt, a self-intoxicated bully from the fictional city of Zenith, is a world away from Dublin's childless cuckold, Leopold Bloom. Similarly, *Babbitt*, a satire on 20s America by the controversial Sinclair Lewis, was a bestselling entertainment (the antecedents of which are found in

Mark Twain), with an artistic intention far removed from Joyce's "silence, exile and cunning".

Yet, in his own way, Lewis took his writing very seriously, researching and annotating his subjects to the point where imagination often got forced aside. Introducing the novel to English readers, Hugh Walpole, a now forgotten literary figure of the 20s, declared that the first 50 pages are "difficult, the dialogue strange, the American business atmosphere obscure". But once the book takes hold, it becomes enthralling. *Babbitt* may be short on structure and narrative guile, but it's full of larger-than-life characters and vivid satire. "Babbittry", denoting a certain kind of bogus sales pitch, became part of the inter-war American lexicon. John Updike, who features later in this series, nods to this in his sequence of novels about "Rabbit" Angstrom, also a salesman. Both are writing about the American dream.

For Lewis, however, it's a socio-economic cul-de-sac from which he wants his heroes – George Babbitt, Elmer Gantry and the rest – decisively to break out. Similar desires might be said to animate the inner lives of some Arthur Miller protagonists, especially Willy Loman.

In *Main Street*, his acclaimed satire on the dullness of life in Gopher Prairie, Lewis had already challenged the romance of small-town America. In *Babbitt* he took on the Midwestern, middle-sized city, and its ecology of American enterprise, celebrated in the term "boosterism".

Lewis recognised that these places, and their inhabitants, were not immune to social instability or economic depression, and that "boosting" these mid-American towns, and their stultifying way of life, offered no guarantee of stability after the upheavals of the First World War. When Babbitt comes to resent the middle-class prison of respectability in which he finds himself, striving to find meaning in an existence made trivial by mammon, the novel takes wing. His revolt resolves itself on his return to society, after a period of defiance and ostracism. He has been purged and renewed and, in the words of his son, is now "really going to be human".

Babbitt's adventures, narrated episodically, are designed to illustrate Lewis's argument and to cohere into a persuasive satire against US bourgeois conformity. Babbitt, like Galsworthy's Forsyte, whom – spoiler alert – I have chosen not to include in this series, is a symbol of American capitalism; Lewis a key transitional figure from Twain, especially, to the great postwar writers of the 1940s and 50s.

A Note on the Text

Babbitt, Lewis's eighth novel, was published in a hardback edition of some 400 pages in 1922. It was an immediate bestseller, and "Babbitt" entered the language to denote a "person and especially a business or professional man who conforms unthinkingly to prevailing middle-class standards".

In its first year of publication, *Babbitt* sold almost 150,000 copies in the United States, becoming a notable bestseller (a term then coming into vogue). Lewis had already enjoyed astonishing success with *Main Street* (1920). Inevitably, both books were contrasted, with opinion fairly equally divided. HL Mencken, the great American critic and columnist from Baltimore, adopted the cause of *Babbitt*, declaring himself "an old professor of Babbittry". Mencken brushed past Lewis's satire to find a passionate work of realism, in which George F Babbitt becomes a crucial archetype, representing those inter-war American city dwellers, sold on Republican conformity. Babbitt, according to Mencken, stood for everything that was wrong with American society.

Nevertheless, *Babbitt* fever swept the American reading public, and also caught the eye of critics, poets and writers. Vachel Lindsay wrote a poem entitled "The Babbitt Jamboree", and in 1927 the English writer CEM Joad published "The Babbitt Warren", a critique of US society. *Babbitt* is part of the reason Lewis was awarded the Nobel prize for literature in 1930, the first American novelist to receive the honour.

– 48 –
A Passage to India
by EM Forster (1924)

In 1957, EM Forster, looking back in old age, wrote that the late-

empire world of *A Passage to India* "no longer exists, either politically or socially". Today, approaching 100 years after its composition, the novel is probably as "dated" as ever. Yet – because Forster's concern is the forging of a relationship between a British schoolteacher and a Muslim doctor, reflecting the larger tragedy of imperialism – *A Passage to India* stands as a strangely timeless achievement, one of the great novels of the 20th century.

The part of *A Passage to India* that most readers remember, of course, is the tortuous romantic drama of the Marabar caves. Thus: when Adela Quested, an English schoolteacher, and her companion Mrs Moore arrive in Chandrapore they enter colonial India, a place obsessed with the promotion of British values and the British way of life. The idea is that Adela will meet and marry Mrs Moore's son Ronny, an eligible but bigoted British civil servant, the city's magistrate. But Miss Quested, as her name implies, has other ideas. Rejecting the prejudice and insularity of the British community, she sets out to investigate the "real" India, assisted in her search by Dr Aziz, a young Muslim doctor who naively wants to promote an entente between the master race and its colonial subjects. Each, in turn, is encouraged by the head of a local government college.

Aziz arranges for Miss Quested and Mrs Moore to visit the famous caves at Marabar. There, in a classic episode of Forsterian "muddle", something happens between Aziz and Adela that disgraces the doctor, and inflames the furious hostility of the British sahibs. In the crisis, Aziz, already disdained as "spoilt westernised", is imprisoned. Eventually, after a trial, Adela withdraws her charges and Aziz, radicalised and angry, moves to the native state of Forster's imagination. "I am an Indian at last," he says, and he stands alone in the monsoon rain. There, in the closing part of the novel, he is visited by Fielding, the British schoolteacher who had been his great confidant and friend. The Aziz-Fielding relationship tormented Forster. In a passage that caused him great creative agony, he wrestled with the complexity of an east-west understanding. "But the horses didn't want it – they swerved apart; the jail, the palace, the birds, the carrion… they didn't want it. 'No, not yet,' and the sky said, 'No, not there.'" It is a bleak but prescient conclusion: the issue of east and west is no nearer a resolution today than it was 100 years ago.

A Note on the Text
EM Forster visited the caves of Barabar in January 1913 on his first visit to India. It was an experience he never forgot, and it was into his fictional caves of "Marabar" that he sent Mrs Moore and her young companion, Adela, in the central and all-important section of his masterpiece, Part II, Caves. On his return from India, he began to write an Indian novel, but abandoned it to write *Maurice*, a novel of

homosexual desire that would not be published until after his death. He did not return to his "Indian" manuscript until 1921, having recently accepted a post as private secretary to the Maharajah of Dewas. Nevertheless, the experience of writing the novel was hardly fulfilling to him. He admitted privately that he was "bored by the tiresomeness and conventionalities of fiction-form", especially "the studied ignorance of the novelist". The last section, "Temple", was Forster's attempt, after a long struggle, to lift the narrative to a higher plane, as well as to resolve the unbridgeable conflict within the Raj.

A Passage to India was published on 4 June 1924 by the British imprint Edward Arnold, and then on 14 August in New York by Harcourt, Brace and Co. Forster borrowed his title from a Walt Whitman poem of the same name in *Leaves of Grass*. By the end of the year, there were 17,000 copies in print in Britain and more than 54,000 in the US. Forster's best-ever sales were matched by enthusiastic reviews. Only in India were critics exercised by his portrait of Anglo-Indian society. Today, he is seen as eerily prescient.

The typescript of *A Passage to India*, with many manuscript revisions, is now held in the library at King's College, Cambridge, Forster's home throughout his later years. As many have noted, Forster never wrote another novel, and lived until 1970, aged 91. For 46 years, his reputation grew with every book he didn't write. *Maurice* (written 1913-14), an explicitly homosexual novel, was published posthumously in 1971.

– 49 –
Gentlemen Prefer Blondes
by Anita Loos (1925)

Anita Loos, a screenwriting Hollywood wunderkind, says she began to draft *Gentlemen Prefer Blondes*, a jazz age classic, on the American railroad, as she crossed from New York to LA in the early 1920s. Travelling on the celebrated Santa Fe Chief with the movie star Douglas Fairbanks and his brainless leading lady, the young Loos became exasperated that a woman so stupid could "so far outdistance me in feminine allure". Could this girl's secret, Loos wondered, possibly be rooted in her hair? "She was a natural blonde and I was a brunette."

Lorelei Lee (aka Mabel Minnow from Little Rock, Arkansas) was born in that nano-second of female rivalry. Whipping out her yellow pad, Loos began drafting *The Illuminating* (originally "Intimate") *Diary of a Professional Lady*, teasing fact and fantasy into an intoxicating depiction of "the lowest possible mentality" in prohibition America, a gold-digging blonde who is not – surprise, surprise – quite as dumb as she looks. No wonder that the part burst into life when Marilyn Monroe starred in the 1953 film version.

Later, Loos joked that the plot of *Gentlemen Prefer Blondes* was "almost as gloomy" as a Dostoevsky novel. Indeed, without Lorelei's *faux-naif* interior monologue, her tale is replete with hints of rape, actual murder, seduction, gangsterism, and courtesanship, spun into airy nothing. When her diary begins, Lorelei is "under the protection" of the millionaire Gus Eisman, a Chicago button manufacturer, but in danger of falling in love with an impecunious British writer who wants to divorce his wife and marry the woman he believes to be his true love.

When Eisman gets wind of this, he sends his mistress on a European tour with her hard-boiled friend Dorothy. Quickly bored with London, despite a dance with the Prince of Wales, they head for Paris ("devine") and its romantic attractions, especially "the Eyeful Tower". Yet the longer Lorelei's sentimental education continues, the more she recognises the truth: continental men are no match for Americans. "I really think," she writes, "that American gentlemen are the best after all, because kissing your hand may make you feel very, very good but a diamond-and-safire [sic] bracelet lasts for ever."

This novella (it is barely 150 pages in my battered Penguin edition) falls into the category of "guilty pleasure", but I think it earns its place on this list, if only for the roll call of its distinguished contemporary fans, its lasting influence, and intensely quotable lines. Long before Helen Fielding's Bridget Jones, Loos hit on a young woman's diary as the perfect medium for satirical romance. *Gentlemen Prefer Blondes*, serialised in *Harper's Bazaar*, became cult reading. Edith Wharton, probably tongue in cheek, hailed it as "the great American novel". Loos, an unreliable witness, claimed that James Joyce, who was losing his sight, saved his reading for Lorelei Lee. Who knows? It's a little book with a broad smile, and a deceptively big heart.

A Note on the Text

In her prime, in the 1920s, Anita Loos was "the Soubrette of Satire" and also boasted that her first screen credit was for an adaptation of *Macbeth* in which her billing followed immediately after Shakespeare's.

The roaring success of *Gentlemen Prefer Blondes* owes an important debt to the celebrated critic and columnist, HL Mencken, a friend of Loos's. "Menck", as she called him, had just left the editorship of *The Smart Set* for *The American Mercury*, and correctly saw that "making fun of sex" was the kind of risqué novelty that would work better in a popular middlebrow publication like *Harper's Bazaar*. So Loos took her Lorelei material to the *Harper's* editor, Henry Sell, who encouraged Loos to extract maximum advantage from Lorelei's European trip. In just a few months, *Gentleman Prefer Blondes* became a magazine sensation. Newsstand sales of *Harper's* doubled, tripled and quadrupled.

Then the publishers Boni and Liveright came calling, and made a contract for a slim hardback, illustrated by Ralph Barton. *Blondes* sold out at once as a runaway bestseller, becoming the second highest-selling book of 1926, and helping to define the jazz age for ever. A second edition of 60,000 copies was exhausted almost as quickly. Some 45 editions later (in the end, 80-plus), the book had passed into classic status. It would be translated into 14 languages, including Chinese. Eventually, Lorelei's most memorable *obiter dicta* found their way into the *Oxford Dictionary of Quotations*. The idea that "diamonds are a girl's best friend" passed into popular culture, and is now repeated without irony too often to be diverting. Loos herself lived long enough (she died in 1981) to describe her book as a "period piece" for the grand-children of its first fans. "May they be diverted by the adventures of Lorelei Lee", she wrote, "and take courage from the words of her favourite philosopher: 'Smile, smile, smile.'"

– 50 –
Mrs Dalloway
by Virginia Woolf (1925)

In the spring of 1924, Virginia Woolf, then in her 40s, gave a famous lecture, later published as the essay Mr Bennett and Mrs Brown, in which she declared that "we are trembling on the verge of one of the great ages of English literature". She might have been speaking about herself. In the next 15-odd years, before her suicide, Woolf would transform the English literary landscape forever. She would innovate (*To the Lighthouse*); she would flirt (*Orlando*); she would provoke (*A Room of One's Own*) and, privately, would dazzle herself and her friends with a stream of letters (and diaries), all of which reveal a writer's mind at full tilt.

Woolf is one of the giants of this series, and *Mrs Dalloway*, her fourth novel, is one of her greatest achievements, a book whose afterlife continues to inspire new generations of writers and readers. Like *Ulysses*, it takes place in the course of a single day, probably 13 June 1923. Unlike Joyce's masterpiece, Woolf's female protagonist is an upper-class English woman living in Westminster who is planning a party for her husband, a mid-level Tory politician.

As Clarissa Dalloway's day unfolds, in and around Mayfair, we discover that not only is she being treated in Harley Street for severe depression, a familiar subject to Woolf, but she also conceals a troubled past replete with unarticulated love and suggestions of lesbianism. Equally troubled is the novel's second main character, explicitly a "double", a Great War veteran who fought in France "to save an England which consisted almost entirely of Shakespeare's plays". Septimus Warren Smith is suffering from shell shock and is on his way to a consultation with Clarissa's psychiatrist. Mingled with the preparations for the party, the stream-of-consciousness exploration of Mrs Dalloway's inner state is broken by an irruption of senseless violence when Septimus, who is waiting to be taken to an asylum, throws himself out of a window. News of Septimus's suicide becomes a topic of conversation at Mrs Dalloway's party, where Woolf indicates Clarissa's deep sympathy for the dead man's suffering. The novel ends unresolved, but on a note of suspenseful menace. "What is this terror?" writes Woolf. "What is this ecstasy?" Her mature work would be devoted to exploring these questions.

A Note on the Text:

Mrs Dalloway, published by the Hogarth Press with a striking Vanessa Bell dust jacket on 14 May 1925, was a novel that grew out of two previous short stories, "Mrs Dalloway in Bond Street" and "The Prime Minister". The latter makes his appearance at the party at the end of the novel. Clarissa also appeared in Woolf's first novel, *The Voyage Out*, as well as in five of her short stories.

Mrs Dalloway's literary influence can be seen in Michael Cunningham's *The Hours* and perhaps also in Ian McEwan's novel *Saturday*, which takes place on a single day, 15 February 2003.

– 51 –
The Great Gatsby
by F Scott Fitzgerald (1925)

In the five years between the publication of his first novel, *This Side of Paradise* (1920) and his masterpiece, *The Great Gatsby* (1925), F Scott Fitzgerald experienced the kind of literary success that can only happen in America. Fitzgerald not only coined the term "the jazz age", he lived and wrote about it with the hedonistic delirium expressed in his second novel, *The Beautiful and Damned* (1922). "I saw the improbable, the implausible, often the 'impossible' come true," he wrote later. His career as the celebrity spokesman for the inter-war generation brought him money, fame, and the love of women. Looking back, he remembered that "it seemed a romantic business to be a successful literary man".

The Great Gatsby is the American novel on this list that remains, after many readings, one of my all-time favourites, an unquiet masterpiece whose mystery never fails to exert its power. This is perhaps because, as Fitzgerald himself wrote, he is exploring the geography of regret. In a letter to a friend, he said: "That's the whole burden of the novel – the loss of those illusions that give such colour to the world that you don't care whether things are true or false so long as they partake of the magical glory."

The "jazz" side of Gatsby, amply represented by Baz Luhrmann's movie, remains seductive. The plot, ripped from the pages of a tabloid and crossed with a romantic novelette, has the potency of cheap music. The attraction of *Gatsby* intensifies with the text itself, a glittering diamond of brevity less than 60,000 words long. If it was just a lurid tale, its appeal would have faded long ago. But, as well as being a tragic romance, it's also a prose-poem, an elegy to its author's lost love, a hymn to the anxieties of the American dream, and a jazz riff on postwar trauma. Not for nothing did Fitzgerald set it in 1922, the year of *The Waste Land*. Put all these elements together, mix in prohibition, bootlegging and the beginnings of celebrity culture, add a soundtrack from Gershwin, plus the creative ambition of a writer tormented by fame, and you have a literary supernova. When Fitzgerald died in Los Angeles, from a heart attack, aged just 44, his publisher's warehouse still held copies of the first edition. There was, as Fitzgerald had predicted, no second act in this American life. Just immortality. *The Great Gatsby*, in short, becomes a tantalising metaphor for the eternal mystery of art.

A Note on the Text:
Fitzgerald began planning his novel in 1922, hoping to write, as he put it, "something new – something extraordinary and beautiful and simple and intricately patterned". But he made slow progress and in the winter of 1922 worked on magazine stories to pay his debts. One of these, "Winter Dreams", he later described as "a sort of first draft of the *Gatsby* idea".

The other impediment to creative progress was his alcoholism. He was, as Sarah Churchwell writes in *Careless People: Murder, Mayhem and the Invention of the Great Gatsby*, consistently "drunk, tearing drunk, roaring drunk". Indeed, in the party season of 1922-23, Fitzgerald calculated that he averaged barely 100 words a day, and knew he had to get out. In 1924, he and Zelda moved to the Riviera, where he immersed himself in his novel. "Out of the woods at last," he wrote in April 1924, "and starting novel."

By 1925, the book was done. "Like Gatsby, I have only hope," Fitzgerald told Gertrude Stein, as he waited for the world's verdict. In the gaudy myth of the novel, there are two further strands: the cover and the title. The jacket art for the first printing of *The Great Gatsby*, a disembodied face above a dark blue Manhattan skyline by Francis Cugat, is one of the most famous cover illustrations in American literature. Copies of this edition now sell for tens of thousands of dollars.

And then there's the title. Fitzgerald had to be talked into *The*

Great Gatsby by Maxwell Perkins, his editor, and Zelda, his wife. To the author, "the title is only fair, rather bad than good". While he was writing, he had flirted with many alternatives, including: "Among the Ash Heaps and Millionaires", "Under the Red, White and Blue", "The High-Bouncing Lover", and "Trimalchio in West Egg" (his most favoured alternative). An early draft of the book has been published by an academic press under the title *Trimalchio*.

Finally, after publication on 10 April 1925, the fate of the novel and the novelist's own creative rallentando fuse into the *Gatsby* myth. Hemingway wrote: "I did not know the terrible odds that were against him. We were to find out soon enough."

The reviews were not as bad as people claim, and the sale of 20,000 copies was above average. Eliot, for one, was full of praise, but the novel did not match the expectations inspired by Fitzgerald's celebrity. Thereafter, Scott and Zelda's lives began to unravel. She had a breakdown and would end up in an asylum. He went to Hollywood to reverse his fortunes, completed *Tender is the Night*, and sold some confessional *Esquire* pieces, later published as *The Crack-Up*. "My God," he wrote to Zelda, "I am a forgotten man."

– 52 –
Lolly Willowes
by Sylvia Townsend Warner (1926)

In prose, as much as poetry, the Great War had many consequences. A year after *Mrs Dalloway*, a startling literary voice with Bloomsbury connections appeared on the London scene with a highly original satire on postwar England. Sylvia Townsend Warner was a young poet who told her editor at Chatto & Windus that she had written a "story about a witch". Within a year, *Lolly Willowes* had become the talk of the town. Today, Townsend Warner holds her place in this series as a proto-feminist who is also a major minor classic.

Laura "Lolly" Willowes is a twenty-something, middle-class Englishwoman who, on the death of her father, at first becomes a conventional maiden aunt living with her brother in London. Then, "groping after something", she makes a bid for personal freedom, an escape to Great Mop, "a secluded hamlet in the heart of the Chilterns", where she finds herself happily becoming a witch in communion with the devil.

In the 1920s, the search for a life (or room) of one's own was a topical theme. The war had liberated millions of women (Townsend Warner had worked in a munitions factory) and wiped out a generation of young men. The role and responsibilities of widows and spinsters was a subject taken up by many writers, from Vera Brittain to DH Lawrence. Lolly addresses it when, having embraced her witchy self, she has a long conversation with a middle-aged country gent who turns out to be Satan. "The one thing all women hate," she tells him, "is to be thought dull."

Sylvia Townsend Warner's whimsical take on postwar womanhood and the quest for meaning, subtitled "The Loving Huntsman", has a sharp edge, a satirical eye and a covert, untamed, eroticism. Townsend Warner was an unconventional lesbian. For her, inter-war women's potential was what mattered most. Women, says Lolly to the devil, "know they are dynamite" and simply long for "the concussion that may justify them".

For Townsend Warner, this "concussion" came a few years after the triumphant publication of *Lolly Willowes*. She fell in love with the poet Valentine Acland, and spent the rest of her life in Dorset. From the 1930s to 70s, she contributed short stories to the *New Yorker*. She died in 1978.

A Note on the Text:

On publication *Lolly Willowes* did well with the London critical establishment, but made a special hit in France (shortlisted for the Prix Femina) and the US, where it was selected as an inaugural Book-of-the-Month title for the newly launched book club. Sylvia Townsend Warner's relationship with her American readers was cemented in 1929 when she was appointed guest editor of the *New York Herald Tribune* and subsequently became a long-term contributor of short stories to the *New Yorker*. The MS of *Lolly Willowes* was kept on display in the New York Public Library until the 1960s next to manuscripts by Woolf and Thackeray. The novel remains Townsend Warner's chief claim to fame, though her life as a lesbian and a communist gives her biography a *frisson* of passion and politics. For more about the literary career of this remarkable woman, the essential texts are Claire Harman's biography, *Sylvia Townsend Warner* (London, 1989) and *I'll Stand By You: Selected Letters of Sylvia Townsend Warner and Valentine Acland,* edited by Susanna Pinney (London, 1998).

– 53 –
The Sun Also Rises
by Ernest Hemingway (1926)

In Woody Allen's *Midnight in Paris*, Corey Stoll makes a scene-stealing appearance as the young Ernest Hemingway, tough-guy modernist and friend of Gertrude Stein. It's a cameo grounded in the truth that, for one of America's 20th century greats, Paris in the 20s was a source of artistic liberation. It was also the setting for the first section of Hemingway's first, and best, novel (published in the UK as *Fiesta*).

The novel, a *roman à clef* describing an anguished love affair between the expatriate American war veteran Jake Barnes and Lady Brett Ashley, a *femme fatale* representative in the writer's mind of 1920s womanhood, is mostly located in Spain, Hemingway's favourite country. For some critics, the heart of the novel is the bullfight, and how each character responds to the experience of the *corrida*. At the same time, the escape into the wild is a great American theme that recurs in the works of Hawthorne, Melville, and Twain. In addition, *The Sun Also Rises*, like most novels of the 1920s, is a response to the author's recent wartime service.

The key to Hemingway, the thing that unlocks the most important doors to his creative life, was a deeper, more personal darkness, his complicated experience of the First World War. There are two versions. Either he was rejected for poor eyesight; or he failed to enlist and instead joined up as an ambulance driver. Each way, in the short-term, he was wounded by the shame of rejection and cowardice.

However, once with the Red Cross, Hemingway got as badly injured as if he'd been in combat. Thereafter, throughout his life, he craved the company of risk-takers – bullfighters or big-game hunters – and longed to be accepted by them. Courage, cowardice and manly authenticity in extremis became his themes.

Perhaps this is also the inspiration for his famously hard-boiled prose. The best of Hemingway's fiction, at its purest and most influential, is found in his stories, but this first novel is also a literary landmark that earns its reputation as a modern classic.

A Note on the Text:
Hemingway began writing the novel with the working title of *Fiesta* on his birthday, 21 July, in 1925. He completed the draft manuscript about eight weeks later, in September, and went on to revise it further during the winter of 1926.

The novel is based on a trip he made from Paris to Pamplona, Spain in 1924 with his wife, Hadley Richardson, and the American writer John Dos Passos. Hemingway returned again in June 1925 with another group of American and British expats. Their experiences and complex romantic entanglements became absorbed into the manuscript of *The Sun Also Rises*.

In the US, Scribner's published the novel on 22 October 1926. Its first edition, just over 5,000 copies, sold well. The Hellenistic-style cover illustration by Cleonike Damianakes showed a seated, robed woman, head bent, eyes closed, shoulders and thigh exposed. Hemingway's editor, the celebrated Maxwell Perkins, wrote that "Cleon's respectably sexy" artwork was designed to attract "the feminine readers who control the destinies of so many novels". Within two months, *The Sun Also Rises* was in a second printing, with many subsequent printings to follow. In 1927 the novel was published in the UK by Cape under the title *Fiesta*. In fact, *The Sun Also Rises* has been in print continuously since its publication in 1926, and is said to be one of the most translated titles in the world.

– 54 –
The Maltese Falcon
by Dashiell Hammett (1929)

Raymond Chandler, who has yet to appear in this series, once said: "Hammett is all right. I give him everything. There were a lot of things he could not do, but what he did, he did superbly." He added, in a summary that helps define Hammett's achievement: "He was spare, frugal, hard-boiled, but he did over and over again what only the best writers can ever do at all. He wrote scenes that seemed never to have been written before." He also gave his characters a distinctive language and convincing motivations in a genre that had grown stereotyped, flaccid and uninvolving.

Although some readers prefer *Red Harvest, The Maltese Falcon* is the Hammett novel that jumps from the pages of its genre and into literature. It's the book that introduces Sam Spade, the private detective who seduced a generation of readers, leading directly to Philip Marlowe. Dorothy Parker, never a pushover, confessed herself "in a daze of love" such as she had not known in literature "since I encountered Sir Lancelot" and claimed to have read the novel some 30 or 40 times.

What is Hammett's appeal? The hard-boiled detective was not really his invention, but he made him a character readers could identify with: the beady-eyed loner who coolly puts himself in harm's way out of a fierce determination to redress wrong and achieve justice. That's a winning insight into the character of any great protagonist. Spade's involvement in the world is not cynical but passionate, and yet his successes are always shadowed by hints of loss and failure. This has filtered down into the work of countless genre writers from Chandler to Le Carré, to Sara Paretsky. Moreover, like Hammett himself, Spade is vivid, physical, and highly sexed. He also shares many elements of Hammett's career and character. Strangely, from a writer with a keen eye on the market, Spade makes only this one appearance in a full-length fiction.

The three principal women at the heart of *The Maltese Falcon*, especially Brigid O'Shaughnessy, all respond to Spade's sexual magnetism. But he, in the end, will always subordinate his desires to the greater good. So he will surrender Brigid, the murderer, to the cops. "You'll never understand me," he says to her, an almost existential statement about the relations of men and women.

Chandler said that Hammett took the murder out of the drawing room and put it back in the alley, where it belongs, adding that "Down these mean streets a man must go who is not himself mean, who is neither tarnished nor afraid." Like Wilkie Collins and Arthur Conan Doyle Hammett was an original who created a profoundly influential literary template that gives him classic status.

A Note on the Text:

The Maltese Falcon was originally serialised in HL Mencken's "pulp" magazine, *Black Mask*, from September 1929. Then it was published in book form by Alfred A Knopf in February 1930. For publication,

Blanche Knopf, his editor, tried to tone down the overt sexuality of the magazine version (she feared the references to Joel Cairo's homosexuality would alienate readers) but Hammett prevailed.

The story has been adapted several times for the cinema, and the 1941 version, starring Humphrey Bogart, Mary Astor, Peter Lorre and Sydney Greenstreet, is generally thought to be a *film noir* classic.

Raymond Chandler, who owes so much to Hammett, deserves the last word. He said of *The Maltese Falcon*: "If you can show me 20 books written approximately 20 years back that have as much guts and life now, I'll eat them between slices of Edmund Wilson's head." Nearly 100 years later, the "guts and life" of Hammett's prose still puts some of his etiolated heirs to shame.

– 55 –
As I Lay Dying
by William Faulkner (1930)

This is the first, and probably the most popular, of Faulkner's Yoknapa-tawpha County stories, a short, dark and compelling novel set in what he called "my apocryphal county", a fictional rendering of Lafayette County in his native Mississippi. It was his ambition, he said, after the comparative failure of *The Sound and the Fury*, "deliberately to write a tour de force". Apart from Mark Twain no other American writer before Faulkner had ever immersed his readers so completely in the vernacular language and culture of a society that was, and perhaps still is, so deeply foreign to mainstream American experience.

The death and burial of a southern matriarch, Addie Bundren, is told from some 15 viewpoints, including that of the dying woman herself. The Bundren family's demanding stream-of-consciousness narrative (Faulkner was a modernist pioneer) is intercut with the voices of the local doctor and preacher, together with neighbours and friends. From the first line, the reader is pitched into the deep south: "Jewel and I come up from the field, following the path in single file… anyone watching us from the cotton-house can see Jewel's frayed and broken straw hat a full head above my own." Welcome to a brutal, backwoods community of impoverished cotton farmers in 1920s Mississippi.

Addie's dying wish is to be buried among her own people, "a hard day's ride" away. So her family are carting her coffin to Jefferson, Miss., for the funeral. The Bundrens' journey to these last rites becomes itself a rite of passage punctuated with fire (a burning barn) and water (a dangerous river crossing). The brilliance of this sometimes difficult novel lies in Faulkner's compulsive, bleak unfolding of Addie's history and her relationship with her beloved son, Jewel, the result of her affair with Rev Whitfield, the local minister.

In counterpoint to this, we also meet her family, an extraordinary cast of weird southerners – Cash, Darl, Dewey Dell and Vardaman Bundren. Perhaps it's the measure of Faulkner's originality that his work seems so incomparably more contemporary than his great contemporaries, Fitzgerald and Hemingway. For some, he is greater than either.

A Note on the Text:

Faulkner claimed he wrote *As I Lay Dying* from midnight to first light in six weeks while working at a power plant to make ends meet, and moreover that he did not change a word of it. This claim is now seen as apocryphal as Yoknapatawpha County itself. According to many sources, the title of his seventh novel derives from Book Eleven of *The Odyssey*, a passage where, with "As I lay dying…", Agamemnon tells Odysseus about his murder.

As I Lay Dying has also directly influenced a number of other critically acclaimed books, including Graham Swift's Booker prize-winning novel *Last Orders* and an African-American retelling by Suzan-Lori Parks, *Getting Mother's Body*. The Australian novelist Peter Carey has often told interviewers that he was inspired to become a writer through reading Faulkner, whose other contemporary admirers include Mario Vargas Llosa. Richard Ford, the Pulitzer prize-winning author of *Canada* and *The Sportswriter*, is another, among many American writers, who also acknowledges a debt to Faulkner, not least because he grew up in Faulkner's home state.

– 56 –
Brave New World
by Aldous Huxley (1932)

The grandson of TH Huxley, an eminent Victorian scientist, and scion of a famous family of public intellectuals, Aldous Huxley was a precociously gifted young man who grew up on the fringes of the Bloomsbury set. In the 1920s, Huxley acquired a reputation for the kind of heartless, satirical fiction that appealed to the Waste Land generation. Today, he is rather out of favour, and mostly read as a curiosity of his time. I've put him into this series for the vivacity of his imagination as much as his prose, which is often top-heavy with ideas, and stylistically rather thin.

Huxley's most famous novel, a dystopian fable set in the seventh century AF (After Ford), began as a parody of HG Wells, specifically of *Men Like Gods,* whose optimism Huxley disdained. A *jeu d'esprit* quickly became a vehicle for Huxley's obsession with the consequences of mass industrialisation and the Americanisation of consumer society. But it retains a satirical edge and is also strikingly aphoristic, with a vivid sense of the power of language and ideas in changing human society. "Words can be like x-rays if you use them properly," says one character. "They'll go through anything. You read and you're pierced." Huxley, the scholarship boy, was steeped in the English classics, and shaped by his education. In *Brave New World* (the title is just the most visible of countless Shakespeare references in the text), we find the world in the hands of 10 World Controllers who administer a global society, bred in test tubes, tranquillised by the mind-numbing drug soma, and graded according to English public school custom (Huxley was an Old Etonian) from alpha plus to epsilon minus. Huxley revels in his invention of a future world, especially the celebrated "feelies" and also in many adventitious moments of light comedy reminiscent of his early work. The plot, such as it is, turns on the relationship of sexy Lenina Crowne and Bernard Marx, a disgruntled alpha plus who imports John, a "Savage", from New Mexico to London. Here, implausibly, the alien tourist clashes with the World Controller, Mustapha Mond, on the place of the individual in a scientifically controlled society, a theme Huxley would explore for the rest of his career.

Much of the incidental detail of everyday life in AF632 derives from England in an age of all-conquering US materialism, the aftermath of America's intervention in the First World War. It would be for another Old Etonian, Eric Blair (aka George Orwell), whom Huxley actually taught briefly, to recognise that the bigger threat came less from bourgeois consumers than from totalitarian dictators like Hitler and Stalin. Orwell's *Nineteen Eighty-Four* would be the dystopia whose nightmare vision would become an essential text for the second half of the 20th century. And yet Huxley's picture of global capitalism, fuelled by the soft power of consumer advertising, is every bit as prescient as Orwell's, and its influence lingers on.

A Note on the Text:
Brave New World was first published by the Bloomsbury-conscious imprint, Chatto & Windus, in London, in 1932 with a striking, and highly collectible, jacket by Leslie Holland. In the US, where Huxley later retired, his humanism and pacifism, combined with his experimentation with LSD, would be taken up by subsequent generations of socially radical innovators. As the author of a radical future vision of society, he was always in demand and became something of a guru. His death on 22 November 1963, the day of President Kennedy's assassination, was rather overshadowed by that domestic political tragedy.

Huxley's dystopian vision has been widely adapted for radio and cinema and has also influenced many writers, notably Ray Bradbury *(Fahrenheit 451)*, Margaret Atwood (*The Handmaid's Tale*) and Kurt Vonnegut (*Piano Player*).

– 57 –
Cold Comfort Farm
by Stella Gibbons (1932)

Stella Gibbons, who was born in the same year as Georgette Heyer and Stevie Smith, 1902, wrote more than 20 novels, and thought of herself as a poet. But she continues to be remembered, and in some quarters revered, for just one title, a *jeu d'esprit* that's a brilliant parody of an inter-war genre of provincial, rural melodrama typified (at the high end) by DH Lawrence and, much lower down, by Mary Webb, author of titles such as *Precious Bane* and *The Golden Arrow*. Part of its immediate success was probably also due to the merciless contempt in which the young Gibbons (she was barely 30) held many generations of romantic/pastoral fiction. Or, indeed, the brisk way (with one, two or three asterisks) in which she humorously drew attention to the best bits in her narrative.

Gibbons wrote *Cold Comfort Farm* while working for the books pages of *The Lady*. Inspired, or perhaps provoked, by the fashion for novels set in remote rustic villages about sensitive young men with names like "Micah", she set about demolishing a piece of treasured literary real estate whose origins can be traced to the late-Victorian novels of Thomas Hardy.

From its opening line – "The education bestowed on Flora Poste by her parents had been expensive, athletic and prolonged" – to Aunt Ada's celebrated recollection of "something nasty in the woodshed", *Cold Comfort Farm* has the air of a novel written, as it were, in one joyous exhalation, according to Gibbons, somewhere between Lyons Corner House and Boulogne-sur-Mer during the year spanning 1931/32.

The plot is simple. Flora Poste, orphaned at 19 when her parents are both carried off by the 1919 Spanish flu epidemic, is penniless. Her only option is to throw herself on the charity of her remote Sussex relatives, the Starkadders – Judith, her preacher husband Amos, their sons Seth and Reuben, several other cousins (Harkaway, Urk, Ezra, and Caraway) including the dominant matriarchal figure of aunt Ada Doom – all living, or partly living, in Cold Comfort Farm, Howling, Sussex. The Starkadders' farm is an ominous place with a priapic bull, Big Business, and a hopeless herd of Jersey cows – Graceless, Pointless, Aimless, and Feckless – attended by several taciturn, brooding rustic inhabitants. Among some memorable comic set-pieces, cousin Amos preaching hellfire and damnation to the congregation of the Church of the Quivering Brethren is a high point.

As the rustic mayhem unfolds, Miss Poste, who is definitely a modern, metropolitan bossyboots, decides that it's her mission to bring a metropolitan "higher common sense" to this benighted spot, and sets about trying to redeem the lives of her relatives. Aunt Ada will go flying to Paris. The memories of the woodshed will become domesticated, Miss Poste herself will eventually marry her country cousin, Charles Fairford, and everyone live happily ever after. Sort of. (It's a comedy, remember?)

A Note on the Text:
Stella Gibbons humorously disparaged her first novel as the work of a journalist trespassing on a higher calling from "the meaningless and vulgar bustle of newspaper offices". *Cold Comfort Farm* was first published by Longmans in 1932, and was, according to the critic Lynne Truss, labelled "middlebrow", to Gibbons's disadvantage among the critics. But the book sold very well: 28,000 copies in hardback and 315,000 in paperback in its first 15 years. It won the 1933 Prix Étranger of the Prix Femina Vie Heureuse, and joined an informal canon of accidental English comic masterpieces. Unlike, for instance, *Three Men in a Boat,* another one-off classic, it found fans mainly in the British Isles. Its afterlife has influenced many writers and it is not fanciful, I think, to see in the film Withnail & I the novel's lingering influence on later generations. Gibbons herself, in a Punch essay, "Genesis of a Novel", compared her book to "some unignorable old uncle, to whom you have to be grateful because he makes you a handsome allowance, but who is often an embarrassment and a bore". Looking back, she was, she said, "filled by an incredulous wonder that I could once have been so light-hearted".

Gibbons twice returned to the scene of her triumph, with *Christmas at Cold Comfort Farm* (1940), and again in 1949 with *Conference at Cold Comfort Farm*. Both flopped, and remain largely unread. Her *Collected Poems* appeared in 1950. She died in 1989 and there's also a biography, *Out of the Woodshed: The Life of Stella Gibbons* by Reggie Oliver (1998).

– 58 –
Nineteen Nineteen
by John Dos Passos (1932)

John Dos Passos is largely forgotten now but, as we'll see, his influence continues to reverberate throughout 20th century American literature. He was born in 1896, contemporary with F Scott Fitzgerald and a year before Thornton Wilder and William Faulkner. His response to the great war (in which, like Hemingway, he served as an ambulance driver) and communist revolution, to which he was passionately attached as a young man, was to become a novelist with the instincts of a journalist, and a fictional reporter with the insight of a storyteller. His friend, the great critic Edmund Wilson, wrote that Dos Passos was "the first American novelist to make the people of our generation talk as they actually did".

His masterpiece, published in 1938 as *USA*, is a massive (1,300-page) trilogy that recounts the evolution of American society during the first three decades of the 20th century, and whose best volume, *Nineteen Nineteen*, first appeared in 1932. By then, the thrills and glamour of the jazz age had become soured by the crash, the depression, and the rise of fascism. Dos Passos, however, was still a committed communist who wanted to depict the gulf between rich and poor in America, as well as to explore the lives of ordinary people in the aftermath of the great war. *Nineteen Nineteen*, which is partly set in the Paris of the 1920s, develops the narrative techniques of the first volume, *The 42nd Parallel,* with its "Newsreel" and "Camera Eye", devices inspired by modernist innovation and emerging mass communications. There is also a lot of sex and violence, described with raw, documentary candour.

Dos Passos, like his innovative contemporary e.e. Cummings, played with typography and layout. To the reader, his books are works of art. As an accomplished artist himself, Dos Passos also painted his own book jackets, with striking modern images. Some sections (Camera Eye) are stream-of-consciousness evocations of mood and place, based on Dos Passos's own experience, and intercut with biographical essays on contemporary American figures, great and small. The momentum is relentless, the reportage vivid and brilliant. *USA* is as jerky and authentic as an old newsreel, and just as much of its time. Today, in

2014, Jane Smiley's trilogy, *The Last Hundred Years,* is a more conventional, mainstream attempt to explore aspects of the American century from the point of view of an Iowa farming family, the Langdons. Deliberate or not, Smiley's book is an unconscious tribute to John Dos Passos.

A Note on the Text:

I first read *USA* as an impressionable teenager, in a massive and battered, I think, Penguin. This must have been an offset from the Harcourt Brace edition which first published *The 42nd Parallel, Nineteen Nineteen* and *The Big Money* in a single volume titled *USA* in January 1938. This volume came at a turning point in the author's life. He had travelled to Spain with Ernest Hemingway and found his communist beliefs challenged by the murderous behaviour of some communist elements associated with the republican side in the civil war. Indeed, Dos Passos and Hemingway fell out over their differing responses to this. After their disagreement, the author of *For Whom the Bell Tolls* wrote to his friend F Scott Fitzgerald that Dos Passos was a second-rate writer with no ear, and "also a terrible snob".

After the Second World War, Houghton Mifflin published *USA* in a deluxe edition in three volumes with colour endpapers and illustrations by Reginald Marsh. (I have a cheap paperback version of this in which the majesty of Dos Passos's intentions is still evident.) The first printing of the illustrated edition was fewer than 1,000 copies, but in due course the mass-market edition sold in thousands.

Dos Passos has had some unlikely champions. Jean-Paul Sartre considered him the greatest writer of his time and was heavily influenced by *Manhattan Transfer* in the writing of *The Reprieve* (1947). In America, Dos Passos's attention to documentary detail in fiction was taken up and reinterpreted in many different ways by Gore Vidal, Truman Capote and Norman Mailer. In the Library of America edition of 1996, Dos Passos's masterpiece found its permanent home.

– 59 –
Tropic of Cancer
by Henry Miller (1934)

In American literature, the renegade strand had found its richest expression in the genius Mark Twain, who went out of his way to oppose the "genteel tradition" of Emerson and Longfellow. By the 20th century, however, the renegade frontier was to be found not in the wild west, but in Paris. Miller, the down-and-out literary *enragé*, revelled in a new frontier of seedy desperation, where there were "prostitutes like wilted flowers and pissoirs filled with piss-soaked bread". He and his muse Anaïs Nin flourished here – resolute, isolated and stoical in pursuit of their new aesthetic. Nin memorably recalled that, while her lover was mellow in his speech, there was always a "small, round, hard photographic lens in his blue eyes".

The shabby, 38-year-old American with unblinking camera vision who arrived on the Left Bank of Paris in 1930 was the quintessence of abject failure. All he had going for him was creative rage, mixed with the artistic vision of the truly *avant garde*. "I start tomorrow on the Paris book," wrote Henry Miller. "First person, uncensored, formless – fuck everything!"

Miller was as good as his word, within the opening pages of the novel whose working title was "Crazy Cock", he was celebrating Tania's "warm cunt", declaring that he "will ream out every wrinkle" with his "prick six inches long". His obsessive reporting of his sexual exploits, and his low-life rootlessness, is the novel's subject (there is no plot), a merciless assault on convention. Next to Fitzgerald's *Tender Is the Night* (1934) and even Faulkner's *Absalom, Absalom!* (1936), Miller's visceral candour was off the charts of contemporary taste, in tone as much as language. Miller's delight in rubbing the reader's face in filth was intoxicating and influential. His "fuck everything" would inspire Kerouac, Genet, Burroughs, Mailer and Ginsberg, among others. Not bad for a man who had once written: "Why does nobody want what I write?"

A Note on the Text:
Miller's sprawling masterpiece was launched by the Obelisk Press, a French publisher of soft pornography, as *Tropic of Cancer,* with a cover by Maurice Girodias, who would later become famous as the leading French publisher of erotic literature. Wrapped in an explicit warning ("Not to be imported into Great Britain or USA"), it set a new gold standard for graphic language and explicit sexuality. From the outset, Miller's "barbaric yawp" shook US censorship and inflamed American literary sensibility to its core. *Tropic* would remain banned for a generation, by which time it had become part of postwar cultural folklore, smuggled into the US wrapped in scarves and underwear. Rarely has a book had such thrilling and desperate underground beginnings.

The outsider status of Miller's novel combined with its subject (life and love at the extremes of existence) recommended the book to writers like Orwell and Beckett. In his essay "Inside the Whale" (1940), Orwell wrote: "I earnestly counsel anyone who has not done so to read at least *Tropic of Cancer.* With a little ingenuity, or by paying a little over the published price, you can get hold of it, and even if parts of it disgust you, it will stick in your memory ... Here in my opinion is the only imaginative prose-writer of the slightest value who has appeared among the English-speaking races for some years past."

For his part Samuel Beckett described it as "a momentous event in the history of modern writing". In the US, as an outright challenge to the censor, Edmund Wilson noted that "The tone of the book is undoubtedly low. *Tropic of Cancer...* is the lowest book of any real literary merit that I ever remember to have read."

Miller's vision prevailed, in the end. Finally, in 1961, the year after *Lady Chatterley's Lover* secured the right to be published in the UK, *Tropic of Cancer* triumphed in its battle with the US censor and was published by the Grove Press. The timing of this landmark verdict did not favour the ageing iconoclast. At first, his book was treated as the fruit of Miller's complex relationship with Anaïs Nin, who was an object of veneration within the American feminist movement. Later, feminists like Kate Millett denounced Miller as a male chauvinist, while Jeanette Winterson asked, perceptively: "Why do men revel in the degradation of women?" This question still hangs over the pages of *Tropic* like a rebuke, but (with a few misgivings) I'm still going to add it to this series.

– 60 –
Scoop
by Evelyn Waugh (1938)

Evelyn Waugh once said that journalism was the enemy of the novel,
 and urged all novelists who were serious about their art to get out of newspapers as soon as they could afford it. Perhaps only a writer and satirist so alert to the corruptions of newspaper life could have written a book as sublimely entertaining as Waugh's tale of nature columnist William Boot, an innocent abroad, like many of his protagonists.

Subtitled "a novel about journalists", *Scoop* is the supreme novel of the 20th century English newspaper world, fast, light, entertaining and lethal. Remarkably, it's a satire revered among successive generations of British hacks, the breed so mercilessly skewered by Waugh, a one-time special correspondent for the *Daily Mail*. Even in the age of online journalism, with many old practices facing extinction, its insights into the British press remain sharp, pertinent and memorable.

It was Waugh's experiences in Ethiopia, during the Abyssinian crisis of 1935-36, that provided the raw material for a wicked romp through the more absurd byways of Fleet Street in the 1930s. Actually, in its combination of farce and pathos, Scoop derives less inspiration from Ethiopia than from the world of Waugh's brilliant early fiction such as *Decline and Fall* and *Vile Bodies*.

But there is a difference. As Cyril Connolly wrote in *Enemies of Promise:* "The satire of Evelyn Waugh in his early books was derived from his ignorance of life. He found cruel things funny because he did not understand them, and he was able to communicate that fun." Later, Waugh's comic vision would mature and darken into books such as *Brideshead Revisited* and the *Sword of Honour* trilogy. So, published in the late 30s, *Scoop* is a kind of farewell to his beginnings as a literary enfant terrible.

As *Scoop* opens, it's the other Boot, John, a self-serious literary novelist, author of *Waste of Time*, who is introduced as the confidant of Mrs Algernon Stitch, a classic Waugh hostess from Mayfair. It's La Stitch's dinner party gossip with Lord Copper, the megalomaniac press magnate, and proprietor of the Daily Beast, that inspires the blunder that will animate the plot: the herbivorous Boot at large in the surreal mayhem of Ishmaelia's civil war.

Waugh had already satirised colonial Africa in *Black Mischief* (1932), and Boot's adventures occur within the privileged bubble of the foreign press corps. *Scoop*, as its title suggests, is a satire not on colonial sideshows, but on the eternal quest for breaking news, the endless competition between the Brute and the Beast. It remains celebrated in newsrooms across the English-speaking world for its portraits of Lord Copper, Mr Salter, and the thrill-seeking foreign correspondent, Jakes, together with those deathless hacks, Corker and Pigge.

Many of these caricatures might remind some readers of Waugh's debt to Dickens, but Scoop remains fiercely modern. So little has really changed. The six words of "Up to a point, Lord Copper" conjure a marrow-freezing universe of corporate fear. Most famous of all, there's the glorious parody of the "feather-footed" vole questing through the "plashy fen", a pointed reminder of the deep sentimentality always to be found in the Street of Shame.

A Note on the Text:
Scoop was published by Chapman & Hall in 1938, and almost at once there was a quest for models. Fleet Street folklore says that William Boot was based on William Deedes, and that Lord Copper derives from Lord Northcliffe and Lord Beaverbrook. In fact, for the origins of all Waugh's characters, the truth is probably more complicated.

Scoop was made into a BBC serial in 1972 and also a television film scripted by William Boyd in 1987, starring Denholm Elliott, and directed by Gavin Millar. The fictional newspaper owned by Lord Copper in *Scoop* has also been the inspiration for the title of Tina Brown's online American publication, *The Daily Beast*.

– 61 –
Murphy
by Samuel Beckett (1938)

 "The sun shone, having no alternative, on the nothing new." Samuel Beckett's entry into this series with his characteristically bleak, nihilistic humour, marks another milestone: the first appearance since Shakespeare of a writer who will innovate as brilliantly in theatre as much as in poetry and prose. Beckett, indeed, is one of the giants of 20th century literature, in any language.

Murphy is an absurdist masterpiece, a first novel that emerged from a long literary apprenticeship, mainly conducted in post-first world war Paris. It was the first substantial work by a young man – Beckett was born on Good Friday, 13 April, 1906 in Foxrock, just south of Dublin – who had been experimenting for years with poetry and prose, partly influenced by James Joyce, for whom he also worked as an unconventional secretary.

Murphy, which would soon become overshadowed by the international success of "Waiting for Godot", is the first in a series of novels whose titles – *Molloy*; *Malone Dies* – begin with the 13th letter of the alphabet. Beckett, always nomadic, had returned to London from Dublin in September 1934 and taken lodgings in Gertrude Street, West Brompton. The novel draws extensively on his experience of living in London and the character of Murphy has plenty of Beckett in him.

The workshy eponymous hero, a "seedy solipsist", adrift in the alienating metropolis, realises that his desires can never be fulfilled conventionally. He withdraws from life in search of a personal stupor. When the novel opens, Murphy has tied himself to the rocking chair in his flat with seven scarves and is rocking to and fro in the darkness. This practice, apparently habitual, has become Murphy's way of achieving an existential state of being that gives him deep private satisfaction. Even his lover, Celia, cannot lure him back into the world. As Murphy's comico-philosophical meditation unfolds, we meet his circle of fellow eccentrics, notably Mr Neary, from Cork, who has the ability, through what he calls "Apmonia", to achieve a philosophy of "harmony" and "attunement".

Murphy is a showcase for Beckett's uniquely comic voice, his command of absurdist narrative, and fascination with existential, mind-body issues of being and nothingness. Eventually, after many vicissitudes, Murphy finds refuge in the Magdalen Mental Mercy-seat (an asylum). Foreshadowing the title of Beckett's second play *Endgame,* the novel ends with a game of chess between Murphy and Mr Endon in which Murphy resigns and then soon after dies, having accidentally set fire to himself in his lonely room and reducing himself to dust and oblivion.

A Note on the Text:

Murphy was written in manuscript in six small exercise books over 10 months from mid-August 1935 to early June 1936. Beckett sent the typescript to his editor Charles Prentice at Chatto & Windus, the London publishers of *Proust* (1931) and a collection of stories, *More Pricks Than Kicks* (1933). After some inevitable prevarication, on 15 July 1936, Chatto turned *Murphy* down, followed by Heinemann on 4 August. The novel now entered the bleak limbo of serial rejection on both sides of the Atlantic, during the rest of 1936 and most of 1937. Occasionally, there were flurries of interest mixed with suggestions for the changes Beckett might do to his text to make the book more commercial. Beckett, however, refused to revise what he had written. Eventually, having returned to Paris, he heard on 9 December 1937 that, thanks to the recommendation of Jack Yeats, *Murphy* had been accepted by Routledge whose editor T Murray Ragg's enthusiasm was subsequently confirmed by Herbert Read.

Then, echoing the random absurdism of his novel, on 7 January 1938, Beckett was stabbed in the chest and nearly killed in a Paris street when he refused the solicitations of a notorious pimp, named "Prudent". Joyce arranged for medical treatment, and Beckett received his page proofs in hospital where he made a few alterations and insertions. Fifteen hundred copies were printed and *Murphy* went on sale on 7 March 1938 price 7s 6d. The reviews were mixed. Dylan Thomas, writing in the *New English Weekly* combined approval with criticism but did Beckett the favour of taking his work seriously. The *Spectator's* critic wrote: "Rarely… have I been so entertained by a book, so tempted to superlatives and perhaps hyperboles of praise." Predictably, the sales of *Murphy* were not good. Routledge records show 568 copies sold in 1938, 23 in 1939, 20 in 1940 and 7 in 1941. In March 1943, *Murphy* was allowed to go out of print.

Within months of publication, however, Beckett was hard at work translating his novel into French, partly to liberate his imagination from the shackles of the mother tongue, but mainly because his future seemed to lie in Paris. Then the war came, and the French translation would not be published until 1947 by Bordas, a publisher with whom Beckett subsequently fell out. Finally, after the success of *En attendant Godot,* Beckett's main publishers, Editions de Minuit, took over the publication of *Murphy* and absorbed this edition into his oeuvre as a whole.

My reading of *Murphy* for this series has been based on the 2009 Faber & Faber edition, edited by Professor JCC Mays, a text derived from the first Routledge edition of 1938, but expertly corrected with reference to several typescript versions. None of the above should obscure the fact that Murphy is a deeply original, comic masterpiece by a giant of 20th century European prose.

– 62 –
The Big Sleep
by Raymond Chandler (1939)

Enter Philip Marlowe, one of the great characters in the Anglo-American novel, a protagonist to rival and possibly surpass Sherlock Holmes. Marlowe holds the key to the enduring appeal of this novel and the six that followed. In 1951, Chandler told his publisher, "It begins to look as though I were tied to this fellow for life."

Maybe he should not have been surprised. Chandler fully understood the archetypal fictional detective, and had been polishing the character for years. In *The Simple Art of Murder* (1950) he describes such a man in a famous passage:

"He must be a complete man and a common man and yet an unusual man... He is a lonely man and his pride is that you will treat him as a proud man or be very sorry you ever saw him. He talks as the man of his age talks, that is, with rude wit, a lively sense of the grotesque, a disgust for sham, and a contempt for pettiness."

Chandler might have been describing Philip Marlowe, who made his debut in this first novel, after several appearances in Chandler's pulp fiction stories. He once observed of his celebrated style: "I'm an intellectual snob who happens to have a fondness for the American vernacular, largely because I grew up on Latin and Greek."

Chandler, like PG Wodehouse, who will feature later in this series, had been educated at Dulwich College, a school founded by Edward Alleyn, the great actor-manager whose company, the Admiral's Men, included the poet and playwright Christopher Marlowe, Shakespeare's great rival. In Chandler's stories, his protagonist also appears as "Mallory". He is a 20th century knight who treads the mean streets of Hollywood and Santa Monica, and who also visits the houses of the stinking rich, with their English butlers, corrosive secrets and sinister vices. Chandler plays with this medieval conceit in surreal metaphors. For instance: "It was a blonde to make a bishop kick a hole in a stained-glass window."

In *The Big Sleep* – the title refers to the gangster euphemism for death – Marlowe is summoned to the home of old General Sternwood whose wild daughter, Carmen, is being blackmailed by a seedy bookseller. But *The Big Sleep* transcends its genre, moving WH Auden to write that Chandler's thrillers "should be read and judged, not as escape literature, but as works of art".

The plot, notorious for its complexity, soon spirals into a world of pornography, gambling and Hollywood lowlife. It's not flawless, and there are some loose ends. When Howard Hawks filmed the novel he asked, "Who killed the chauffeur?" and Chandler replied that he had no idea. To him, plot was always subordinate to character, mood and atmosphere.

A Note on the Text:
Chandler published his first detective story, in the pulp fiction magazine *Black Mask*, at the end of 1933. He explained this departure to his British publisher: "Wandering up and down the Pacific coast in an automobile I began to read pulp magazines, because they were cheap enough to throw away and because I never had at any time any taste for the kind of thing which is known as women's magazines. This was in the great days of the *Black Mask*... and it struck me that some of the writing was pretty forceful and honest." Between these beginnings and 1938, when he began to write *The Big Sleep,* he wrote 21 *Black Mask* stories, developing and honing the qualities of his mature work. A late starter, he came to this world as an outsider, a

middle-aged English public schoolboy adrift in California. However, he caught on quick. The early stories have several Marlowe prototypes, LA settings, good and bad cops mixed into the regular crime cocktail of violence, drugs, sex and booze.

When he came to write *The Big Sleep,* Chandler "cannibalised" (his own description) his stories. The central plot of the novel comes from two stories, "Killer in the Rain" (published in 1935) and "The Curtain" (published in 1936). Both stories were standalone tales, sharing no common characters, but they had similarities. In each, there's a strong father distressed by his wild daughter. Chandler melded the two fathers to make a new character and also did the same for the stories' two daughters. There are other sources, too. Like Carmen Sternwood, his own much-loved wife Cissy had posed nude as a young woman and, like Carmen, taken opium. Marlowe's alcohol problems reflect Chandler's own latent alcoholism. In virtually every scene of a Chandler novel, someone is lighting a cigarette, or having a drink.

The Big Sleep was published in the spring of 1939. Despite collecting an impressive retinue of literary admirers, including Somerset Maugham and, later, Edmund Wilson, the Knopf (US) edition sold barely 13,000 copies, though it did better in France and England. It did not begin to attract serious international attention until after the appearance of Howard Hawks's film starring Humphrey Bogart.

In 1959, the year of Chandler's death, his great English admirer Ian Fleming permitted himself a discreet nod of homage. Towards the end of James Bond's confrontation with Goldfinger, he passes through an airport and buys a book about golf – and the latest Chandler.

– 63 –
Party Going
by Henry Green (1939)

Henry Green is the pseudonym of Henry Yorke, an Oxford friend of Evelyn Waugh. Precociously gifted, Green/Yorke wrote an avant-garde novel, *Blindness*, while still at Eton, but never enjoyed anything close to Waugh's success.

His first mature fiction, *Living*, was a modernist tour de force, partly inspired by his experience on the shop-floor of his family's Midlands bottle factory. There's an irony in the success of this debut. Yorke was, as he put it in his memoir, *Pack My Bag*, "born a mouthbreather with a silver spoon in 1905". Growing up in the inter-war years, he was part of a highly gifted generation that included Christopher Isherwood, Graham Greene and Anthony Powell.

Party Going, published on the brink of the Second World War, reflects that experience. It's the polar opposite of *Living*, but quite as dazzling in the poetry of its prose, a masterpiece of literary impressionism. I came to read it, as a respite from my first job in the book world, sitting against the radiator, on the floor of the Hogarth Press library in William IV Street, in the West End.

Party Going offers the last word on that "low, dishonest decade", the 1930s. A group of bright young things – Max, Amabel, Angela, Julia, Evelyn and Claire – are on their way to a house party in France, by train. But fog is rolling in from the Channel. England is cut off, and the railway paralysed; their train has been delayed. So the party – quintessentially shallow, vapid and spoilt – holes up in the station hotel to wait for the fog to lift, a brilliant fictional premise.

Outside, in the metropolitan gloom, people come and go like spectres. "It's terrifying," says one of the girls, in a line that could have come from Waugh, "I didn't know there were so many people in the world."

A shadowy old woman, Miss Fellowes, retrieves a dead pigeon from the street, and washes it in a strange and disturbing act of piety.

In another brilliant scene that's cinematic in its intensity, Amabel takes a bath in the hotel. Meanwhile, she and Max struggle with their feelings, at once flirting with, and then avoiding, intimacy.

The critic VS Pritchett wrote that Green's special subject is "the injury done to certain English minds by the main, conventional emphases of English life". There, for me, is where the fascination of *Party Going* lies. Green paints an unforgettable portrait of a doomed, amoral world whose characters, trapped in the fog, are somehow waltzing blithely towards oblivion. The weather outside the hotel represents the menacing blur of the future. Sebastian Faulks wittily describes aspects of *Party Going* as if "a scene from *Private Lives* has been revised by Samuel Beckett".

Once war comes, it will be time for end-game, not carousel. Strikingly, Green's later fiction becomes increasingly difficult and austere with *Loving*, a tale of life in an Anglo-Irish country house, his outstanding late achievement.

A Note on the Text:
Party Going, Henry Green's second novel, followed his acclaimed modernist debut, *Living*, and marked the high point of his literary career. *Party Going* was published by Virginia and Leonard Woolf's imprint, the Hogarth Press, in 1939, just before the outbreak of war. Within a few years it had acquired a distinguished retinue of literary admirers – including Auden, Isherwood and Eudora Welty – but never quite moved beyond a cult audience. Thereafter, encroaching deafness and a reclusive temperament cut him off from the world, and slowly stifled his creativity. After the age of 47, he never wrote again. Indeed, his most entertaining contribution to literary life was the hilarious interview he gave to Terry Southern for an early edition of the *Paris Review*.

In the 1970s, *Party Going*, *Living* and *Loving* were collected into a single paperback volume published by Picador, an imprint of Pan Books. The experiment did not prosper. Nevertheless, the same combination was repeated first by Penguin in 1993, and again by Vintage (Random House) in 2005, with similarly dismal results. Despite the passionate advocacy of John Updike in America, and Sebastian Faulks in Britain, among many critics, Henry Green remains what the *Paris Review* described as "the writer's writer's writer". I'm probably not alone in thinking he deserves a better posterity.

– 64 –
At Swim-Two-Birds
by Flann O'Brien (1939)

Flann O'Brien is an Irish writer with many aliases and parallel lives, a legend of the Irish literary scene in the generation after the death of James Joyce. As a student, he wrote as "Brother Barnabas". As Brian O'Nolan, or Ó Nualláin, he worked for the Irish civil service until his retirement. As Myles na Gopaleen, he wrote, in English and Irish Gaelic, Cruiskeen Lawn, a weekly column, part satire, part exuberant blarney, for the *Irish Times*. As Flann O'Brien, he published one of the funniest first novels of the 20th century, *At Swim-Two-Birds*.

This exhilarating and intoxicatingly self-referential extravaganza was admired by the ageing Joyce for its "true comic spirit" and subsequently championed by Anthony Burgess whose own multifarious creativity and anarchic imagination equalled O'Nolan's.

From a longer perspective, *At Swim-Two-Birds*, a mixture of autobiography, fantasy, farce and satire, is the love child of Sterne's *Tristram Shandy* and Joyce's *Portrait of the Artist*, while also being a mad elegy for an Irish culture apparently threatened with oblivion.

Swim-Two-Birds is an Irish public house of the kind that is fast disappearing, the home of music, folklore and every kind of gossip, in poetry and prose, while also being the quotidian HQ of its narrator, who may or may not be an idle young Dublin student named Dermot Trellis. Our narrator, who likes to harangue the reader, and declares that "a good book may have three separate openings entirely dissimilar", lives with his disapproving uncle, a grumpy Guinness employee.

"Tell me this," his relative complains, "do you ever open a book at all?" Actually, our narrator is juggling all kinds of literature in his head. Beneath the top line of the story, a portrait of lower-middle-class Dublin inevitably influenced by Joyce, there is a novel-within-the-novel, the tale of John Furriskey, a young man "born at the age of twenty-five", the work of "eccentric author Dermot Trellis" that quickly spins off into farcical riffs on Irish folklore, focused on the Celtic hero Finn MacCool, the Pooka MacPhellimey and two rustic nitwits, Lamont and Shanahan, loquacious cowhands.

From here on in, as the various characters gang up on Flann

O'Brien's various "authors", *At Swim-Two-Birds* becomes what John Updike nailed as "a many-levelled travesty of a novel", a description that would have delighted both Brian O'Nolan and Myles na Gopaleen.

A Note on the Text:
It was Graham Greene, moonlighting as a reader for Longman's, who first spotted the potential of an unsolicited manuscript, oddly titled *At Swim-Two-Birds,* just before the outbreak of the Second World War, coincidentally the publication year of *Finnegans Wake.* The idea of a pseudonym came up in the contractual negotiations between author and publisher. O'Nolan wrote: "I have been thinking over the question of a pen-name and would suggest Flann O'Brien. I think this invention has the advantage that it contains an unusual name and one that is quite ordinary. 'Flann' is an old Irish name now rarely heard."

The novel first appeared on 13 March 1939, but sold barely 200 copies in the first few months of publication. In 1940, Paternoster Row, the London home of many publishers, was destroyed by bombing. Longman's warehouse, containing the unsold copies of the novel, was reduced to smoking rubble. O'Nolan would later claim that Hitler hated his work so much he had contrived the Second World War to stop it.

Generally, however, the reviews were poor, and the book was sustained by the enthusiastic support of writers such as Graham Greene and Dylan Thomas. The latter came up with a line that for many years adorned various paperback reprints: "This is just the book to give your sister – if she's a loud, dirty, boozy girl." Another champion was Jorge Luis Borges who, in 1939, described Flann O'Brien's masterpiece in the following terms: "I have enumerated many verbal labyrinths, but none so complex as the recent book by Flann O'Brien, *At Swim-Two-Birds...* [which] is not only a labyrinth, [but also] a discussion of the many ways to conceive of the Irish novel and a repertory of exercises in prose and verse which parody all the styles of Ireland."

Borges went on to note that "the magisterial influence of Joyce... is undeniable, but not disproportionate".

After the war, in America, *At Swim-Two-Birds* was republished by Pantheon Books in 1950, but sales remained low. Longman's, meanwhile, had turned down O'Nolan's second novel, *The Third Policeman,* to his great dismay. This would not be published, posthumously, until 1968. Previously, in May 1959, a now defunct London publishing house MacGibbon & Kee, persuaded O'Nolan to allow them to reissue *At Swim-Two-Birds*. Thereafter, the novel was taken up by Penguin Books, which was the edition I first read in 1971, an unforgettable moment.

– 65 –
The Grapes of Wrath
by John Steinbeck (1939)

I began this series with the suggestion that the enduring classics of English and American fiction were novels written either from a burning need for self-expression, often in extremis (*Pilgrim's Progress*), or from a passionate desire to entertain an audience with bravura storytelling (*Tom Jones*). Of course, over time, as the idea of the novel matured, and its readership developed, these comparatively raw instincts would become more sophisticated, getting softened, deepened and tamed. More subtle considerations would come to dominate the genre. Yet this domesticated bourgeois pet would never, as it were, lose a capacity to bare its teeth and drag the reader back into the wild. *The Grapes of Wrath*, is a novel with blood on its teeth.

This is the "American book" Steinbeck always longed to write, a realist tour de force which exemplifies the quite primitive instincts that originally governed the Anglo-American novel, a cry of rage – mixing blue-collar bitterness, prairie folk wisdom and regular left-wing politics – from a bestselling writer inspired to pick up his pen by a deep sense of social injustice, in this case the dreadful conditions of immigrant farmhands in the American south-west. Steinbeck's exposé of the social and economic horrors of farming life in the American dust bowl was a campaigning document by a writer with a conscience who had, as it happened, been born on a farm. The starkness of his narrative, and his sense of injustice, echoed the haunting photos of Dorothea Lange. Like her, he was not afraid to devote his art to the scandal of the Okies (Oklahoma migrants) who trekked to the fruit fields of the Golden State (California) in search of a better life, and suffered horribly in their search for a promised land.

"To the red country and part of the gray country of Oklahoma, the last rains came gently, and they did not cut the scarred earth...." In quasi-Biblical cadences, Steinbeck introduces to reader to the wretched of the earth, the Joad family, dispossessed farmers fleeing dust bowl conditions. Tom Joad has just been paroled from prison. Simultaneously, his family have lost their farm to the bank. The Joads are about to set out west in search of work, down Route 66 to California, the promised land. Nothing goes right. The Joads are exploited, bullied and torn apart. Their grandparents die en route, and have to be buried by the roadside.

As the family begins to disintegrate, it is the women who are strong, like the pioneers of the 19th century. Old Ma Joad takes over. "Women can change better than a man," she says. Tom gets implicated in another killing, and must flee into a landscape bereft of hope and opportunity. In the controversial conclusion to a bleak and pitiless narrative, Tom's sister, Rose of Sharon Joad, loses her daughter and offers her breast to a fellow Okie who is dying of starvation. "She squirmed closer," writes Steinbeck, "and pulled his head close. 'There!' she said. 'There.'" The novel ends with Rose of Sharon's mysterious smile at this shocking gesture of self-sacrifice.

A Note on the Text:
The Grapes of Wrath grew out of a series of newspaper articles on the California migrant workers entitled "The Harvest Gypsies" that Steinbeck published in the *San Francisco News* (illustrated with photographs by Dorothea Lange) from 5 to 12 October, 1936. Writing at the height of the Depression, Steinbeck was on fire with his subject. Like some of the greatest novels in this series, the book was written in a white heat. He said, "I want to put a tag of shame on the greedy bastards who are responsible [for the Great Depression]." The novel – 200,000 words on 165 cramped, handwritten pages in a 12in x 18in lined ledger book – was completed in five months at the rate of 2,000 words a day. "Never worked so hard in my life nor so long before," he told a friend. It was, said Steinbeck, his ambition to "rip a reader's nerves to rags" from page to page. To achieve added drama and tempo, he borrowed the jump-cut technique of Dos Passos' *USA* trilogy. At his wife Carol's suggestion, he took his title from "The Battle Hymn of the Republic" by Julia Ward Howe: "Mine Eyes have seen the glory of the coming of the lord/ He is trampling out the vintage where the grapes of wrath are stored..."

Steinbeck told his literary agent that he liked the title "because it is a march, and this book is a kind of march – because it is in our own revolutionary tradition." On 26 October, 1938, Steinbeck reported he was "so dizzy" he could "hardly see the page." He scrawled "END" in large letters on the manuscript, and then wrote in his journal "Finished this day, and I hope to God it's good."

The first reactions of Steinbeck's agent and editor were excited. *The Grapes of Wrath* was rushed into print, going from typescript to page proof in four months, and published on 14 April 1939 by the Viking Press in New York. The novel at once became a national sensation, possibly the most reviewed and publicised, and even the most controversial, American novel of the 20th century – discussed on the radio, denounced by angry readers, and even banned in some libraries. The Associated Farmers of California were particularly incensed, complaining about "a pack of lies" and "Jewish propaganda", though Steinbeck was not Jewish. A certain Ruth Comfort Mitchell attempted to refute the novel in a vindication of California's treatment of its immigrant workers, in a now-forgotten book entitled *Of Human Kindness.* Joining battle from the other side, both Pearl Buck, author of *The Good Earth,* and the First Lady, Eleanor Roosevelt, who said she never thought the novel was exaggerated, supported Steinbeck. As did the US Senate, which judged that, if anything, the novelist had underestimated the violation of human rights on the west coast.

Despite, or perhaps because of, this furore *The Grapes of Wrath* became the best-selling book of 1939, selling almost half a million copies (at $2.75 a copy) in the first year of publication alone. In 1940, the novel also won the Pulitzer prize for fiction, and would subsequently be taught in schools and colleges across the United States. In that year, John Ford directed a hastily put-together movie of the same name starring Henry Fonda, a rare case of an opportunistic movie equalling its fictional source. When Steinbeck was awarded the Nobel prize for literature in 1962, the prize committee identified this "great work" as a principal reason for awarding the prize. Not everyone was a Steinbeck fan. For example, F Scott Fitzgerald writing to his friend the critic Edmund Wilson, described Steinbeck as "a rather cagey cribber". Posterity has taken a different view. *The Grapes of Wrath* features on many "100 best" lists, including TIME, the Modern Library, *Le Monde*, and the BBC's "Big Read" of 2003. Informal estimates suggest that it has sold about 15 million copies in the 75 years since its publication. There's an American classic for you.

– 66 –
Joy in the Morning
by PG Wodehouse (1946)

For PG Wodehouse, this novel, completed amid the horrors of wartime
 Germany, was something of a miracle, "the supreme Jeeves
novel of all time", he wrote. Defying gravity, English literature's "performing flea" effortlessly reminded his postwar
readers of a world whose day was done and also of a literary
sensibility that had entranced a generation now facing
retirement. A late-season masterpiece, *Joy in the Morning* is
both an elegy and an encore.

"The super-sticky affair of Nobby Hopwood, Stilton Cheesewright,
Florence Craye, my uncle Percy…" is one of those imbroglios that
Bertie Wooster believes his biographers will refer to as "The Steeple
Bumpleigh Horror".

A more brilliant example of Wodehouse's literary escapism, his
capacity to conjure sweetness and light out of airy nothing, would be
hard to find. Not only does he weave together many of his best characters and themes around the old plot of a Wodehouse heroine (Florence
Craye) and her matrimonial designs upon Bertie ("She was one of those
intellectual girls, steeped to the gills in serious purpose, who are unable
to see a male soul without wanting to get behind it and shove"), it
was also conceived and written during the "phoney war", and all but
completed during the Nazi occupation of Le Touquet (Wodehouse's
interwar home).

Joy in the Morning is an anthology of Wodehouse's favourite comic
situations: the impending doom of a mésalliance; a blazing country
cottage; a nocturnal confrontation; a fancy-dress ball. Style and content
achieve a perfect union when a running gag about "the fretful porpen-
tine" culminates with "a hidden hand" concealing a hedgehog in Bertie's
bed. The novel also contains some of Wodehouse's most immortal similes,
including the moment when one of the characters, caught in the act,
spins round "with a sort of guilty bound, like an adagio dancer surprised
while watering the cat's milk". There's also, for readers troubled by
Wodehouse's terrible wartime gaffes, a line of oblique self-justification.
"I doubt," says Bertie, speaking of the writer Boko Fittleworth, "if you
can ever trust an author not to make an ass of himself."

A Note on the Text:

Joy in the Morning was the novel Wodehouse was working on at home in Le Touquet when the German army burst into France with the blitzkrieg of May 1940. Two months later, he was interned as an "enemy alien" and had to leave his unfinished MS in the care of his wife Ethel.

During his internment in Upper Silesia ("If this is Upper Silesia," he joked, "what must Lower Silesia be like?") Wodehouse wrote another novel, *Full Moon*, and did not return to the final chapters of his incomplete Jeeves and Wooster novel until 1943, after his release from captivity, and more especially, after his disastrous radio broadcasts from wartime Berlin. Battered, and embarrassed, but unbowed, he took for his title a quotation from Psalm 30, verse 5: "Weeping may endure for a night, but joy cometh in the morning." This, perhaps, was a coded affirmation of his determination to ride out the controversy surrounding his wartime behaviour.

Eventually, *Joy in the Morning* would be completed in the idyllic rural solitude of Degenershausen, a country house deep in the Harz mountains. From there, the typescript was shipped back to his American publisher, Doubleday Doran, who launched it, with some misgivings about its reception after the scandal of the broadcasts, on 22 August 1946. An English edition from Herbert Jenkins followed on 2 June 1947. In the event, the reviews were good, and the hardback sales respectable, some 20,000 copies at first.

For a writer who preferred to give little away, and (as he put it) "wear the mask", Wodehouse's preface to *Joy in the Morning* is surprisingly candid, revealing his creative anxiety about the effect of the Second World War on his art and his audience. "The world of which I have been writing since I was so high…" he conceded, "has gone with the wind and is one with Nineveh and Tyre. In a word, it has had it." Although he would go on writing about silly young men in spats, butlers, posh girlfriends, and country houses for another 30 years, he never recovered his vintage prewar form (with the possible exception of *The Mating Season*, 1949). His best work was done. Some Wodehouse fans may want to dispute this, but *Joy in the Morning* stands, for me, as his masterpiece, rivalled only by *Uncle Fred in the Springtime, The Code of the Woosters* and *Heavy Weather*.

– 67 –
All the King's Men
by Robert Penn Warren (1946)

Robert Penn Warren was a southern poet and novelist, the only writer to win Pulitzer prizes for both his fiction and his poetry. In 1986, he was appointed America's poet laureate.

All the King's Men is one of American literature's definitive political novels, as well as a profound study of human fallibility in politics. Set in the 1930s, it describes the dramatic rise to power, as state governor, of Willie Stark, a one-time radical attorney.

The novel is narrated by Jack Burden, a political reporter who comes to work as the governor's most trusted aide. The passage of Stark's career is interwoven with Burden's life story and philosophical reflections. As he says: "This has been the story of Willie Stark, but it is my story, too. It is the story of a man who lived in the world, and to him the world looked one way for a long time and then it looked another and very different way."

Stark, or "the Boss", is shown becoming transformed from an idealistic lawyer into a powerful state governor, who quickly adopts all kinds of corruption to build a political machine rooted in graft and intimidation.

Stark's politics earn him many enemies, but his constituents love his fiery, populist manner. The governor is surrounded by a typical southern political gallery of allies and thugs, as well as Burden, who had turned his back on his genteel upbringing to become Stark's amanuensis.

In the process, Burden betrays both his ideals and his career as a historian, and loses the love of his life, Anne Stanton, the daughter of a former state governor.

All the King's Men has a complex narrative structure: events are described out of sequence to demonstrate the relationship between the past and the present. By showing how and why the characters developed as they did, and how events were shaped, the novel gives the reader the means by which to measure the characters and the events they shape.

Robert Penn Warren's great novel is at once a political tragedy, a study of individual corruption, and a compelling southern drama with a long afterlife. In *Primary Colors,* by "Anonymous" (1996), homage is paid to its influence in the character of Governor Stanton.

A Note on the Text:

All the King's Men, the novel, began life in 1936 as a verse play entitled "Proud Flesh". One of the characters in "Proud Flesh" was named Willie Talos, referring to the brutal character Talus in Spenser's *The Faerie Queene.*

All the King's Men was published in 1946, in a 464-page hardcover edition from the New York imprint Harcourt Brace & Company, and took its immediate title from the children's nursery rhyme Humpty Dumpty. Among various critical responses, the *New Republic* praised it as a novel "in the tradition of many classics", and compared it favourably with *Moby-Dick*.

The *New York Times* critic snootily observed that it wasn't "a great novel or a completely finished work of art. It is as bumpy and uneven as a corduroy road, somewhat irresolute and confused in its approach to vital problems and not always convincing. Nevertheless, [it] is magnificently vital reading, a book so charged with dramatic tension it almost crackles with blue sparks; a book so drenched with fierce emotion, narrative pace and poetic imagery that its stature as a 'readin' book,' as some of its characters would call it, dwarfs that of most current publications."

Willie Stark was possibly inspired by the life of senator Huey Long, the aggressively populist governor of Louisiana and the state's senator in the mid-1930s. Long was at the peak of his career when he was assassinated in 1935. A year earlier, Penn Warren had been teaching at Louisiana's state university. Stark, like Long, is shot to death in the state Capitol building. The title of the book was possibly inspired, in part, by Long's populist motto, "Every man a king."

Penn Warren, however, was always troubled by the identification of Willie Stark with Huey Long. He once complained that this had led to nonsensical and "contradictory interpretations of the novel". He continued: "On one hand, there were those who took the thing to be a not-so-covert biography of, and apologia for, Senator Long, and the author to be not less than a base minion of the great man. There is really nothing to reply to this innocent boneheadedness or gospel-bit hysteria. As Louis Armstrong is reported to have said, there's some folks that, if they don't know, you can't tell 'em...

But on the other hand, there were those who took the thing to be a rousing declaration of democratic principles and a tract for the assassination of dictators. This view, though somewhat more congenial to my personal political views, was almost as wide of the mark. For better or worse, Willie Stark was not Huey Long… The difference between the person Huey P Long and the fictional Willie Stark may be indicated by the fact that in the verse play ["Proud Flesh"] the name of the politician was Talos — the name of the brutal, blank-eyed 'iron groom' of Spenser's *Fairie Queene,* the pitiless servant of the knight of justice. My conception grew wider, but that element always remained, and Willie Stark remained, in one way, Willie Talos. In other words, Talos is the kind of doom that democracy may invite upon itself. The book, however, was never intended to be a book about politics. Politics merely provided the framework story in which the deeper concerns, whatever their final significance, might work themselves out."

Half a century after the first printing of *All the King's Men*, a southern academic, Noel Polk, undertook a "restored" edition. This version proved almost as controversial as the original. Writing in the *New York Times*, Joyce Carol Oates declared that "the 1946 text, for all its flaws, is superior to the 'restored' text, which primarily restores distracting stylistic tics and the self-consciously mythic name Willie Talos, which Warren had dropped in favour of the more plausible Willie Stark.

"That Robert Penn Warren, novelist, poet, essayist, and shrewd literary critic, not only approved the original 1946 edition of his most famous novel but oversaw numerous reprintings through the decades, including a special 1963 edition published by Time Inc with a preface by the author, and did not 'restore' any of the original manuscript, and did not resuscitate 'Willie Talos,' is the irrefutable argument that the 1946 edition is the one Warren would wish us to read.

"That Noel Polk should make a project of 'restoring' a text in this way, and that this text should be published to compete with the author-approved text, is unconscionable, unethical, and indefensible."

For some critics, Robert Penn Warren remains hard to categorise (an otherwise comprehensive recent study of Anglo-American fiction, *The Novel: A Biography* by Michael Schmidt, almost ignores him), but his work lives on in the minds of his devoted readers, including this one, who first read him on an Amtrak train between Washington and Philadelphia in the autumn of 1974.

– 68 –
Under the Volcano
by Malcolm Lowry (1947)

It is November 1939, the Day of the Dead in Quauhnahuac, Mexico. Two men in white flannels, one a film-maker, are looking back to last year's fiesta. It was then, we discover, that Geoffrey Firmin – the former British consul, ex-husband of Yvonne, a rampant alcoholic and also a ruined man – embarked on his *via crucis*, an agonised passage through a fateful day, that would end in Firmin's killing.

Lowry himself, a refugee from the Fitzrovia of his contemporary George Orwell and the young Dylan Thomas, described *Under the Volcano* as "a prophecy, a political warning, a cryptogram, a preposterous movie, and a writing on the wall". At the back of his mind, he was inspired by Melville and the capacious majesty of *Moby-Dick*. Lowry's Captain Ahab, however, is fighting a more nebulous nemesis than a whale. In 12 chapters corresponding to the 12 hours of the consul's last day on earth, Lowry takes Firmin on a colossal bender, fuelled by beer, wine, tequila and mescal ("strychnine" to our protagonist). He is drinking himself to death, like Lowry himself, though *Under the Volcano* is about much more than alcoholism. Halfway through, the consul decides that "It was already the longest day in his entire experience, a lifetime". Formally, then, the novel's narrative technique owes a huge debt to Joyce, Conrad, and Faulkner. Lowry's text also teems with allusions to classical and Jacobean tragedy, echoing the cadences of Christopher Marlowe and the Elizabethans.

One of mescal's side-effects is a highly lucid, almost brilliant, depression: this is a dominant mood throughout much of Lowry's introverted, strangely compulsive narrative. Again and again, he insists that he is present in all his characters, an assertion of complex consciousness that is also a deranged kind of solipsism provoked by tropical drink and drugs. We are in the Mexico that attracted many interwar English literary travellers, notably Lawrence, Waugh and Greene, but it's a Mexico that has become a hell on earth.

The background to the consul's Day of the Dead is the drumbeat of conflict, both public and private. Germany is re-arming. Yvonne, Firmin's divorced wife, has come back to challenge his drinking. "Must you go on and on forever into this stupid darkness?" she asks. At the edge of darkness there is death. *Under the Volcano* began in Lowry's mind when, arriving in Mexico, he saw a local Indian bleeding to death by the roadside, which is how Firmin will end, shot in a cheap bar before being tossed into a ravine with a dead dog. The last moments of the consul at the end of the "Day of the Dead" (chapter 12) become one of the greatest passages of English prose on the eve of the Second World War.

A Note on the Text:
No writer in this series had as much trouble as Malcolm Lowry, from inside and out, with his work-in-progress. For the struggling author, in the making of his masterpiece, over nearly a decade, almost nothing went right. At first, in 1936, living in Cuernavaca, Mexico, in the shadow of two volcanoes (Popocatépetl and Iztaccihuatl), galloping alcoholism and a failing marriage, Lowry wrote a short story (not finally published until the 1960s) entitled "Under the Volcano", a sketch of the bigger canvas that was to follow, including a horse branded with the number seven.

The first, raw draft of *Under the Volcano* followed soon after. He considered this to be the "Inferno" element of a trilogy, *The Voyage that Never Ends*, modelled on Dante's *Divine Comedy*. Ultimately, fate determined that only the first part of this ambitious project would ever be completed to its author's satisfaction. In 1940, Lowry commissioned a New York literary agent, Harold Matson, to find a publisher for this manuscript, which was roundly rejected, up and down Manhattan.

Next, between 1940 and 1944, Lowry revised the novel, with crucial editorial assistance from the actress Margerie Bonner, who saved him from the worst of his alcoholism and later became his second wife. This process absorbed him completely: during those years Lowry, who had previously preferred to address himself to several projects at the same time, worked on nothing but his manuscript. In 1944, the current draft was nearly lost in a fire at Lowry's beach house (a squatter's shack) in British Columbia. Bonner rescued the unfinished novel, but the rest of Lowry's works in progress were consumed in the blaze.

The novel was finished in 1945 and immediately submitted to a number of publishers. In late winter, while still travelling abroad, Lowry heard that his novel had been accepted by Reynal & Hitchcock in the United States and Jonathan Cape in Britain. Cape had reservations about publishing and asked for drastic revisions. He added that if Lowry didn't make the changes "it does not necessarily mean I would say no". Lowry's reply, written in January 1946, was a prolonged, vehement, slightly mad defence of the book as something to be considered a work of lasting greatness: "It can be regarded as a kind of symphony," he wrote, "or in another way as a kind of opera – or even a horse opera. It is hot music, a poem, a song, a tragedy, a comedy, a farce and so forth ... Whether it sells or not seems to me either way a risk. But there is something about the destiny of the creation of the book that seems to tell me it just might go on selling a very long time."

Cape published the novel without further revision. To Anthony Burgess it was "a Faustian masterpiece". Yet, *Under the Volcano* was remaindered in England, and out of print when Lowry died of alcoholism in 1957. Thanks to a better response in North America, especially Canada, its afterlife has been lusty and international, featuring regularly on several "best novels" lists. Now it's recognised as a classic.

– 69 –
The Heat of the Day
by Elizabeth Bowen (1948)

London in the blitz influenced the creative lives of many important English writers, from Graham Greene to Rose Macaulay. But none captured wartime London as memorably as Elizabeth Bowen (1899-1973), an Anglo-Irish writer who first attracted critical attention with a collection of short-stories in 1923.

Like *The Death of the Heart*, her prewar masterpiece, *The Heat of the Day* opens in Regent's Park, on "the first Sunday of September 1942", with the sinister figure of Harrison, a counterespionage agent posing as an airman, chatting up a woman at an open-air concert. He's killing time till his evening "date" with Stella Rodney, the novel's protagonist, an attractive, independent woman "on happy sensuous terms with life" who works for a government agency called XYD and is described as a "camper in rooms of draughty dismantled houses".

Stella is dispossessed, but she has in her lover Robert, a Dunkirk survivor, someone with whom she can share mutual passion and "the continuous narrative of love". But even this is in jeopardy. Harrison, who has been watching Robert, advises Stella that her lover is suspected of passing information to the enemy. He offers Stella a bargain: his silence about Robert's treachery for an impossible price – herself. Once Robert confesses, his love will be doomed.

Trapped between spy and spycatcher, Stella struggles to keep her life in balance while recognising she's adrift in dark times. Occasional passages of great beauty capture the atmosphere of the nightly bombing of London: "Out of mists of morning charred by the smoke from ruins each day rose to a height of unmisty glitter; between the last of sunset and first note of the siren the darkening glassy tenseness of evening was drawn fine."

Like many writers who come to the novel through the short story, Bowen's fiction is highly symbolic and tightly wound with acres of meaning crowded into the disjunctions and silences of everyday conversation. Harold Pinter was a natural for the screenplay of the 1989 TV version of the novel. *The Heat of the Day* is both of its time and timeless. A spy story and a haunting love story. Bowen catches the provisional, precarious atmosphere of a society facing the threat of imminent destruction. More than just a great writer of the blitz, she is the supreme mid-century anatomist of the heart, with a unique sensitivity to the lives of ordinary English men and women in extremis.

The best account of this subject, in addition to Victoria Glendinning's important biography of Bowen, is Lara Feigel's *The Love-Charm of Bombs*, an exploration of the blitz as a metropolitan trauma. Feigel's absorbing and well-researched group portrait of five prominent writers caught up in the nightly routine of sirens and barrage includes Elizabeth Bowen, Graham Greene, Rose Macaulay, Hilde Spiel (an Austrian writer trapped in wartime Wimbledon) and Henry Yorke (better known as the novelist Henry Green). Nevertheless, the blitz remains a comparatively under-explored literary terrain. Sarah Waters's 2006 novel *The Night Watch* is a rare example of a serious attempt to make popular literature out of this crucial episode from the Second World War.

A Note on the Text:
The Heat of the Day was favourably compared, on publication, to the work of EM Forster, Virginia Woolf and Henry Green. It was first published by Jonathan Cape in 1948 in the United Kingdom, and in 1949 in the United States of America by Alfred A Knopf.

Some critics place it beneath *The Death of the Heart* (1938) in importance. I've chosen it both because it has always been a favourite of mine and also because it helps to make a bridge in this list between the fiction of the 1930s and the transformed literary landscape of the postwar world.

Not everyone was enthralled by *The Heat of the Day*. Raymond Chandler, unfairly, described it as "a screaming parody of Henry James". The New Statesman's critic, more judicious, wrote: "Unerringly, exquisitely, Miss Bowen has caught the very feel of her period… The novel is the most completely detailed and most beautiful evocation of it that we have yet had." Anthony Burgess, writing later, concurred. "No novel has better caught the atmosphere of London during the Second World War."

– 70 –
Nineteen Eighty-Four
by George Orwell (1949)

"It was a bright cold day in April, and the clocks were striking thirteen."

Time is out of joint, and everyday life has no comfort any more: from *Down and Out in Paris and London* (1933) to *Animal Farm* (1945), George Orwell had been incubating a profound inner dissonance with his society. Even as a child, he had been fascinated by the futuristic imagination of HG Wells (and later, Aldous Huxley). Finally, at the end of his short life, he fulfilled his dream. *Nineteen Eighty-Four,* arguably the most famous English novel of the 20th century, is a zeitgeist book. Orwell's dystopian vision was deeply rooted both in its author's political morality, and in its time, the postwar years of western Europe. Its themes (the threat of the totalitarian state, censorship and the manipulation of language) continue to reverberate, with prophetic menace, like distant gunfire, into the present.

After the third world war, Britain is now Airstrip One in the American superstate of Oceania, permanently in conflict with Eurasia and Eastasia. Winston Smith, a former journalist employed by the Ministry of Truth to rewrite old newspaper articles so that the historical record always supports state policy, decides to launch his own hopeless private rebellion against the oppression of "the Party" and its all-seeing, all-powerful dictator, Big Brother. Winston's revolt gets added impetus from his association with Julia, another dissident, who wants to use her rampant sexuality to defy the repression of "the Party".

When Winston and Julia's brief affair is discovered by the Thought Police they are subjected to the torments of Room 101 at the hands of the merciless O'Brien. "If you want a picture of the future," says this demonic figure, "imagine a boot stamping on a human face – for ever." At the end, now brainwashed into submission, Winston awaits his execution as "the last man in Europe", the working title of Orwell's first draft.

The plot of *Nineteen Eighty-Four* is one thing; its ideas are something else. In the 65 years since its publication, "Big Brother is watching you", "newspeak", "doublethink" "prole", "thoughtcrime", "unperson", "reality control" and "the Two Minutes Hate" have become inseparable from the English language. Orwell himself, in the words of one critic, "the wintry conscience of his generation", has become a kind of secular saint, which is an incarnation that might surprise his former colleagues on the *Observer*.

A Note on the Text:
The circumstances surrounding the writing of *Nineteen Eighty-Four* make grim reading, and help to explain the persistent bleakness of Orwell's dystopia. The idea for "The Last Man in Europe" had been in Orwell's mind since the Spanish civil war. His novel, which owes something to Yevgeny Zamyatin's dystopian fiction *We*, probably began to acquire a definitive shape during 1943-44, around the time he and his wife, Eileen, adopted their only son, Richard, whom I was once lucky enough to interview about his father. Orwell was also partly inspired by the meeting of the allied leaders at the Tehran Conference of 1944. Isaac Deutscher, a colleague on the *Observer*, for which Orwell was working as a foreign correspondent, reported that Orwell was "convinced that Stalin, Churchill and Roosevelt consciously

plotted to divide the world" at Tehran.

Orwell had been attached to David Astor's *Observer* since 1942, first as a book reviewer and later as a correspondent. His editor professed great admiration for Orwell's "absolute straightforwardness, his honesty and his decency", and would be his patron throughout the 1940s. The closeness of their friendship is crucial to the backstory of *Nineteen Eighty-Four.*

Orwell's creative life had already benefited from his association with the *Observer* in the writing of *Animal Farm.* As the war drew to a close, the interaction of fiction and journalism would contribute to the much darker and more complex novel he had in mind. There were other influences at work. Soon after Richard was adopted, Orwell's flat was wrecked by a doodlebug. The atmosphere of random terror in the everyday life of wartime London became integral to the mood of the novel-in-progress. Worse was to follow. In March 1945, while on assignment for the *Observer* in Europe, Orwell received the news that his wife, Eileen, had died under anaesthesia during a routine operation.

Now David Astor stepped in. His family owned an estate on the remote Scottish island of Jura, next to Islay. There was a house, Barnhill, seven miles outside Ardlussa at the northern tip of this desolate part of the Inner Hebrides. Initially, Astor offered it to Orwell for a holiday. In May 1946 Orwell, still picking up the shattered pieces of his life, took the train to Jura, a risky move. He was not in good health. The winter of 1946-47 was one of the coldest of the century, and he had always suffered from a bad chest. At least, cut off from the irritations of literary London, he was free to grapple unencumbered with the new novel. "Smothered under journalism," as he told one friend, "I have become more and more like a sucked orange."

Part of Orwell's difficulties derived from the success of *Animal Farm.* After years of neglect, the world was waking up to his genius. "Everyone keeps coming at me," he complained to Koestler, "wanting me to lecture, to write commissioned booklets, to join this and that, etc – you don't know how I pine to be free of it all and have time to think again."

On Jura he would be liberated from these distractions but the promise of creative freedom on an island in the Hebrides came with its own price. Years before, in the essay "Why I Write", he had described the struggle to complete a book: "Writing a book is a horrible, exhausting struggle, like a long bout of some painful illness. One would never undertake such a thing if one were not driven by some demon whom one can neither resist or [sic] understand. For all one knows that demon is the same instinct that makes a baby squall for attention. And yet it is also true that one can write nothing readable unless one constantly struggles to efface one's personality." Then that famous Orwellian coda: "Good prose is like a window pane."

From the spring of 1947 to his death in 1950 Orwell would re-enact every aspect of this struggle in the most painful way imaginable. At first, after "a quite unendurable winter", he revelled in the isolation and wild beauty of Jura. "I am struggling with this book," he wrote to his agent, "which I may finish by the end of the year – at any rate I shall have broken the back by then so long as I keep well and keep off journalistic work until the autumn."

Life at Barnhill was simple, even primitive. There was no electricity. Orwell used Calor Gas to cook and to heat water. Storm lanterns burned paraffin. In the evenings he also burned peat. He was still chain-smoking black shag tobacco in roll-up cigarettes: the fug in the house was cosy but not healthy. A battery radio was the only connection with the outside world. Once his new regime was settled, Orwell could finally make a start. At the end of May 1947 he told his publisher, Fred Warburg: "I think I must have written nearly a third of the rough draft. I have not got as far as I had hoped to do by this time because I really have been in most wretched health this year ever since about January (my chest as usual) and can't quite shake it off."

Mindful of his publisher's impatience for the new novel, Orwell added: "Of course the rough draft is always a ghastly mess having very little relation to the finished result, but all the same it is the main part of the job." Still, he pressed on, and at the end of July was predicting a completed "rough draft" by October. After that, he said, he would need another six months to polish up the text for publication. In late October 1947, oppressed with "wretched health", Orwell recognised that his novel was still "a most dreadful mess and about two-thirds of it will have to be retyped entirely". Just before Christmas, he broke the news that he had been diagnosed with TB.

In 1947 there was no cure for TB – doctors prescribed fresh air and a regular diet – but there was a new, experimental drug on the market, streptomycin. Astor arranged for a shipment from the US. The side-effects were horrific (throat ulcers, blisters in the mouth, hair loss, peeling skin and the disintegration of toe and fingernails) but in March 1948, after a three-month course, the TB symptoms had disappeared. "It's all over now, and evidently the drug has done its stuff," Orwell told his publisher. "It's rather like sinking the ship to get rid of the rats, but worth it if it works."

As he prepared to leave hospital, Orwell received the letter from his publisher that, in hindsight, would be another nail in his coffin. "It really is rather important," wrote Warburg to his star author, "from the point of view of your literary career to get it [the new novel] by the end of the year and indeed earlier if possible."

Just when he should have been convalescing, Orwell was back at Barnhill, deep into the revision of his manuscript, promising Warburg to deliver it in "early December", and coping with "filthy weather" on autumnal Jura. Early in October he confided to Astor: "I have got so used to writing in bed that I think I prefer it, though of course it's awkward to type there. I am just struggling with the last stages of this bloody book [which is] about the possible state of affairs if the atomic war isn't conclusive."

The typing of the fair copy of "The Last Man in Europe" became another dimension of Orwell's battle with his book. The more he revised his "unbelievably bad" manuscript, the more it became a document only he could read and interpret. It was, he told his agent, "extremely long, even 125,000 words". With characteristic candour, he noted: "I am not pleased with the book but I am not absolutely dissatisfied… I think it is a good idea but the execution would have been better if I had not written it under the influence of TB."

He was still undecided about the title: "I am inclined to call it NINETEEN EIGHTY-FOUR or THE LAST MAN IN EUROPE," he wrote, "but I might just possibly think of something else in the next week or two." By the end of October, Orwell believed he was done. Now he just needed a stenographer to help make sense of it all.

In a desperate race against time, Orwell's health was deteriorating, the "unbelievably bad" manuscript needed retyping, and the December deadline was looming. Warburg promised to help, and so did Orwell's agent. At cross-purposes over possible typists, they somehow contrived to make a bad situation infinitely worse. Orwell, feeling beyond help, followed his ex-public schoolboy's instincts: he would go it alone.

By mid-November, too weak to walk, he retired to bed to tackle "the grisly job" of typing the book on his "decrepit typewriter" by himself. Sustained by endless roll-ups, pots of coffee, strong tea and the warmth of his paraffin heater, with gales buffeting Barnhill, night and day, he struggled on. By 30 November 1948 it was virtually done.

Now Orwell, the old campaigner, protested to his agent that "it really wasn't worth all this fuss. It's merely that, as it tires me to sit upright for any length of time, I can't type very neatly and can't do many pages a day". Besides, he added, it was "wonderful" what mistakes a professional typist could make, and "in this book there is the difficulty that it contains a lot of neologisms".

The typescript of George Orwell's latest novel reached London in mid-December, as promised. Warburg recognised its qualities at once ("among the most terrifying books I have ever read") and so did his colleagues. An in-house memo noted "if we can't sell 15 to 20 thousand copies we ought to be shot".

Nineteen Eighty-Four was published on 8 June 1949 (five days later in the US). Secker & Warburg in the UK, and Harcourt Brace in New York were eager to get it out into bookshops as soon as possible. Orwell's American editor, Robert Giroux, whom I remember with fondness from the 1980s, did not wait for the English page proofs from which to set his edition, as was customary. Instead, he prepared a fresh copy for the American printer, with the result that the two first editions are significantly different in many small ways.

The novel was almost universally recognised as a masterpiece, even by Winston Churchill, who told his doctor that he had read it twice. Orwell's health continued to decline. In October 1949, in his room at University College hospital, he married Sonia Brownell, with David Astor as best man. It was a fleeting moment of happiness; he lingered into the new year of 1950. In the small hours of 21 January he suffered a massive haemorrhage in hospital and died alone.

Orwell's title remains something of a mystery. Some say he was alluding to the centenary of the Fabian Society, founded in 1884. Others suggest a nod to Jack London's novel *The Iron Heel* (in which a political movement comes to power in 1984), or perhaps to one of his favourite writers GK Chesterton's story, *The Napoleon of Notting Hill,* which is set in 1984.

In his edition of the *Collected Works* (20 volumes), Peter Davison notes that Orwell's American publisher claimed that the title derived from reversing the date, 1948, though there's no documentary evidence for this. Davison also argues that the date 1984 is linked to the year of Richard Blair's birth, 1944, and notes that in the manuscript of the novel, the narrative occurs, successively, in 1980, 1982 and finally, 1984. There's no mystery about the decision to abandon "*The Last Man in Europe*". Orwell himself was always unsure of it. It was his publisher, Fred Warburg, who suggested that *Nineteen Eighty-Four* would be a more commercial title. It remains one of the all-time classics of the 20th century.

– 71 –
The End of the Affair
by Graham Greene (1951)

There are many Greenes, and almost all of them – the thriller writer (*The Third Man*), the entertainer (*Our Man in Havana*), the contemporary political novelist (*The Quiet American*), the polemicist (*The Comedians)* and the serious religious writer (*The Power and the Glory*) – deserve consideration in this series. I've chosen *The End of the Affair* because it blurs the line he drew between his "entertainments" and his more serious work. The novel owes its inspiration to the conventions of romantic fiction while at the same time transcending genre. Crucially, it dates from Greene's best years, the age of postwar austerity that also nurtured the previous author in this series, George Orwell.

Set in Clapham during the blitz (before the war, Greene owned a house in Clapham), it's a story of adultery. Maurice Bendrix, a second-rank novelist, wants to write about a civil servant, and makes the acquaintance of his neighbour's wife, Sarah. They fall in love and have an affair tortured by his jealousy and her guilt. When Bendrix is nearly killed by a bomb (Greene's house was similarly wrecked during the blitz), his mistress suddenly breaks off relations. Only in retrospect will the meaning of this inexplicable act of rejection become apparent.

Two years pass. Sarah's husband, Henry, who is ignorant of the affair, approaches Bendrix about his wife's infidelity with "a third man". Intrigued, the novelist employs a private detective to investigate. Having said, at the outset, that "a story has no beginning or end", Greene now employs a dizzy mix of flashback, stream-of-consciousness and conventional narrative, partly based on Sarah's diary, to relate how she, having prayed for a miracle, "catches belief like a disease", and then subsequently dies. The "third man", a recurrent figure with Greene, turns out to be God, for whom Sarah has become "a bride in Christ". This supernatural, Roman Catholic element of the plot has not worn well, but the portrait of wartime London, and the agony of two people caught in an illicit love affair, remains compelling.

A Note on the Text:

The best clue to the emotional freight carried by *The End of the Affair* is probably to be found in its differing dedication pages. The English edition, published by William Heinemann in September 1951, reads "To C". But the American edition, much less cryptic, reads "To Catherine with love". Catherine Walston, the wife of the Labour peer Harry Walston, had been quite explicitly Greene's mistress for several years, in a relationship that tormented all concerned. Few women ever touched Greene as deeply, however, and his novel became the sad record of their ultimately doomed relationship. "It was," writes Norman Sherry in his very unsatisfactory three-volume biography, "a love affair of dangerous proportions", and one wracked, as the novel is, with Catholic guilt.

The End of the Affair is the fourth and final Greene novel with an overtly Roman Catholic dimension. (The others are *Brighton Rock, The Power and the Glory* and *The Heart of the Matter.*) About a year after its publication Greene told Evelyn Waugh that he wanted to write a political novel. It would be fun to deal with politics, he said, "and not always write about God". Waugh's response was characteristically sharp and practical. "I wouldn't give up writing about God at this stage if I was you," he replied. "It would be like PG Wodehouse dropping Jeeves halfway through the Wooster series."

Waugh's review of *The End of the Affair* of 6th September 1951 in the magazine *Month* stands up well to the test of time. In his new novel, writes Waugh, "Mr Greene has chosen another contemporary form, domestic, romantic drama of the type of Brief Encounter, and has transformed that in his own inimitable way." Waugh added that the story was "a singularly beautiful and moving one".

This, perhaps, explains its continued appeal. The novel has been filmed twice (in 1955 and 1999). William Golding, ignored the religion and accurately described Greene as "the ultimate chronicler of 20th century man's consciousness and anxiety".

– 72 –
The Catcher in the Rye
by JD Salinger (1951)

JD Salinger's Holden Caulfield is to the 20th century what Huckleberry Finn is to the 19th: the unforgettably haunting voice of the adolescent at odds with a troubling world. Holden, the opposite of Huck, is an unhappy rich boy who has done a bunk from his posh secondary school, Pencey Prep, in Agerstown, Pennsylvania. He begins his first-person narrative in words that echo the famous opening of Twain's novel, a frank disavowal of "all that David Copperfield kind of crap".

Holden declares that he isn't going to tell us "about this madman stuff that happened to me around last Christmas just before I got pretty run-down". Actually, that's just what he does, writing (apparently in retrospect from California) about three days in December 1949 when, having been chastised by his school "for not applying myself", he plays truant over a long and memorable weekend in Manhattan. Holden is tortured by the battle to come to terms with himself, with his little sister Phoebe, and their dead brother Allie. Like many adolescents, he feels that the world is an alien, hostile and comfortless place run by "phonies".

One of the many remarkable things about Salinger's portrayal of Holden Caulfield is that he seems to be fully inside the head of this troubled 16-year-old when the author himself was almost twice that age. Salinger had fought in Europe as an infantryman, after landing at Utah Beach on D-day, and later saw action at the Battle of the Bulge. Quite a lot of the downtown action in *The Catcher in the Rye* (a night out in a fancy hotel; a date with an old girlfriend; an encounter with a prostitute, and a mugging by her pimp) might almost as well describe a young soldier's nightmare experience of R&R.

That's just one reading. Salinger's masterpiece (he published comparatively little after its appearance) has also influenced later writers with angry protagonists, from Martin Amis's Charles Highway to Philip Roth's Portnoy and many others besides. *The Catcher in the Rye* remains the crazy, and often very funny, distorting mirror in which generations of British and American teenagers will examine themselves. At the same time, it instructs them to give nothing away to "the phonies" who ruin all our lives. "Don't ever tell anybody anything," says Holden Caulfield, echoing Huck Finn again. "If you do, you start missing everybody."

A Note on the Text (and its afterlife):
The Catcher in the Rye had some difficulty finding a publisher. One editor judged its protagonist simply "crazy". *The New Yorker*, which had favoured Salinger's stories, stalled with indecision. Eventually, it was published on 16 July 1951, by Little, Brown in Boston, with a famous, award-winning cover designed by E Michael Mitchell.

Salinger had been working towards his masterpiece, in sketches and drafts, for a decade and more. Some of his earliest short stories, written as a student, contain characters reminiscent of those in *The Catcher in the Rye*. Indeed, while still at Columbia, Salinger wrote a story, "The Young Folks", that included a character described as a prototype of Sally Hayes (Holden's old flame). In November 1941, Salinger also sold a story ("Slight Rebellion Off Madison"), featuring a disaffected teenager with "prewar jitters" named Holden Caulfield, to the *New Yorker*. After the outbreak of war, in which Salinger served as an infantryman, the piece was considered unpatriotic and did not get published until December 1946. Meanwhile, another story entitled "I'm Crazy", containing material that was later used in *The Catcher in the Rye,* appeared in *Collier's* magazine on 22 December 1945. Another long story about Holden Caulfield was accepted by the *New Yorker* for publication, although it never appeared.

The Catcher in the Rye continues to hold its place as the defining novel of teenage angst and alienation. My friend, the critic Adam Gopnik, says it is one of the "three perfect books" in American literature (the others are *The Adventures of Huckleberry Finn* and *The Great Gatsby*). Gopnik says that "no book has ever captured a city better than *The Catcher in the Rye* captured New York in the 50s". Book and author quickly acquired a mystique, partly abetted by Salinger, who cultivated his obscurity to the point of mania, becoming as secretive and self-obsessed as Holden Caulfield, in the words of the *New York Times*, "the Garbo of letters". Apart from this novel, Salinger published just one collection of stories and two short books about the Glass family, which some readers prefer.

However, between 1961 and 1982, *The Catcher in the Rye* became more studied in the high schools and libraries of the United States than any other novel. By 1981, it was the second most taught book in the United States. Teenagers especially loved the book for what is taken as Holden Caulfield's sponsorship of rebellion, combined with his promotion of drinking, smoking and sex. More seriously, there is the grimmer association of *The Catcher in the Rye* with the murder of John Lennon by Mark Chapman, and John Hinckley's failed assassination of Ronald Reagan.

Salinger himself remained sequestered from the world in New Hampshire. "There is a marvellous peace in not publishing," he said, some 20 years after he first fell silent.

– 73 –
The Adventures of Augie March
by Saul Bellow (1953)

From the get-go – "I am an American, Chicago-born" – this turbo-

charged masterpiece declares itself to be a heavyweight contender; and for some, *The Adventures of Augie March* is a knockout. Delmore Schwartz called it "a new kind of book". Forget *Huckleberry Finn* (nodded at in the title); forget *Gatsby*; even forget *Catcher in the Rye*. This, says Martin Amis, one of many writers under Bellow's spell, is "the Great American Novel. Search no further". Well, maybe.

In retrospect, both JD Salinger and Saul Bellow, who declared their originality at the beginning of the 1950s, stand head-and-shoulders above a rising generation of young contenders, from Norman Mailer and Gore Vidal to Kurt Vonnegut, and James Salter. No question: the great American postwar fiction boom starts here.

Augie March opens in 1920s Chicago during the Great Depression. Augie is "the by-blow of a travelling man", and his adventures, loosely patterned after Bellow's experience, are picaresque. This odyssey, in Bellow's own words, traces "a widening spiral that begins in the parish, ghetto, slum and spreads into the greater world", much as his own life did. Augie finds his feet through his engagement with a kind of America that had not been run to earth in fiction before. A sequence of brilliant set pieces narrates the footloose Augie's upward drift. He becomes a butler, a shoe salesman, a paint-seller, a dog-groomer and a book thief, even a trades union shop steward.

He also revels, like Dickens, in some memorable characters – Augie's Jewish mother; Einhorn, the fixer and surrogate father – and some seductive women: Sophie Geratis, Thea Fenchel (and her eagle, Caligula), and finally, Stella, whom Augie will marry. It's a long book, some 500 pages. "It takes some of us a long time," says Augie, "to find out what the price is of being in nature, and what the facts are about your tenure." Quite so.

Augie enlists in the merchant marine during the Second World War. When his ship, the Sam MacManus, is torpedoed, Augie experiences a long quasi-surreal episode on board a lifeboat in which he confronts matters of life and death in the company of Basteshaw, a weirdo. In the end, with persistent questions about identity and reality unresolved, Augie, the "travelling man", declares himself to be "a sort of Columbus", one who discovered a new world but who may himself be a flop. "Which," as Bellow jokes in a brilliant closing line, "doesn't prove there was no America".

A Note on the Text:
Saul Bellow published his first novel, *Dangling Man* in 1944, followed by *The Victim* (1947) – two works of fiction that reflect his marginal status as a Canadian Jew living in the US – but did not find his true voice as a novelist until he wrote *The Adventures of Augie March*. Later, looking back, he recalled: "I was turned on like a fire hydrant in summer." He had begun to write the novel in Paris, having won a Guggenheim fellowship. According to his first biographer, James Atlas, from whom he became estranged, Bellow found the spectacle of water flooding down a Parisian street to be the inspiration for the "cascade of prose" that gushed after his famous opening line: "I am an American, Chicago born – Chicago, that sombre city – and go at things as I have taught myself, free-style, and will make the record in my own way…"

He was, he said, revelling in "the relief of turning away from mandarin English and putting my own accents into the language. My earlier books had been straight and respectable. But in *Augie March* I wanted to invent a new sort of American sentence. Something like a fusion between colloquialism and elegance." Philip Roth, who would sometimes struggle with Bellow's influence, noted that this new style "combined literary complexity with conversational ease". It was, like many literary innovations, from Mark Twain onwards, a high-low hybrid, and linked, in Roth's words, "the idiom of the academy with the idiom of the streets (not all streets – certain streets)".

The great, unfulfilled, hope of American fiction in the 1930s, Delmore Schwartz, put this explicitly: "For the first time in fiction America's social mobility has been transformed into a spiritual energy which is not doomed to flight, renunciation, exile, denunciation, the agonised hyper-intelligence of Henry James, or the hysterical cheering of Walter Whitman." Other critics, notably James Wood, have celebrated something equally universal – "the beauty of this writing, its music, its high lyricism, its firm but luxurious pleasure in language itself".

The Adventures of Augie March encountered only one serious pre-publication critique (from Bellow's British editor, John Lehmann, the celebrated founder of Penguin New Writing). The upshot of this clash was Bellow's determination to prevail. And he did. *Augie March* spoke directly to the new postwar generation, and would go on to influence writers as various as Cormac McCarthy, Martin Amis, Jonathan Safran Foer and Joseph Heller.

Bellow's third novel was published by the Viking Press in 1953. In 1976 he was awarded the Nobel prize for literature, which identified this book as an important "novel and subtle analysis of our culture, of entertaining adventure, drastic and tragic episodes in quick succession interspersed with philosophic conversation, all developed by a commentator with a witty tongue and penetrating insight into the outer and inner complications that drive us to act, or prevent us from acting, and that can be called the dilemma of our age…"

– 74 –
Lord of the Flies
by William Golding (1954)

Like all the recent novels in this list, *Lord of the Flies* owes much of its dark power and impetus to the Second World War, in which Golding served as a young naval officer. His experiences at Walcheren in 1944 nurtured an appetite for quasi-medieval extremes, mixing fiction and philosophy, which is not always a recipe for success in novels. However, *Lord of the Flies* remains both universal and yet profoundly English, with nods to Defoe, Stevenson and Jack London.

By the 1950s, now teaching at a boys' grammar school, Golding was struggling to make his way as a novelist, having had a volume of poems published in 1934. His wife, Ann, who played a crucial role in his creative life, suggested RM Ballantyne's *Coral Island* as a source of inspiration. The upshot: a post-apocalyptic, dystopian survivor-fantasy about a bunch of pre-teen and teenage boys on a remote tropical island. But this is a far cry from the world of Robinson Crusoe or Long John Silver.

Lord of the Flies (whose title derives from one transcription of "Beelzebub") is the work of an English teacher with a taste for big themes, and engages the reader at three levels. First, it's a brilliantly observed study of adolescents untethered from rules and conventions. The main players – Ralph, Jack and Piggy – represent archetypes of English schoolboy, but Golding gets under their skin and makes them real. He knows how they tick, and draws on his own experience to explore the terrifying breakdown of their community.

Second and third, *Lord of the Flies* presents a view of humanity unimaginable before the horrors of Nazi Europe, and then plunges into speculations about mankind in the state of nature. Bleak and specific, but universal, fusing rage and grief, *Lord of the Flies* is both a novel of the 1950s, and for all time. A strange kind of Eden becomes a desolate portrait of life in a post-nuclear world. Perhaps it's no surprise that it should become a cult classic of the 60s, to be read as avidly as *Catcher in the Rye*, *To Kill a Mocking Bird* and *On the Road*.

A Note on the Text:

Before completing this novel, William Golding had been "Scruff", the shy, oddball English teacher at Bishop Wordsworth's school in Salisbury. *Lord of the Flies,* written during 1952-53, suffered successive rejections before its triumphant publication in 1954. At first titled Strangers from Within, the novel not only endured almost universal disdain, it was also the desperate last throw of an awkward schoolmaster who had struggled for years to find an audience.

His daughter, Judy, born at the end of the war, was too young to remember her father writing *Lord of the Flies* but she told me in an interview some years ago: "I do remember the parcels [of manuscript] going off and coming back. We lived on a very tight budget, so the postage must have been a significant expense."

The legend of this iconic postwar novel has become hoary with many tellings. When it first arrived at Faber & Faber (its eventual publisher), it was a dog-eared manuscript that had obviously done the rounds. Its first in-house reader, a certain Miss Perkins, famously dismissed it as an "absurd and uninteresting fantasy about the explosion of an atom bomb on the Colonies. A group of children who land in jungle country near New Guinea. Rubbish & dull. Pointless." However, a newly recruited young Faber editor, Charles Monteith, disagreed. He saw that the first chapter (about the aftermath of the bomb) could be dropped, fought for the book, and then, having persuaded Golding to cut and rewrite, steered it through to publication. Monteith, whom I came to know well, and admire, was doing what Maxwell Perkins did for Thomas Wolfe or Gordon Lish for Raymond Carver. It's a skill that is rarely found in publishing today.

Eventually, the novel would sell more than 10m copies, but fame and success did not come overnight. The first printing of about 3,000 copies sold slowly. Gradually, the book's qualities won serious attention. A turning-point occurred when EM Forster chose *Lord of the Flies* as his "outstanding novel of the year." Other reviews described it as "not only a first-rate adventure but a parable of our times". Judy Golding told me it was only "five years later, after the film came out [directed by Peter Brook], that I noticed parents of my friends suddenly becoming interested in Daddy".

Thereafter, the novel became cult reading. When I worked at Faber in the 1980s, we used to reprint it, 100,000 copies at a time, year after year. I believe this still goes on. That's one definition of classic, a book which even when we read it for the first time gives us the sense of re-reading something we have read before. In the words of Italo Calvino, "A classic is a book which has never exhausted all it has to say to its readers."

Lord of the Flies has had a wide influence on many English and American writers, including Alex Garland, whose *The Beach* pays homage to Golding's original. Nigel Williams also adapted *Lord of the Flies* for the stage in a strikingly powerful version that has helped sustain the novel's afterlife.

– 75 –
Lolita
by Vladimir Nabokov (1955)

In 1962, almost a decade after its first appearance, Nabokov told the BBC that "*Lolita* is a special favourite of mine. It was my most difficult book – the book that treated a theme which was so distant, so remote, from my own emotional life that it gave me a special pleasure to use my combinational talent to make it real."

The author's passion for this erotic tragi-comedy is part of its charm and its appeal. Nabokov knows he is crossing boundaries of good taste but he exults in his truancy from convention anyway. Everything, and everyone, is up for grabs. From the famous opening line, *Lolita* is the work of a writer in love with the potentiality of the English language: "Lolita, light of my life, fire of my loins. My sin, my soul. Lo-lee-ta: the tip of the tongue taking a trip of three steps down the palate to tap, at three, on the teeth. Lo. Lee. Ta." Nabokov's novel is both a comic tour de force and a transgressive romp. As Martin Amis, a devoted advocate, has written, *Lolita* is "both irresistible and unforgivable".

Subtitled "the confessions of a white widowed male", the novel is an intoxicating mix of apologia, prison diary and urgent appeal to the members of a jury by a 38-year old defendant, Dr Humbert Humbert, a professor of literature. Humbert, who is obsessed with "nymphets" (Nabokov's coinage), girls on the edge of puberty, has been charged with the murder of Clare Quilty, a playwright. As Humbert's confession unfolds, in two unequal parts – the latter a travelogue that prompted Christopher Isherwood to joke that it was "the best travel book ever written about America" – the reader discovers that his defence is "crime of passion": he slaughtered Quilty out of love for Dolores Haze, his "Lolita".

Although we see him drugging the love object of his dreams, Humbert is hardly debauching an innocent. In a twist that makes for uncomfortable reading in the context of contemporary anxieties about child abuse, Nabokov establishes that Lolita is sexually precocious already. When it comes to the moment when she and Humbert are "technically lovers", it was, in Nabokov's brilliant and clinical reversal, "she who seduced me".

A Note on the Text:
Nabokov's mother tongue was Russian, just as Joseph Conrad's was Polish. But, like Conrad, he takes his place here as a master of the English (and American) language. Nabokov's own retrospective account, dated 12 November 1956, "On a book entitled *Lolita*", provides the essential narrative of his novel's gestation.

He writes that "the first little throb of *Lolita* went through me late in 1939, or early in 1940, in Paris." At the time, he says, he was "laid up with a severe attack of intercostal neuralgia". The upshot of this "little throb" was "a short story some 30 pages long", written in Russian. But Nabokov was displeased with this preliminary sketch and says he "destroyed it some time after moving to America in 1940".

But the fever-germ of his masterpiece was lodged in his imagination. In 1949, he continues, "the throbbing, which had never quite ceased, began to plague me again". Now writing in English as a would-be American, he began a new version. Progress was painfully slow. "Other books intervened," he writes, but still he could not reconcile himself to consigning his unfinished draft to the incinerator.

Meanwhile, the exiled Nabokov, a distinguished lepidopterist, could never resist the lure of errant butterflies. "Literature and butterflies," he once said, "are the two sweetest passions known to man." Every summer he and his wife would head out west to Colorado, Arizona or Wyoming in pursuit of Variegated Fritillaries and Polyommatus Blues. It was there, out in Telluride, that he resumed writing *Lolita* "in the evenings, or on cloudy days". By the spring of 1954 he had completed a longhand draft and "began casting around for a publisher".

It was now that the fun started. The immediate response of the four American publishers to whom it was submitted (Farrar Straus, Viking, Simon & Schuster and New Directions) was that they would not touch it with a bargepole. One editor, a timid soul, exclaimed "Do you think I'm crazy?" Others expressed fears about prosecution, and hinted darkly at the risk of prison. In despair, Nabokov turned to publication in France with Maurice Girodias's Olympia Press, an imprint specialising in what has been described as a list of "pornographic trash". Nabokov duly signed a contract with the Olympia Press for publication of the book, which would not appear anonymously (as had been mooted in America) but came out in volume form (two volumes, actually) under his own name.

Lolita was published in September 1955, as a pair of green paperbacks littered with typographical errors. Nevertheless, the first printing of 5,000 copies sold out, though virtually no one had reviewed it. Then, towards the end of 1955, Graham Greene, choosing his books of the year for the *Sunday Times*, described it as one of the best books of the year. This statement provoked a reaction from the *Sunday Express,* whose editor called it "the filthiest book I have ever read" and "sheer unrestrained pornography". The novel became a banned book, in a manner unthinkable today. For two years, copies of *Lolita* were proscribed by the authorities and hunted down by British customs. Eventually, the young publisher George Weidenfeld saw his chance. In 1959 he brought out a British edition, challenging the law. After a tense standoff, the attorney general decided not to prosecute. Weidenfeld made his first fortune, and *Lolita* entered British literary mythology. In America, the first US edition was issued by Putnam's in August 1958. The book went into several printings and it is said that the novel became the first since Margaret Mitchell's *Gone With the Wind* to sell more than 100,000 copies in its first three weeks.

One of *Lolita's* first supporters, the great critic Lionel Trilling, addressed what is perhaps a central issue at the heart of this controversial novel, when he warned of the moral difficulty in interpreting a book with such an eloquent narrator: "We find ourselves the more shocked when we realise that, in the course of reading the novel, we have come virtually to condone the violation it presents… We have been seduced into conniving in the violation, because we have permitted our fantasies to accept what we know to be revolting." Time and format do not permit this entry to explore the many fascinating literary critical reactions to this book. It will never cease to horrify some readers and delight others. *De gustibus non est disputandum.*

Looking back, Nabokov declared *Lolita* to be a record of his "love affair with the English language". His private tragedy, he declared, tongue in cheek, was that "I had to abandon my natural idiom, my untrammelled, rich, and infinitely docile Russian tongue for a second-rate brand of English, devoid of any of those apparatuses – the baffling mirror, the black velvet backdrop, the implied associations and traditions – which the native illusionist, frac-tails flying, can magically use to transcend the heritage his own way."

Second-rate ? We should be so lucky.

– 76 –
On the Road
by Jack Kerouac (1957)

In 1855, a young American poet named Walt Whitman announced, with typical gusto, that "the United States themselves are essentially the greatest poem", and made good on this claim in a landmark collection of poems, *Leaves of Grass,* transforming America's literary imagination for ever. When, exactly 100 years later, Jack Kerouac began to hammer out the typescript of his own masterpiece, he was consciously responding to Whitman's challenge "to express the inexpressible". This would become Kerouac's lifelong ambition and it expressed itself as *On the Road.* The book would be an urtext for the James Dean decade.

To Kerouac, Whitman's "I hear America singing" was almost an epigraph. *On the Road* pulsates to the rhythms of 1950s America: jazz, sex, drugs, and the desperate hunger of a new generation for experiences that are passionate, exuberant and alive to the heartbreaking potential of the present moment. Kerouac was an artist, but he was not immune to the charms of the American dream. *On the Road* is perhaps the supreme American romance, a contemporary version of Huck Finn's longing to "light out for the territory". Indeed, although acclaimed as a prophet of 1960s counterculture, Kerouac's own idea of himself and his work was to reclaim the gritty individualism and frontier spirit of the pioneering days of the American past.

The narrative opens in the depths of winter in New York City, 1947, with Salvatore Paradise "feeling that everything was dead". Sal, an Italian-American, is hanging out near Columbia University with a bunch of fellow "Beats" (a new term), restless and disaffected bohemians who include Carlo Marx (aka the poet Allen Ginsberg) and Dean Moriarty (aka the original Beat himself, Neal Cassady). Everyone is feeling the call of the wild, aching to hit the road and head out west. That, in a sentence, is what *On the Road* is all about: the quest for ultimate fufilment before the sun goes down. Kerouac called this magic moment "It", and devoted his life, through free association, and literary improvisation, to the pursuit of ecstatic inspiration. For the Beats, it's the journey, not the arrival, that matters. Sal Paradise will chase girls, drink late into the night, and walk on the wild side, but "It" will always elude him. The reader follows him (and the charismatic Dean Moriarty) as a mystical and poignant reminder of lost youth, and those sublime years when everyone feels immortal.

A Note on the Text:
Perhaps no manuscript of any book in this series had such a strange artistic and physical history as the famous text of *On the Road*. Jack Kerouac, who was born in Lowell, Massachusetts, in 1922, had begun to write fiction while working as a merchant seaman in the Second World War. In 1943, he completed a novel entitled *The Sea Is My Brother,* and first met some of the characters, young "Beats", who would eventually find their way into *On the Road*. It was always Kerouac's fictional method ruthlessly to plunder his autobiography.

In 1948, he completed his first novel to be published, *The Town and the City,* an account of his life from 1935-45. It was published in 1950, but drew poor reviews and did not sell. However, the writing of this novel introduced him to Beat avatar Neal Cassady, the model for Dean Moriarty. Their meeting in Harlem early in 1947 is described in the opening chapter of *On the Road*. Soon after completing *The Town and the City,* Kerouac began one of the first versions of *On the Road*, using a "factualist" way of writing in imitation of Theodore Dreiser. Kerouac began to revel in what he described as "a greater freedom in writing" than hitherto.

At this stage in its long gestation, *On the Road* (the title hardly ever varied) was planned as a quest novel like Bunyan's *The Pilgrim's*

Progress. The narrator who would eventually become the Italian-American Salvatore ("Sal") Paradise, was no longer called Ray Smith but "Smitty", while Dean Moriarty was now Red Moultrie. Kerouac was deep into this version when Harcourt Brace offered to publish *The Town and the City,* demanding some substantial editorial cuts. So he put his "road book" aside to meet this request, and did not return to it until June 1949. At this point, coming back to it afresh, he was dissatisfied with what he had done, and headed out to San Francisco to join Cassady, an excursion that became absorbed into part three of *On the Road.* Then, in March 1950, Cassady took him to Mexico (part four of the novel), where Kerouac got married to Joan Haverty. He continued, meanwhile, to slog away at *On the Road*, and developed his friendships with William Burroughs, Allen Ginsberg and Cassady, all of whom would have a decisive influence on the published text of the novel. Occasionally, his new wife, Joan, would ask about his exploits with Cassady, and he began to fashion his "road book" as a kind of explanation, a first-person narrative of what had happened before their marriage.

At this time, Kerouac also developed the non-stop typing style he pioneered to get the "kickwriting" momentum he needed to achieve the literary effect he was after. It was now, crucially, that he taped together 12ft-long pieces of drawing paper, trimmed them to fit, and fed them into his typewriter as a continuous roll. (This may not make much sense to readers who have grown up with laptops.) It was essential to the non-stop typing method not to have to pause to insert new paper. This, said Kerouac, was the start of "a new trend in American literature". Sweating profusely, changing his T-shirts throughout the day, fuelled by pea soup and benzedrine, he embarked on a typing marathon – three weeks in April 1951 – in which the essential draft (nearly 90,000 words) of *On the Road* would be completed. Perhaps only the Faulkner of *As I Lay Dying* had such an intense creative experience.

But Kerouac was still not done. After that spring frenzy, he would continue to revise and retype the original MS roll many times. In October 1951, he was still reworking it in the belief that his "wild form" of narrative had not captured his subject to his satisfaction. This became an alternative version, entitled *Visions of Cody*, in which Cassady became "Cody Pomeray".

In March 1953, Kerouac's struggles with his masterpiece reached a turning-point when Malcolm Cowley, an editorial adviser at Viking, expressed interest in Kerouac's work and then, having read it, told him frankly that he preferred the typescript roll version to all others. By now, Kerouac's work and originality were beginning to attract attention, and, after many more vicissitudes, in December 1956, Kerouac again revised his text for Viking. Publication, finally, was scheduled for September 1957. His publishers knew they were dealing with a writer trapped in an obsession: they never sent him galley proofs and Kerouac was dismayed by some of the editorial changes wrought by Cowley.

It hardly mattered. On publication, Kerouac awoke to find himself famous. Just before midnight on 4 September 1957, Kerouac left his apartment on New York's Upper West Side to wait at the 66th street news-stand for the next day's edition of the *New York Times*. He had been tipped off that his novel was going to be reviewed by Gilbert Millstein, but he cannot have anticipated the critic's excitement. Millstein declared that *On the Road*'s publication was "a historic occasion in so far as the exposure of an authentic work of art is of any great moment in an age in which the attention is fragmented and the sensibilities are blunted by the superlatives of fashion". The novel, Millstein continued, was "the most beautifully executed, the clearest and the most important utterance yet made by the generation Kerouac himself named years ago as 'Beat', and whose principal avatar he is."

The rest is literary history.

– 77 –
Voss
by Patrick White (1957)

The lone rider on his journey to self-realisation, the plot of many
westerns, is perfectly suited to the Australian outback, and it gives Patrick White's monumental novel an archetypal power that still dominates the Australian literary landscape. Only Christina Stead (*The Man Who Loved Children*) rivals White's achievement.

Voss is based on the story of Ludwig Leichhardt, the Prussian naturalist who made several explorations of the Australian interior in the mid-1840s. Leichhardt aimed to pioneer an overland route from Brisbane to Perth but he vanished without trace in the infinite vastness of the interior.

White focuses on two characters: *Voss*, the German explorer, and Laura, a naive and lovely orphan recently arrived in New South Wales, who meet for the first time in the house of Laura's uncle, the patron of Voss's expedition. Their complex and passionate relationship, a mutual obsession based on separation, is set against the merciless landscape of Voss's trek towards oblivion.

White, who in 1973 became the first Australian to win the Nobel prize for literature, was a difficult man, notorious for his abrasive relationship with a society that, high and low, did its best to alienate him. Much of White's prickly rage went into Voss, who is misanthropic, wilful and doomed. "The map?" says the explorer, when asked about navigation. "I will first make it."

White was a literary map-maker, too. He is both of his time (sharing many preoccupations with Saul Bellow and William Golding), and a cultural pioneer, asserting the need for a richer and more complex understanding of a great country. Until the 1950s Australian poetry and fiction, like American literature in the 19th century, was in thrall to dusty English models. Angry and often obscure, deeply intellectual and gay, Patrick White liberated his readers from a cultural prison. Parts of *Voss*, notably the treatment of indigenous Australians – "black swine" to the explorer – remain contentious but White is a founding father of the literary independence movement that followed in the 1970s and 80s. His work paved the way for David Malouf, Murray Bail, Peter Carey, Tim Winton, Christos Tsiolkas, Julia Leigh and many more. He is also a pioneer in "Commonwealth Literature", a genre that's now virtually redundant, having been overtaken by the influence of global media and global English.

A Note on the Text:
Voss was published by Eyre & Spottiswoode, a London-based imprint with strong Australian connections, in 1957. The first edition had jacket art by Sidney Nolan, and although it was the novel that established White's profound originality, not everyone was convinced. One hostile newspaper review declared White to be "Australia's most unreadable novelist". The distinguished Australian poet AD Hope once said of White that, although he "shows on every page some touch of the born writer", he nevertheless lacked style, choosing "as

his medium this pretentious and illiterate verbal sludge". To the end of his life, White would never quite shake off a reputation for "difficulty".

The indispensable study of Patrick White and his work comes from David Marr in *Patrick White: A Life* (1991). *Voss* has also been adapted into an opera with a David Malouf libretto. White himself wanted *Voss* to be produced for the cinema, directed by Ken Russell and, later, Joseph Losey, but the film was never made.

– 78 –
To Kill a Mockingbird
by Harper Lee (1960)

Earlier in this series, I excluded *Uncle Tom's Cabin* by Harriet Beecher Stowe (1852) from this series on the grounds that, in the 19th century, much of its phenomenal popularity derived from its timely advocacy of Abolition in the run-up to the American Civil War. Similarly, *To Kill A Mockingbird*, owed some of its success to extra-literary circumstances: it was published in the year JFK went the White House, caught the mood of the Civil Rights movement, achieved sales of more than thirty million copies, and inspired a movie classic, starring Gregory Peck. But, where *Uncle Tom* is a simple tale with an explicit moral, intended to change hearts and minds, Harper Lee's first published book (succeeded, controversially, in 2015 by *Go Set A Watchman*) is a complex and subtle work of literature that has inspired and influenced generations of schoolchildren in the US and, most especially, in the UK. It's that rare thing: a truly popular classic.

Narrated by Jean Louise "Scout" Finch, at the outset the 6-year-old tomboy daughter of widowed small-town lawyer Atticus Finch, *To Kill a Mockingbird* is ostensibly about race prejudice in the American South. At the core of its main plot is the trial of Tom Robinson, an African-American accused of raping a white girl. When Atticus Finch is instructed to conduct Robinson's defence, his fortune cookie declaration that "You never really understand a person until... you climb inside his skin" becomes the rhetorical heart of a novel based on Harper "Nelle" Lee's formative years in the Alabama of the 1930s. Scout's coming-of-age, another major strand in the story, will involve her realisation that "Boo" Radley is a benign mystery in her life and that many childhood terrors have mature meaning.

For all Atticus Finch's noble defence, Robinson is convicted by an all-white jury, condemned to death, and shot dead while attempting a jail-break. The death of an innocent man is linked to the dominant metaphor expressed in the novel's title. The mockingbird (*Mimus polyglottos*), a thrush-like bird with a long tail, creamy grey breast and white flashes, is a popular creature in American folklore. For Harper Lee it is the quintessence of innocence and the goodness of the natural world. Mockingbirds, says one character, "don't do one thing but sing their hearts out for us. That's why it's a sin to kill a mockingbird."

A Note on the Text:

To Kill A Mockingbird was published by Lippincott on July 11, 1960. It was initially titled *Atticus*, but Lee renamed it to represent a novel that went far beyond a character study. Her editor at Lippincott warned Lee to anticipate a modest sale of a few thousand copies. She herself once said, "I never expected any sort of success ......" and claimed that she was "hoping for a quick and merciful death at the hands of the reviewers." This is disingenuous. She also remarked that "at the same time, I sort of hoped someone would like it enough to give me encouragement. I hoped for a little, but I got rather a whole lot, and in some ways this was just about as frightening as the quick, merciful death I'd expected." Instead of a "quick and merciful death", a Reader's Digest reprint gave the novel an immediate audience, which would eventually top a thirty million copy sale worldwide (and counting). Despite her publisher's warnings, the book soon brought acclaim to Lee in her hometown of Monroeville, and throughout Alabama.

Critical reactions varied. To the *New Yorker* it was "skilled, unpretentious, and totally ingenious". *Time* magazine declared that the novel "teaches the reader an astonishing number of useful truths about little girls and about Southern life". Some reviewers lamented the use of poor white Southerners, and one-dimensional black victims. The great Southern writer, Flannery O'Connor, said that "I think for a child's book it does all right. It's interesting that all the folks that are buying it don't know they're reading a child's book. Somebody ought to say what it is."

Within a year of its publication *To Kill a Mockingbird* had been translated into ten languages. In the years since then, it has been translated into more than 40 languages, has never been out of print in hardcover or paperback, and has become part of the standard school curriculum. A 1991 survey by the Book of the Month Club found that *To Kill a Mockingbird* was rated behind only the Bible in books that are "most often cited as making a difference". Chimamanda Ngozi Adichie writing in *The Guardian* stated that Lee writes with "a fiercely progressive ink, in which there is nothing inevitable about racism and its very foundation is open to question", and compared her to Faulkner, who wrote about racism as an inevitability.

American literature has several examples of one-book writers who burned out fast. In 1946, for instance, *Raintree Country* by Ross Lockridge and *Mister Roberts* by Thomas Heggen both became bestsellers and got the Hollywood treatment. But then Lockridge and Heggen became hopelessly "blocked". By the end of the 50s, both had committed suicide.

Until 2015, Harper Lee was famous as the quintessential one-book author, often the subject, over many years, of wild rumours. One of the most bizarre was that her friend Truman Capote (whose *In Cold Blood* she helped research) was true author of *Mockingbird*. More seriously, she claimed to be working on another novel "ever so slowly", a manuscript entitled "The Long Goodbye". But it remained unseen, and the rumours continued to ebb and flow.

But now there's a prequel – a new novel, and a literary curiosity. The main thing about *Go Set A Watchman* (a title derived from Isaiah 21.vi) is that its author was born in Monroeville, Alabama in 1926. The new book, an odd mixture of good, bad and indifferent, shows Lee stuck on the race politics of the deep south like a feather on a tar barrel.

In the late 1940s, while in her 20s, Lee made her one bid for another life among the Yankees, and moved to New York City where she began to write. The Jean Louise Finch of *Go Set A Watchman* who comes home to Maycomb, Alabama, to visit her ageing, arthritic father is no longer "Scout Finch, juvenile desperado, hell-raiser extraordinary" but someone much closer to her creator. Lee's first novel cost her dear. At one point, she threw the manuscript out of her apartment window into the snow. The genesis of *Go Tell A Watchman* is mysterious but in 1957, Lee's agent submitted it to publishers as "an eye-opener for many northerners in the segregation battle", and it was signed up by Tay Hohoff, an editor at Lippincott's.

This manuscript was a "fish out of water" story about a young woman from the deep south who, going home, is confronted by the racist attitudes of Atticus Finch, her father, and Henry ("Hank") Clinton, her "white trash" boyfriend. Told in the third person, the novel traces Jean Louise's painful coming-to-terms with her roots. The most vivid passages, which are fleeting, concern twenty-something Miss Finch's recollections of childhood and her brother Jem, who is now dead.

On page 109, the reader learns that Atticus had once "accomplished what was never before or afterwards done in Maycomb County: he won the acquittal for a coloured boy on a rape charge. The chief witness for the prosecution was a white girl."

This is still a debut: stilted, uneven, and awkward. At the end, Jean Louise's uncle Jack reveals, in a novelettish twist, the dark truth of his obsession with her. *Go Set A Watchman* has a certain promise, but not much more. Harper Lee, who described it as "a pretty decent effort", seemed to know this.

But then, in an inexplicable creative leap that will bring hope to the world's creative writing classes, something happened. Tayhoff, who recognised the true heart of *Go Set A Watchman*, asked Lee to focus on Scout's childhood, opening a secret door in her imagination. Harper Lee found her voice. A new novel, entitled "Atticus Finch", was born, and would become *To Kill A Mockingbird*.

– 79 –
The Prime of Miss Jean Brodie
by Muriel Spark (1960)

The Prime of Miss Jean Brodie is probably the shortest novel on this list, a sublime miracle of wit and brevity, and a Scots classic that's a masterclass in narrative construction and the art of "less is more". The action centres on the romantic, fascinating, comic and ultimately tragic schoolmistress Jean Brodie who will, in the most archetypal sense, suffer for the sin of hubris, her excessive self-confidence. At first, her ideas about beauty and goodness, her mysterious glamour and charm will dazzle and seduce her girls – "the crème de la crème" – at the Marcia Blaine School, but in the end the same gifts will cause her downfall. "Give me a girl at an impressionable age," she boasts, "and she is mine for life." Eventually that prediction will be fulfilled in the saddest way imaginable.

It is, as Miss Brodie says, "nineteen-thirty-six. The age of chivalry is dead." The novel's theme, deftly laid out in a narrative that flashes backwards and forwards, to and from the 1930s, is the education of six wonderfully distinctive, heartless and romantic 10-year-old girls (Monica, Sandy, Rose, Mary, Jenny, and Eunice) and the covert class-room drama that leads to Miss Brodie's "betrayal", her peremptory dismissal from Marcia Blaine by her great enemy, the headmistress, Miss Mackay. That, of course, has nothing to do with school, and everything to do with sex, and the art teacher, Teddy Lloyd, with whom Miss Brodie (defiantly in her "prime") is hopelessly in love.

It had been Miss Brodie's plan to control and manipulate the lives of "her girls". But finally, it is Sandy who, before she becomes Sister Helena of the Transfiguration, exacts the decisive revenge that will doom her teacher to a bitter and solitary spinsterhood. Miss Brodie will never get over it, and die quite soon. "'Whatever possessed you?' said Miss Brodie in a very Scottish way, as if Sandy had given away a pound of marmalade to an English duke."

My paperback edition runs to just 128 pages. The elfin spirit of Robert Louis Stevenson hovers over every line, and Muriel Spark nods to this influence by having some of the girls read *Kidnapped*.

A Note on the Text:

Muriel Spark occupies a special place in the *Observer's* literary history. As a young woman, she had made her way as a poet, literary editor and literary biographer in postwar London. But it was as a short-story writer that she first came to prominence at the very end of 1951, when she won the *Observer* short story competition for her surreal and, in places, richly poetic "The Seraph and the Zambesi". Her novels followed soon after; by the late 1950s, she was fully estab-lished as a writer to watch.

Spark's method of composition became quite famous. She composed her fiction in a copperplate hand, usually a single draft with very few corrections, in spiral-bound school notebooks from the Edinburgh stationer and bookseller James Thin. It was in such a volume that she began to write about a middle-aged schoolteacher, drawn from her own school memories.

The Prime of Miss Jean Brodie is so short that it was first published, in its entirety, in the *New Yorker*, and then reissued in volume form by Macmillan in the UK in 1961. The character of Miss Jean Brodie became Spark's "milch cow", and brought her international fame, especially after the novel was made into a film starring Maggie Smith, who won an Academy (best actress) award for her performance.

In real life, the character of Miss Brodie was based in part on Christina Kay, a teacher of Spark's for two years at her Edinburgh school, James Gillespie's School for Girls. The author would later write of her thus: "What filled our minds with wonder and made Christina Kay so memorable was the personal drama and poetry within which everything in her classroom happened." Miss Kay was the basis for the good parts of Brodie's character, but also some of the more bizarre. For example, Miss Kay did hang posters of Renaissance paintings on the wall, and also of Mussolini marching with Italian fascists.

Another Scottish writer, Candia McWilliam, identified the novel's lasting appeal when she wrote that it is "sublimely funny, and also very short, with much to say about sex". She adds that it is "technically beyond praise. The pressure it exerts upon the mind is controlled by a guiding spirit that reveals to us the moral universe while affording the refreshment of laughter and revelation." What better definition of a classic?

– 80 –
Catch-22
by Joseph Heller (1961)

In 1962, writing in the *Observer,* Kenneth Tynan saluted *Catch-22* as "the most striking debut in American fiction since *Catcher in the Rye.*" Within a year, he had been joined, in a chorus of praise, by writers as various as Harper Lee, Norman Mailer and Graham Greene. More than 50 years later, this brilliant novel still holds an unforgettable comic grip on the reader.

"It was love at first sight," Heller begins, setting the tone for everything that follows. "The first time Yossarian saw the chaplain he fell madly in love with him."

Bombardier Yossarian is in a military hospital with a pain in his liver that's not quite jaundice. Hinting at the famous "catch" of the title, Yossarian can be treated if he's got jaundice, but discharged if he hasn't. If neither, then he's in a Kafkaesque limbo, where he's at the mercy of fate.

This anticipates the notorious conditions under which a combat airman can be grounded: you have to be insane before you're excused flying combat missions, but if you don't want to fly any more missions that proves you are not insane. The OED defines this "Catch-22" as "a difficult situation from which there is no escape, because it involves mutually conflicting or dependent conditions", which is a very dull way to describe the absurd crux whose mad logic exhilarates every page of one of the greatest war novels of all time.

Bombardier Yossarian, who is at odds with his own side as much as with the enemy, is an unforgettable Second World War Everyman, whose cat-and-mouse relationship with a cast of deranged oddballs – Milo Minderbinder, Major Major and Doc Daneeka – is played out, amid mounting absurdity, on the island of Pianosa in the Mediterranean. It's 1944, and Yossarian has figured out that "the enemy is anybody who is going to get you killed, no matter which side he's on".

Inevitably, the high comedy with which the novel opens eventually modulates into a darker, bleaker humour, and movingly, it's the tragic death of rear-gunner Snowden which reminds us that Heller's merriment is the kind of gallows laughter that's inspired by the horror of war.

A Note on the Text:

Heller first began to write the novel that became *Catch-22* in 1953, while working as a copywriter in New York. Once he'd found the famous opening – "It was love at first sight" – he had the voice he needed for the narrative.

The rest followed slowly in manuscript, and by 1957 he had about 270pp in typescript. Eventually his literary agent Candida Donadio sold an incomplete version of *Catch-22* to Simon & Schuster, where it was taken up with enthusiasm by a young editor, Robert "Bob" Gottlieb, who would eventually move to Alfred A. Knopf. Gottlieb, who is now retired, after a distinguished career that included editing the *New Yorker,* oversaw all aspects of the novel's appearance, and was instrumental in its launch. Heller later dedicated the novel to him as a "colleague".

Gottlieb's enthusiasm inspired him to send out advance copies, a strategy that (as so often) did not always work. Evelyn Waugh wrote back: "You are mistaken in calling it a novel. It is a collection of sketches

– often repetitious – totally without structure."

Structure aside, the main pre-publication debate was to do with Heller's title, which had at first derived from the opening chapter of the novel, published in magazine form (next to an extract from Jack Kerouac's *On the Road*), as "Catch-18" in 1955. Subsequently, Candida Donadio requested a change in the title, to avoid confusion with another recently published Second World War novel, *Mila 18* by Leon Uris, who was a bestselling literary name at the time.

Initially, "Catch-11" was proposed, but then the release of the Holly-wood movie *Ocean's 11* (1960) raised more anxieties, and this was also rejected. So was "Catch-17" (deemed too similar to the film *Stalag 17*), and also "Catch-14". Apparently, Simon & Schuster did not think that "14" was "a funny number". Eventually author, agent and publisher settled on *Catch-22*.

Joe Heller's first novel was officially launched on 10 October 1961, priced $5.95 in hardcover. The book was not a bestseller in hardcover in the US. Despite selling 12,000 copies before Thanksgiving, it never entered the NYT bestseller list. However, *Catch-22* got good notices (and bad: Heller later said that "the disparagements were frequently venomous").

There were positive reviews from the *Nation*, which saluted "the best novel to come out in years"; the *Herald Tribune* ("A wild, moving, shocking, hilarious, raging, exhilarating, giant roller-coaster of a book"), and the *New York Times* ("A dazzling performance that will outrage nearly as many readers as it delights"). Elsewhere, for example in the *New Yorker*, there was critical rage: attacks on a book which "doesn't even seem to be written; instead, it gives the impression of having been shouted onto paper... what remains is a debris of sour jokes".

Nevertheless, it was nominated for the National Book Award, and went through four printings in hardcover, selling especially well on the East Coast. The book never established itself nationally until it was published in paperback, and benefited from a national debate about the pointlessness of the Vietnam war. Abroad, Heller had better luck, and in the UK his novel did become a bestseller. During the 1960s, the book acquired a cult following, especially among teenagers and college students. Although *Catch-22* won no awards, it has remained consistently in print and, since publication, has sold more than 10m copies.

– 81 –
The Golden Notebook
by Doris Lessing (1962)

"Everything's cracking up", says Anna, the protagonist of Lessing's masterpiece, a novel that takes its place in this list for its odd, visionary engagement with the issues and anxieties of its time and also for its extraordinary grip on the literary imagination of the late 20th century, when Lessing (who lived to November 2013) was in her prime.

The Oxford Companion to English Literature describes this novel as "one of the key texts of the women's movement of the 1960s", a reductive description that would have infuriated Lessing, partly because she hated to be pigeonholed, and also because she understood fiction to be infinitely more varied and complex than one "movement". Lessing's work has always been difficult to define: a mix of classical realism, science-fiction, parable, memoir, fantasy and polemic. *The Golden Notebook* has many of these elements.

Anna Wulf is a divorced single mother, and a novelist afflicted with writer's block, who keeps four notebooks – black, red, yellow, and blue – in which she explores her literary/childhood, political, emotional, and everyday/psychological lives. She does this, says Lessing, "to separate things off from each other, out of fear of chaos, of formlessness – of breakdown".

This is a novel that hovers compellingly on the edge of madness, exploring the idea that a writer who fashions a unified narrative somehow betrays the truth of existence. In the closing part of the blue notebook describing her emotional life, Anna falls in love with her American lodger, Saul Green, a cathartic crisis that will finally release her from writer's block. Now she resolves, in her own words to "put all of myself into one book".

This becomes *The Golden Notebook*, the one coherent volume that will liberate Anna and her lover, and hold the key to her recovery. This theme of "breakdown" or "crack up" and psychic "self-healing" is Lessing's declared "central theme". Her novel, she insisted, was never intended to be "a useful weapon in the sex war".

The Golden Notebook is about one woman's search for personal and political identity, told in several voices. A tour de force of multiple narratives, it is not exactly a masterpiece of English style, but a great fictional rooming-house with many inhabitants, heartbreaks and arguments – a defiant and ambitious work that remade many readers' idea of fiction and its uses.

A Note on the Text:

In June 1971, Doris Lessing wrote a fascinating preface to a new edition of *The Golden Notebook* in which she did something typically contrarian, and something most novelists don't like ever to do: she explained herself. "The shape of this novel is as follows," she wrote. "There is a skeleton, or frame, called Free Women, which is a conventional short novel, about 60,000 words, and which could stand by itself. But it is divided into five sections and separated by stages of the four notebooks, black, red, yellow and blue. The notebooks are kept by Anna Wulf, a central character of Free Women…"

Lessing continues: "I was so immersed in writing this book that I didn't think about how it might be received… The actual time of writing, then, and not only the experiences that had gone into the writing, was really traumatic: it changed me… My major aim was to shape a book which would make its own comment, a wordless statement: to talk through the way it was shaped. As I have said, this was not noticed. One reason for this is that the book is more in the European tradition than in the English tradition of the novel. Or rather, in the English tradition as viewed at the moment. The English novel after all does include *Clarissa* and *Tristram Shandy* – and Joseph Conrad. But there is no doubt that to attempt a novel of ideas is to give oneself a handicap: the parochialism of our culture is intense… Finally, this novel continues to be, for its author, a most instructive experience."

Lessing also devoted a substantial part of this preface to repudiating any association with the feminist movement. She never saw herself as anything but a writer who worked in many genres, for herself alone. As she expressed it to the *New York Times* in July, 1982: "What the feminists want of me is something they haven't examined because it comes from religion. They want me to bear witness. What they would really like me to say is, 'Ha, sisters, I stand with you side by side in your struggle toward the golden dawn where all those beastly men are no more.' Do they really want people to make oversimplified statements about men and women? In fact, they do. I've come with great regret to this conclusion."

The Golden Notebook probably explains why, in 2007, Lessing was awarded the Nobel prize for literature. In its prize citation, the Swedish academy described her as "that epicist of the female experience, who with scepticism, fire and visionary power has subjected a divided civilisation to scrutiny". Less grandiose, it's also worth noting that Doris Lessing was the 11th woman and the oldest person ever to receive the Nobel prize for literature.

– 82 –
A Clockwork Orange
by Anthony Burgess (1962)

There are two possible approaches to *A Clockwork Orange* and it's best to address this up front. There's the novel, written in 1961 by Anthony Burgess; a short, brilliant, dystopian polemic intended, he said, as "a sort of tract, even a sermon, on the importance of the power of choice". The second, Stanley Kubrick's *A Clockwork Orange*, is the brilliant cinematic adaptation; a controversial masterpiece, released in 1971, that everyone remembers. But the book, not Kubrick's script, is the essential text, a stunningly original novel that opened many literary doors for the work of subsequent British writers such as Martin Amis, JG Ballard and Will Self, and a volume bursting with linguistic energy that continues to startle and inspire generations of new readers.

According to the Burgess scholar, Andrew Biswell, *A Clockwork Orange* was originally set in 1980 and is animated by an internal debate with another great dystopia, Orwell's *Nineteen Eighty-Four*. Burgess's novel – sometimes described as "a novella" – also addresses, but in less ideological terms, the corruptions of state power while also debating free will and human responsibility. Self-consciously trangressive (the title probably comes from some cockney slang for "queer", though not in any sexual sense), *A Clockwork Orange* tells the story of Alex, a Beethoven-mad thug with a lovely internal monologue. Eloquent in Nadsat, his teen argot, a heady mix of Russian, Romany and rhyming slang, Alex narrates his career as the leader of a gang of "droogs", Peter, Georgie and Dim. It is often said that these brutes derive from the mods and rockers, but Biswell shows conclusively that a deeper inspiration comes from Burgess's wartime experience.

A brilliant and sinister opening of horrific "ultra violence" describes the gang on the rampage: terrorising a school teacher, beating a drunk, carving up a rival gang, stealing a car, and ransacking a country cottage, having tortured a harmless literary man and gang-raped his wife. After the sick brio of this opening, the novel settles into Alex's subsequent incarceration in State Jail 84F and the mind-altering aversion therapy inflicted on him by the authorities. It also explores, with some subtlety, the relationship of free will and individual responsibility in Burgess's inimitable style.

A Clockwork Orange ends with Alex admitting: "I was cured, all right." This is followed by a quasi-redemptive final chapter that was cut from the US edition, and consequently ignored by Kubrick in his script. So the book and the film go forward together, like dysfunctional, conjoined twins.

A Note on the Text:

According to his biographer, Andrew Biswell, Burgess began planning a series of novels about imaginary futures in 1960. In "the earliest surviving plan" for the novel, Burgess sketched a book of about 200 pages, divided into three sections of 70 pages apiece. He himself liked to say he wrote the book in three weeks, to make money. Whatever the truth, and with Burgess you never quite know what's for real and what he's invented on the spur of the moment, the first draft of *A Clockwork Orange* was completed in the English south coast town of Hove in 1962. It's interesting to note that a generation earlier Graham Greene similarly explored the themes of evil, as expressed in teenage rebellion and social delinquency, in his own "south-coast" entertainment, *Brighton Rock*.

Burgess had returned to Britain in 1959 after some years abroad in Malaya to find, to his dismay, that much had changed. A vibrant and violent youth culture, with coffee bars, pop music and teenage gangs, had become the subject of newspaper headlines and widespread middle-class "state-of-the-nation" anxiety.

Actually, a lot of the source material in *A Clockwork Orange* dates to the 40s, not the 50s or 60s. Burgess said that the novel's inspiration was his pregnant first wife Lynne's beating by a gang of drunk American servicemen stationed in England during the war. She subsequently miscarried. Burgess attributed his arresting title to various possible origins: he often claimed that he had overheard the phrase "as queer as a clockwork orange" in a London pub in 1945.

Later, on television in 1972, once his novel had become notorious, he said, more vaguely that "the title is... a phrase which I heard many years ago". He said he fell in love with it and wanted to use it as a book title. He resisted suggestions that he had made it up: "The phrase 'as queer as a clockwork orange' is good old east London slang. Now, obviously, I've given it an extra meaning. I've implied an extra dimension. I've implied the junction of the organic, the lively, the sweet – in other words, life, the 'orange' – and the mechanical, the cold, the disciplined. I've brought them together in this kind of oxymoron." We have also to record several sources stating that there is "no other record of the expression being used before 1962".

The book has three parts, each with seven chapters – an intentional nod to the age of 21 as the age of majority. The 21st chapter was omitted from the editions published in the US before 1986, sacrificing philosophical completeness for narrative convenience. When Burgess first sold the book to an American publisher, WW Norton, he was told by his editor, Eric Swenson, that US audiences would never go for this final chapter in which Alex sees the error of his ways, decides he has lost the thrill of violence, and resolves to turn his life around. Burgess allowed Swenson to cut the redemptive final chapter from the US version, so that the tale would end on a darker note, with Alex succumbing to his violent, reckless nature.

Stanley Kubrick's film adaptation, which Burgess used to refer to as "Clockwork Marmalade", was based on this US edition. Kubrick called chapter 21 "an extra chapter", claimed that he did not read the full version until he had finished his screenplay, and never gave serious consideration to using it. In my recollection of the writer, Burgess spent his last years regularly denouncing the film version of his novel and all those associated with the contract, including his literary agent, the late Deborah Rogers.

Burgess was an extraordinary man, a mixture of polymath and charlatan. Life around him was never dull and he was one of the most original people I've ever encountered.

– 83 –
A Single Man
by Christopher Isherwood (1964)

Christopher Isherwood made his famous declaration of artistic intent in 1939: "I am a camera with its shutter open, quite passive, recording, not thinking… Some day all this will have to be developed, carefully printed, fixed." This cool, blank, dispassionate gaze, which often disturbed the critics, characterises all Isherwood's writing, some of the finest English prose of the 20th century, whose decades are shadowed by his own life and work. Indeed, there are several "Christophers" competing for a place in this list. The choice is not easy. His genius was spotted early by the Woolfs, who published *The Memorial* (1932) at the Hogarth Press. Later in the 1930s, he became celebrated for his Berlin fiction, especially *Mr Norris Changes Trains* (1935) and *Goodbye to Berlin* (1939), which introduced the world to "Sally Bowles" of *Cabaret* fame.

Isherwood's third act, creatively speaking, is set in Los Angeles, where he worked in Hollywood, and also pioneered American gay fiction. This could be seen as a fulfilment of Edmund Wilson's sharp critical insight that Isherwood's "real field is social observation". *A Single Man* is widely recognised as his supreme achievement, as much a work of compressed brilliance as Chopin's *Ballade No 4*. It is also, Isherwood said, "the only book of mine where I did more or less what I wanted to do. It didn't get out of control." His fiction was always a transistorised reorganisation of his own self. As he developed, his fictional persona became progressively more complex, yet truer to himself. In this novel, it emerges as a character that's both independent, yet deeply connected to its author.

Dedicated to Gore Vidal, *A Single Man* is set in 1962, just after the Cuban missile crisis, and describes a day (the last day) in the life of George Falconer, a 58-year-old expat Englishman who is living in Santa Monica and teaching at a university in LA, just as Isherwood did. The narrative is edgy, subtle, and controlled, with chasms of buried rage. George has recently lost his partner, Jim, in a car crash, and is struggling with bereavement. He tries to make a connection to the world around him, while denying his predicament as a widower. We see him go through the motions of everyday life: teaching a class, fighting with his neighbours, working out at the gym, shopping at a supermarket, drinking with an older woman friend, flirting intellectually with a young student – before fading out on the final page. As a study of grief and a portrait of the aftermath of a gay marriage, *A Single Man* is unique, brilliant, and deeply moving, with not a word wasted.

A Note on the Text:

In December 1952, Isherwood began to develop a film script entitled "The Day's Journey", which would ultimately morph into "A Single Man", a project he first envisaged as a movie. Indeed, some of the novel's dialogue, as the Isherwood scholar Katherine Bucknell has noted, reads like a screenplay.

Thereafter, *A Single Man* was conceived as a novel about an English woman, and modelled on Virginia Woolf's *Mrs Dalloway*, which Isherwood once described as "one of the most truly beautiful novels or prose poems or whatever that I have ever read". There were several decisive moments in the evolution of the text. In September 1962, Isherwood wrote in his diary "this morning we went on the beach and discussed *The Englishwoman*, and Don [Bachardy, his lover], after hearing my difficulties with it, made a really brilliant simple suggestion, namely that it ought to be *The Englishman* – that is, me." He described the consequences of this insight as "very far-reaching".

In its first American (Simon & Schuster) printing, *A Single Man* is just 186 pages long. My Vintage paperback edition runs to a skinny 152 pages. Rarely did Isherwood, the brilliant miniaturist, cram so great a reckoning into such a little room. Privately, over the years, he came to refer to it as his "masterpiece".

One indispensable guide to the making of the novel is the second volume of Isherwood's diaries edited by Katherine Bucknell. She writes that "*A Single Man* draws obviously and significantly on experiences described in the diaries, but also upon Isherwood's life, and upon the process of ageing and the challenge of continuing in his mature identity". Readers of these fascinating volumes will find all kinds of insights. Later, disdaining the personal in the way he preferred, Isherwood himself was publicly matter-of-fact about his intentions for the novel.

In 1985, he gave an interview to the gay writer Armistead Maupin, in which they discussed *A Single Man*. Maupin wanted to know if

"George", the man who has lost his lover, Jim, was an Isherwood creation, or "based on someone you knew?" To which Isherwood replied: "It was an obvious idea, you know, the widower who doesn't present himself as one. That's what it amounted to. No, I was never in that situation myself." At this point his partner, Don Bachardy chips in: "I always suspected he was imagining what it would be like if we split up because I remember that period [1962-3] was a very rough time for us, and I was making a lot of waves. I was being very difficult and very tiresome."

Maupin countered by asking how Bachardy was being tiresome? Bachardy replied: "Just by being very dissatisfied. I was approaching 30, and 30 for me was the toughest age of all. I started suffering from it around 28, and I didn't really get over it until about 32. And since then, every birthday has been a breeze. My 40s were the best time of my life."

Don Bachardy has continued to interpolate himself into his lover's story, and is often essential to it, but it is Isherwood's prose — fiction, diaries, essays and memoir — that holds the key to his genius, and guarantees his posterity.

– 84 –
In Cold Blood
by Truman Capote (1966)

 Some of the greatest books on this list are built on narratives that could have been torn from the pages of a newspaper (*The Great Gatsby* is a good example). *In Cold Blood*, subtitled "A True Account of a Multiple Murder and Its Consequences", grandly described by Capote as "a non-fiction novel", actually began as a *New York Times* murder story that became transformed into a tale of spine-tingling suspense and extraordinary intuition. It was Capote's genius to understand that this Midwest killing had a mythic quality, and that the sinister murderers opened up the dark underbelly of postwar America.

During the early hours of 15 November 1959, in the small prairie community of Holcomb, Kansas, four members of a prosperous farming family, the Clutters, were savagely murdered by shotgun blasts discharged at close quarters into their faces. There was no apparent motive for the crime, and hardly any clues. The local FBI investigator, Alvin Dewey, had never seen a crime so meaningless or "so vicious", and vowed to hunt down and convict the killers, whatever the cost. More darkly, the backstory to Capote's book became a private tragedy, etched between the lines of a brilliant quasi-journalistic investigation, that would haunt Capote throughout his writing life.

Soon after the news of this shocking massacre had broken in the US press, the fashionable and acclaimed author of *Other Voices, Other Rooms* (1948), *Breakfast at Tiffany's* (1958), and some ground-breaking *New Yorker* reportage, arrived in Holcomb in the aftermath of the Clutters' funeral. He was not alone. In one of many unacknowledged deceptions perpetrated on the reader, he was accompanied by his childhood buddy, Harper Lee. She had just finished writing the novel *To Kill a Mockingbird,* that would make her famous. Her role in Capote's bestseller now became crucial.

It was Harper Lee who would help to penetrate the cordon of silence protecting the privacy of a remote Kansas community reeling from the Clutter murders. As a result, Capote was able to conduct his own unforgettable investigation into the manhunt, arrest and trial of the killers, Dick Hickock and Perry Smith, a weird quest that would end just after midnight, 14 April 1965, on the gallows of the Kansas state penitentiary.

"No one will ever know what *In Cold Blood* took out of me," Capote once said. "It scraped me right down to the marrow of my bones. It nearly killed me. I think, in a way, it did kill me."

A Note on the Text:

Truman Capote, describing the composition of *In Cold Blood*, spoke of "maintaining a stylistic and emotional upper hand over your material", asserting that "the greatest intensity in art in all its shapes and sizes is achieved with a deliberate, hard and cool head". Finding the right form for your story, he insisted, was "simply to realise the most natural way of telling the story". As a great literary self-promoter, he also claimed a special originality for *In Cold Blood*. Several critics, unmoved by this hype, preferred to place his "non-fiction novel" in a tradition that could be traced to *The Storm* by Daniel Defoe (1704), in which Defoe used the voices of real people to tell his story. Indeed, this technique would be adopted by many subsequent writers before

Capote, including Dickens, Twain and Steinbeck.

Capote also maintained, at least initially, that he was not writing a crime story. In public, in the early days of the project, Capote stuck to this line. In 1962, he told *Newsweek*: "My book isn't a crime story. It's the story of a town." Well, maybe. But the more he recognised that Hickock and Smith were central to the story he wanted to tell, the more he abandoned this first intention (if that's what it was). Focusing on the killers and their victims gave his narrative a texture and a shape —and some extraordinary pace. The experience of reading the book is still vertiginous. Actually, he composed *In Cold Blood* in brief, self-contained sections, linking them like pieces of a jigsaw puzzle. In the process, Capote began to exploit classic literary crime techniques to heighten the suspense. Several critics have noted the quasi-cinematic style of the first two sections of the novel ("The Last to See Them Alive" and "Persons Unknown"), and the urgent inter-cutting between the Clutters and their killers.

When I worked at Faber & Faber in the 1980s, I was lucky enough to become friends with Capote's editor at Random House, the legendary Joe Fox. He often spoke about working with "Truman" on this manuscript, and some of what follows is owed to my memories of Joe's conversation.

Fox used to say that his author was for a long time rather lost in Kansas, wondering what on earth he had got himself into, and how he was going to fashion a narrative. For the first several weeks, with the police making no progress on the case, as Capote himself said later: "Nothing happened. I stayed there and kept researching it and researching it and got very friendly with the various authorities and the detectives on the case. But I never knew whether it was going to be interesting or not."

Capote fretted to Fox that he was getting nowhere. What if they never caught the killers? Was the projected book just a wild goose chase? But then, by chance, Smith and Hickock were apprehended for a different crime, interrogated and charged. Once the story began to gather speed, Capote found a new set of worries. What if the killers would not co-operate? Or speak to him? To animate the middle and closing sections of the book ("Answer" and "The Corner"), he had to establish a dialogue with Hickock and Smith. Being Capote, this became both intimate and obsessive. As he put it: "I made very close contact with these two boys and saw them very often over the next four years until they were executed."

This relationship, especially with Perry Smith, inspired the later charge that he had somehow coldly waited for the hanging, as a suitably moving climax. This accusation surfaced first in the *Observer* in a row between Capote and the critic Ken Tynan after his review of *In Cold Blood* implied that Capote wanted an execution. Capote always rebutted this. "I never knew," he once said, even when halfway through the book, and after working on it for a year and a half, "whether I would go on with it or not, whether it would finally evolve itself into something that would be worth all that effort."

Capote's literary aesthetic also attracted the criticism of Tom Wolfe in his 1967 Esquire essay "Pornoviolence" in which he argued that *In Cold Blood* manipulates the reader with the promise of disclosing gruesome details about a true crime, thereby reducing the work to a level of sadistic sensationalism, what Wolfe dubbed "pornoviolence".

Eventually, Joe Fox (who actually travelled with Capote to the killers' execution) persuaded his author that the book was done. Random House published *In Cold Blood* early in 1966, after a four-part serialisation the previous September in the New Yorker, whose editor, William Shawn, had first commissioned Capote. *In Cold Blood* was a *succès fou* in the USA and, later, worldwide. But its success blighted Capote's creativity, and his work dwindled to almost nothing in the 1970s. He died in 1984, aged 59, shortly before his 60th birthday.

– 85 –
The Bell Jar
by Sylvia Plath (1966)

Sylvia Plath's only novel was originally published in January 1963 under the pseudonym Victoria Lucas, and became tangled up almost immediately in the drama of her suicide, to the book's detriment among the critics. However, republished under Plath's own name in 1966, it became a modern classic.

"It was a queer, sultry summer, the summer they electrocuted the Rosenbergs, and I didn't know what I was doing in New York." After this brittle, dangerous introduction to the summer of 1953, we meet Esther Greenwood who is, she tells us, "supposed to be having the time of my life". It's a theme that, 40 years on, would become commercialised, even satirised, in *Sex and the City*.

But, in the age of Mad Men, Esther/Sylvia is far too driven, damaged and/or neurotic, and with too much emotional baggage, to have a ball in Manhattan. The story of her life and times, however, is told with blistering honesty, and a vivid attention to detail. It's a raw, unsettling book with flashes of brilliance, a *roman à clef* that's also a long, tormented footnote to Plath's tormented poetry.

Plath herself had won an internship at *Mademoiselle* in New York City in 1953, and her painfully autobiographical novel draws heavily on her experience. The reader discovers, in flashbacks, why Esther cannot give herself wholeheartedly to her new life in the city. With hindsight, it's easy to pick up the smell of death from Esther's account. Hardly a page goes by without a reference to a dead baby, a cadaver, or her late father ("dead since I was nine"). The other man in her life, Yale boyfriend Buddy Willard, troubles her spirit in other ways, too.

Plath's essential theme, a staccato drumbeat, is Esther's obsession with the opposite sex. At first, released from her mother's repressive scrutiny, she decides to lose her virginity (a "millstone around my neck") to Constantin, a UN Russian translator, but he's too sensible to fall for her. Then, having failed on another date, in which she is labelled a "slut", she hurls her clothes off her hotel roof, and returns home for a suicidal summer, a worsening depression which she compares to suffocating under a "bell jar". Esther's predicament, more generally, is how to develop a mature identity, as a woman, and to be true to that self rather than conform to societal norms. It's this quest that makes *The Bell Jar* a founding text of Anglo-American feminism.

Eventually, as Esther spirals lower, with successive suicide attempts, she is given shock treatment (ECT), echoing the Rosenbergs' fate, in horrifying scenes, graphically described. Finally, another doctor gives her the longed-for diaphragm. "The next step," says Esther, "was to find the proper sort of man." Irwin, the maths professor, of course, turns out to be just the opposite, and the consequences of their intercourse dominate the final pages of the book until beautiful and well-adjusted Dr Nolan begins to steer Esther back to sanity, and a return to college.

A Note on the Text:
In her journal for December 1958, Plath lists what she calls "Main Questions", including: "What to do with hate for mother? Why don't I write a novel?" After this latter question, she later added, in her own handwriting: "I have! August 22, 1961: THE BELL JAR." Elsewhere, Ted Hughes has also confirmed that Plath began to write her only novel in 1961, completing it after the couple's separation in 1962. In other words, *The Bell Jar* was written fast and urgently.

Plath told her mother that "What I've done is to throw together events from my own life, fictionalising to add colour – it's a potboiler really, but I think it will show how isolated a person feels when he is suffering a breakdown… I've tried to picture my world and the people in it as seen through the distorting lens of a bell jar."

She also described the book as "an autobiographical apprentice work which I had to write in order to free myself from the past". At first, it was composed as part of the Eugene F Saxton Fellowship, a programme affiliated with the New York publisher Harper & Row whose immediate response to the manuscript was one of disappointment, after which Plath was free to offer it to publishers in London.

William Heinemann published *The Bell Jar* in London on 14 January 1963 under the pseudonym Victoria Lucas, a strategy inspired by her desire to spare the feelings of both her mother and a number of real-life characters in the novel, notably Buddy Willard (Dick Norton). Plath killed herself in her London flat, 23 Fitzroy Road, near Primrose Hill, less than a month later, on 11 February 1963.

– 86 –
Portnoy's Complaint
by Philip Roth (1969)

No 86 marks a milestone: it's the first time in this series that I have listed a living writer. From this (1969) publication date, I shall now be addressing contemporary English and American literature, and many living writers. Inevitably, the choice will become correspondingly more difficult.

Portnoy's Complaint is the novel that made Philip Roth an international literary celebrity, an iconic book that changed everything for the writer, pitching him headlong into a relentless world of banal public curiosity. After *Portnoy,* his working life became dominated by answering questions about the inter-relationship of fact and fiction in his writing. Roth's response has been to take refuge in a variety of alter egos, notably Nathan Zuckerman. He will never again hold forth as brilliantly or as memorably as he does in this novel.

The context of Portnoy's hilarious, ranting monologue is estab-lished on the closing page. "So [said the doctor]. Now vee may perhaps to begin. Yes?"

Alexander Portnoy lies on the couch. Dr Spielvogel sits behind, listening to a subject that is, says Roth, "so difficult to talk about and yet so near at hand". In short, masturbation, and its corollary, satyro-mania.

To facilitate his solitary lust, Portnoy commands a far richer arsenal of sex aids than most horny young men: old socks, his sister's under-wear, a baseball glove and – notoriously – a slice of liver for the Portnoy family dinner.

This is a "talking cure" as Freud never envisaged it, a farcical monologue by – this is Roth again – "A lust-ridden, mother-addicted young Jewish bachelor", a tirade that would "put the id into yid".

Alex is an archetypal Jewish-American son, coincidentally the same age as his creator, and a former "honour student" who's now working in New York as a civil rights lawyer. His mother would have preferred him to become a doctor, marry and have children, but we are all too aware that her wishes will never be part of her son's adult life.

Alex free associates for Spielvogel with a wild frenzy that some have suggested is owed to the standup comics of Roth's youth, and perhaps near-contemporaries such as Lenny Bruce. Roth's response has been to identify his main influence as "a sit-down comic named Franz Kafka".

For all its avowed literary seriousness, this "wild blue shocker" (*Life*), a novel in the guise of a confession, was an immediate bestseller. Taken by hundreds of thousands of American readers as a confession in the guise of a novel, it placed its author inexorably centre stage in the minds of his audience. He's been there ever since.

A Note on the Text:

I interviewed Roth in 2008, the year of his 75th birthday, for the publication of *Indignation*. I recall that part of this interview, never used in the printed version, concerned his persistent frustration with his reputation as the author of a "shocking" novel that's now nearly half a century old. Roth's weary complaint was that some of his readers still haven't got over his controversial and brilliantly comic exploration of sexual desire and frustration, especially as this might relate to a Jewish man's mother.

The origins of the novel are the subject of dispute, and all explanations are vulnerable to Roth's own mischievous taste for throwing literary hounds off the scent. There are many versions. Some derive from Roth himself, always an unreliable narrator, especially in his 1988 "novelist's autobiography", *The Facts*. More credibly, some can be attributed to his literary associates. For many years I was friends with one of his long-time editors, Aaron Asher, who never failed to regale his circle with entertaining tales of working with "Philip".

When I met Roth at his home in upstate Connecticut, I suggested at one point that he might have unconsciously courted outrage with *Portnoy's Complaint*. He disdained this line of inquiry. "I don't have any sense of audience," he said, "least of all when I'm writing. The audience I'm writing for is me, and I'm so busy trying to figure the damn thing out, and having so much trouble, that the last thing I think of is: 'What is X, Y or Z going to be thinking of it?'"

The novel itself occupied Roth for much of the 1960s, the decade in which, to his great distress, his first wife, Margaret Martinson, was killed in a car crash (in 1968, five years after they had separated). It seems likely that the idea of Portnoy's monologue derived from one of Roth's hilarious dinner-party riffs (for which he is famous among his friends). He himself has often said he cannot identify any single experience from which *Portnoy's Complaint* originated.

In early drafts it was "The Jewboy"; then a play (workshopped by Dustin Hoffman); then "Whacking Off"; then a long short story, "A Jewish Patient Begins His Analysis", and finally, with the appearance of his psychoanalyst, *Portnoy's Complaint*. With a lurid yellow Paul Bacon cover it was published as such on 12 January 1969 by Random House in New York. The city's literary community, especially the Jewish elements, were soon up in arms, and even the great critic Lionel Trilling was moved to enter the fray. Roth was unmoved. He took refuge in his writing, and has done so to this day (though he now says he has stopped writing fiction). As his character Peter Tarnopol in *The Great American Novel* puts it: "Literature got me into this, and literature is gonna have to get me out."

Today, Philip Roth is 82, and working with Blake Bailey on an authorised biography, due for publication by the end of this decade. In 2014 Roth told the BBC that "One of the biggest tasks that has come to me is working with the biographer Blake Bailey and ever since then I have been in the employ of Blake Bailey." Although Roth says that he does not expect to live long enough to see the biography's completion, he has submitted vast amounts of newly written material for Bailey.

His biographer told the BBC: "He has supplied me with literally thousands of pages of typed notes that are addressed directly to me. He has turned over all his personal papers to me." This personal archive is so extensive, says Bailey, that it will take him "years to excavate".

We shall see.

Robert McCrum

– 87 –
Mrs Palfrey at the Claremont
by Elizabeth Taylor (1971)

"Laura Palfrey," writes Elizabeth Taylor, in a brilliant, character-defining sentence at the opening of her masterpiece, "would have made a distinguished-looking man and, sometimes, wearing evening dress, looked like some famous general in drag."

Mrs Palfrey, recently widowed, arrives at the Claremont hotel on the Cromwell Road, one rainy Sunday in January. She is asserting her right to be herself after years as a colonial wife, while also acknowledging the inevitability of decline and death. "It was hard work being old," writes Taylor. "Both infancy and age are tiring times."

The hotel becomes a genteel antechamber to oblivion, its spectral inhabitants representative figures from postwar English life. It's the 1960s, and a new society is taking shape. The Claremont symbolises a class and a way of life heading for the dustbin of history. But Taylor, though ruthlessly observant, also delights in exploring the trivial banalities of everyday life.

When she subjects the newest resident of the Claremont to that classic geriatric indignity, a fall, the upshot is not humiliation, but romance. Ludo Myers is a struggling writer who rescues Mrs Palfrey and becomes, through a series of misunderstandings, her grandson "Desmond".

Although this is, at times, a heartbreaking novel, striking many sombre chords, some of it teeters on the edge of sit- or romcom, as Mrs Palfrey strives to do the right thing and also to be true to herself. Much of the reader's joy lies in the exquisite subtlety in Taylor's depiction of all the relationships, the sharp brevity of her wit, and the apparently effortless way the plot unfolds. Among the other residents of the Claremont, Lady Swayne and Mrs de Salis are comic monsters who could have easily enjoyed walk-on parts in Jane Austen.

Finally, Mrs Palfrey rejects an offer of marriage, and has another fall. This time, there is no happy outcome. She dies alone, unwanted and unremembered. That, possibly, was Elizabeth Taylor's commentary on her own fate. She could hardly have been more wrong.

A Note on the Text:

Elizabeth Taylor is a great English novelist who remains a surprisingly well-kept secret. Anne Tyler says she is a "soul sister" to Jane Austen and Elizabeth Bowen, and Sarah Waters has praised her as a writer of "great subtlety, great compassion and great depth". However, the depth of her genius is still only half-recognised. Novels such as *Angel, The Wedding Group* and *Mrs Palfrey at the Claremont* should propel her on to any list of English fiction such as this, but it's notable how often she still gets ignored or overlooked.

Mrs Palfrey at the Claremont is, for me, her masterpiece. My enthusiasm is probably coloured by the fact that I got my first job at Chatto & Windus, Taylor's publisher, just a few months after her death in 1976. So I came to know her editor (Dennis Enright) and her publisher (Norah Smallwood) as friends. It was from them that I heard the stories of the witty, secretive, reclusive and dedicated writer who lived and worked almost all her life in the home counties, particularly Penn in Buckinghamshire.

Mrs Palfrey at the Claremont, a late bloom in Taylor's oeuvre, was published by Chatto in 1971. The novelist Paul Bailey, who has special affection for this novel, has written: "I envy those readers who are coming to her work for the first time. Theirs will be an unexpected pleasure, and they will – if they read her as she wanted to be read – learn much that will surprise them." For the *Daily Telegraph,* "Taylor excels in conveying the tragicomic poignancy of everyday life".

In 1982, *Mrs Palfrey* became a Virago Modern Classic, a move that introduced the novel to a much wider audience. To her fans, of course, she never needed any hype; to the wider world of serious fiction readers, she now slowly began to get the recognition she deserves.

Elizabeth Taylor died from cancer in 1976.

– 88 –
Rabbit Redux
by John Updike (1971)

John Updike is 20th century American literature's blithe spirit, a virtuoso of language whose perfect pitch illuminated every line he wrote with an airy and zestful brilliance. He was always something of a miniaturist. His first hope was to be a poet. When that ambition misfired, he took his delight in the English sentence and made a name for himself as a *New Yorker* short story writer. Finally, he brought his gifts of wit, curiosity and invention to the American novel. By the end of his career, he had become one of the most complete and versatile men of letters in his country's history. Among many possible fiction choices – his debut, *The Poorhouse Fair;* the sensational scandal of *Couples;* the exhilarating magical realism of *The Witches of Eastwick* – I've picked his panoramic masterpiece, the Henry Angstrom series, a portrait of America compiled over four decades: *Rabbit, Run* (1960); *Rabbit Redux* (1971); *Rabbit Is Rich* (1981); and *Rabbit at Rest* (1990).

Harry "Rabbit" Angstrom, who owes something to Sinclair Lewis's *Babbitt*, is as much Updike's fictional alter ego as Zuckerman is Philip Roth's, a college basketball star of Swedish ancestry who has to reconcile himself, after a dazzling start, to the long littleness of life among the American middle class.

On first meeting, Harry is selling a revolutionary vegetable-peeler on commission (later, he will run a Toyota dealership), and wrestling with a miserable suburban marriage. Harry is a good man whose circumstances provoke him to do bad things. In the first volume, he leaves his boozy wife, Janice, to go off with a call-girl (but not for long).

In *Rabbit Redux*, my favourite, which is set in America in 1969 (the Apollo moon landing; race riots; the oil crisis etc), it's Janice who has left Harry. He gets caught up in a sequence of unfortunate events in which he knows he's in the wrong, but will never get found out. In *Rabbit Is Rich*, Harry is middle-aged, with all the stresses of mid-life on his back. Finally, in 1990, with *Rabbit at Rest*, Updike plants his lovably mediocre hero in Reagan's America, a state of anaesthesia that provoked his contemporary and rival Gore Vidal to deplore Updike's "acceptance of authority in any form".

This is unfair. Updike's dominant mood is of grace under pressure, of Lutheran stoicism, and the acceptance of fate. When Harry finally succumbs to cardiac arrest, he confides to his son: "All I can tell you is, it isn't so bad." Ian McEwan, summarising Updike's achievement on his untimely death in 2009, compared him to Saul Bellow as "a master of effortless motion – between first and third person, from the metaphorical density of literary prose to the demotic, from specific detail to wide generalisation, from the actual to the numinous, from the scary to the comic". Updike was, like all the greatest in this series are, aways the supreme entertainer.

A Note on the Text:
Henry "Rabbit" Angstrom, the account of whose life and times adds up to more than half a million words, is often placed with honour, and a measure of irony, next to America's great literary protagonists such as Huck Finn, Jay Gatsby and even Captain Ahab. *Rabbit Redux* was published in the US by Alfred A Knopf, a great literary house and a natural home for a novel that, from the title down, nodded to the Anglo-American literary tradition. Anthony Trollope published *Phineas Redux* in 1873, and Updike, who was steeped in English literature, would have enjoyed the allusion. Others critics have noted its "Dickensian" ambitions.

The Angstrom series had many inspirations, including Sinclair Lewis's *Babbitt*. Updike, who also venerated Lewis, always spoke warmly about his admiration for Marcel Proust, though "Rabbit" has little to do, explicitly, with *À la Recherche du Temps Perdu*. Ian McEwan, quoted above, described Updike's "Rabbit" novels as his "masterpiece". Philip Roth, a sometime rival, declared Updike to be America's "greatest man of letters, a national treasure", while, for Lorrie Moore, Updike is "our greatest writer", though she prefers his short stories.

After the fourth "Rabbit" book appeared in 1990, there were later, and shorter, outings, notably the novella "*Rabbit Remembered*", published in a collection entitled *Licks of Love* (2001). John Updike died from lung cancer in January 2009. His archive of manuscripts, papers and letters is held in the Houghton Library at Harvard University.

– 89 –
Song of Solomon
by Toni Morrison (1977)

I first read Toni Morrison in 1977 when a proof copy of her novel, *Song of Solomon*, was on offer to the then-independent publisher, Chatto & Windus. Part of my background reading for this, her third book, involved discovering, and falling in love with, her debut, *The Bluest Eye* (1970), and its successor, *Sula* (1973). Since then, I have followed most of Morrison's subsequent fiction, notably *Beloved* and *Jazz*, but I remain a diehard fan of the novel that established her name. From 1977 on, she only grew in stature as a contemporary writer of extraordinary power and vision, ultimately becoming, in 1993, the first African-American woman to win the Nobel prize for literature.

Song of Solomon blazed that trail. It was the first book by a black American woman writer to be chosen as a main selection of the all-powerful Book of the Month Club, a recognition unknown to the black community since Richard Wright's *Native Son* (1940).

Song of Solomon takes off, and finally comes back to earth, with an exhilarating leap of danger. The idea of "fly" and "flight" (as an escape, or challenge) runs through the story of Macon "Milkman" Dead III, who gets his nickname from being breastfed into childhood by his dominant mother.

"Who am I ?" is the central premise of many classic novels in this series, including *David Copperfield* and *The Adventures of Huckleberry Finn*. From the arresting first scene of an insurance agent's suicidal leap, to the closing pages, when Milkman hurls himself into the air against his best friend and nemesis, Guitar, the novel traces Milkman's coming of age as an African American in search of a better understanding of his heritage. To achieve this, in a telling reversal of traditional black migration, Milkman makes his way to the warm and nurturing south from the frozen and alienating north.

The novel is partly set in an unspecified Michigan town, and the unfolding story, replete with buried treasure, violent deaths and slavery tales, moves steadily south to Pennsylvania, where Milkman's grandfather had died, and finally to Shalimar in Virginia, the home of his slave ancestors. In the words of the song that Milkman sings:

Solomon done fly,
Solomon done gone
Solomon went across the sky,
Solomon gone home.

Where, in the first and northern half of the novel, Milkman battles his origins, in the south he embraces them, and by the end is at one with his roots.

Song of Solomon is full of characters, especially Milkman's mysterious sister, Pilate, whose symbolic lives play an important role in the weaving of Morrison's narrative. The story loops and swoops, in its evocation of the black American experience in the 20th century, expressing a complex literary surface in a musical and often poetic language that's infused with the rhythms of African American speech and song. Morrison has acknowledged that *Song of Solomon* liberated her from traditional models in her writing. In a style she would perfect in novels such as Beloved, Morrison conjures her tale from many voices and stories. The overall effect is a kaleidoscope of many gorgeous colours and patterns, evocative of memory and history, and actualised through the compelling figure of Macon Dead, one of the great characters of contemporary American fiction.

A Note on the Text:
In her "Forward" to the Vintage edition, Morrison writes that she used to despise "artists' chatter about muses – 'voices' that could speak to them and enable a vision, the source of which they could not otherwise name… I regarded the 'mystery' of creativity as a shield erected by artists to avoid articulating, analysing, or even knowing the details of their creative process – for fear it would fade away."

She goes on: "Writing *Song of Solomon* destroyed all that." She describes how her late father became her "muse", how his voice was absorbed into her writing, and how the challenge of the novel became the management of "a radical shift in imagination from a female locus to a male one".

This use of voices has enabled her, writes Morrison, to break away from what she identifies as "a totalising view". For Morrison, American literature has become "totalised – as though there is only one version. We are not one indistinguishable block of people who always behave the same way… I try to give some credibility to all sorts of voices, each of which is profoundly different. Because what strikes me about African-American culture is its variety."

Song of Solomon was Morrison's first step down a road that would become increasingly original and would lead her to the achievements and mastery of *Jazz* and *Beloved*.

– 90 –
A Bend in the River
by VS Naipaul (1979)

 "*A Bend in the River*," VS Naipaul has written, with that hint of creative inscrutability he cherishes, "remains mysterious." At the same time, however, it is perhaps the novel that most nearly touches the author's inner concerns. Salim, who comes from the east coast of Africa, from a long-established Indian trading family, uproots himself to the heart of an unnamed African country as a merchant and sets up shop in an unnamed town at this "bend in the river". Salim, like Naipaul himself, is under no illusions about his move and declares, in a celebrated opening line: "The world is what it is; men who are nothing, who allow themselves to become nothing, have no place in it."

Is this the Congo? Naipaul says so, conceding "an echo" of a journey he made to Kinshasa in 1975. His brilliantly reimagined fictional landscape conjures a hellish vision of the developing world's endemic dislocation. The town in which Salim, "a man without a side", sets up shop, formerly Arab, then colonial, becomes a microcosm of a society moving towards independence: a place of chaotic and violent change; tribal warfare, ignorance, poverty and human degradation. Salim's story is punctuated by irruptions of violent death, a tormented love affair and his own complex, terror-struck response to the emergence of "the Big Man", an archetypal African dictator.

Naipaul, who is of Indian ancestry like Salim, is drawn to this visceral and dangerous scene while being at the same time disdainful of its crudeness and savagery. Salim's story articulates a vision of disorder and decline in a moment of post-imperial upheaval that has made Naipaul vulnerable to accusations of having reactionary artistic politics.

When, at the end, the character Ferdinand urges Salim to flee for his life, he does so in language that seems to open a window on to Naipaul's inner vision: "We're all going to hell, and every man knows this in his bones. We're being killed. Nothing has any meaning… It's a nightmare – nowhere is safe now." Naipaul's acid contempt for the independence struggle has inspired as much hostile criticism as Conrad for *Heart of Darkness*. Indeed, Naipaul towers next to Conrad, whose work surely inspired this novel. In his prime, Naipaul was the greatest living writer of English prose and this (in my judgment, slightly ahead of *Guerrillas* and *The Enigma of Arrival*) is his masterpiece.

A Note on the Text:

A Bend in the River is set in central Africa, yet Naipaul claims he "knew very little about this part of the world when I settled down to write… I had travelled widely and it might have been said that there was nothing clear in my head."

Nevertheless, the novel seems to have been written fast, from July 1977 to August 1978, with some of it, notably the "easy and complete fabrication" of the character Ferdinand, coming to Naipaul in a dream. He has added subsequently that his dream life has never been as fruitful since.

At first, Naipaul's literary agent (soon to be fired) judged the book too "cerebral" and, as the author sourly notes, "a year's work fetched only \$25,000". However, *A Bend in the River*, published by Knopf in New York in May 1979, immediately won powerful support from reviewers. The critic Elizabeth Hardwick praised "a haunting creation, rich with incident and human bafflement, played out in an immense detail of landscape rendered with poignant brilliance".

John Updike wrote: "Always a master of fictional landscape, Naipaul here shows, in his variety of human examples and in his search for underlying social causes, a Tolstoyan spirit." This was especially generous. Updike had just published his own "African novel", *The Coup,* and was coming under fire for straying into a landscape he could not understand.

Not everyone was so enchanted. Edward Said attacked a novel that, he declared, continued a long tradition of "hostility to Islam, to the Arabs". *A Bend in The River* was shortlisted for the 1979 Booker prize but, perhaps because Naipaul had already won (in 1971) with *In a Free State*, he was passed over.

Politics has always hovered mutinously off stage in response to

Robert McCrum

Naipaul's work. When I interviewed him in 2008, he seemed resigned to the adversity and probably indifferent to it. He was already a Nobel laureate, probably the best riposte to the critics.

– 91 –
Midnight's Children
by Salman Rushdie (1981)

Among the many turning points in the constant remaking of the English novel – the dazzle of Stern, the quieter, witty genius of Austen; the polyvalent brio of Dickens; the vernacular brilliance of Twain, and so on – the appearance of *Midnight's Children* in 1981 now stands out as a particularly significant milestone.

Salman Rushdie's second novel took the Indian English novel, revolutionised it by marrying the fiction of Austen and Dickens with the oral narrative tradition of India, and made a "magical realist" (the label was still in its infancy) novel for a new generation. This emergent global readership would find, in a story set in Bombay, a work of contemporary fiction that mashed up tales of east and west into a self-confessed fabrication narrated by the highly symbolic figure of Saleem Sinai, an Indian boy born on the stroke of midnight, 15 August 1947, a boy whose distinctive nose seems like a miniature embodiment of the sub-continent whose history has just taken him prisoner.

Saleem sets out his stall as the narrator in the novel's third paragraph: "I have been a swallower of lives; and to know me, just the one of me, you'll have to swallow a lot as well. Consumed multitudes are jostling and shoving inside me…" And so, off we go.

Saleem, whom Rushdie inhabits for his own purposes, is a character with many unusual powers, especially a psychic connection to all the other children born as he was, at the very moment of modern India's birth. An equally important, and sometimes neglected, element of the novel is Rushdie's angry response to the repressions of the 1970s "Emergency". With Saleem, the personal and the historical become indistinguishable, and Rushdie makes a further duality when he exchanges his narrator for a second baby, an alter ego who expresses

224

Saleem's dark side. All this is described in Indian English prose that pulsates between the tumultuous and the fantastic.

A page of Rushdie is a rich, jewel-encrusted tapestry of allusions, puns, in-jokes, asides, and the unconsidered trifles of popular culture. Some readers may find this diet close to indigestible, but Rushdie's charm, energy and brilliance, with his sheer *joie de vivre*, justify the critic VS Pritchett's verdict (in the *New Yorker*) that, with *Midnight's Children*, "India has produced a great novelist... a master of perpetual storytelling".

A Note on the Text:

The making of *Midnight's Children* began, by Rushdie's own account, when he travelled to India in 1975, a return home sponsored by a £700 advance for his first novel *Grimus*, a quasi-science fantasy experiment that flopped badly. But his next novel would be different. "I had wanted for some time to write a novel of childhood," he said in 2005. But it was not until this trip that he began to conceive "a more ambitious plan". He would take Saleem Sinai, a minor character from an abandoned novel entitled *The Antagonist*, and link him to the totality of Indian independence by somehow making the history of modern India "all his fault".

The idea was one thing; the writing would be something else. "I was broke," recalls Rushdie. "The novel in my head was clearly going to be long and strange and take quite a while to write and in the meanwhile I had no money." Having briefly been a copywriter for Ogilvy & Mather, he now rejoined the agency on a part-time basis, and settled down to write the book he was beginning to call *Midnight's Children*, having rejected *Children of Midnight* as "banal".

By mid 1979, he was done. The typescript was sent to his friend and editor Liz Calder at Jonathan Cape where, in the best publishing tradition, the first reader's report was brief, hostile and dismissive: "The author should concentrate on short stories until he has mastered the novel form."

Thereafter, wiser readings prevailed. The novel was bought by both Cape in the UK and Alfred Knopf in the US. Calder, says Rushdie, saved him from "two bad mistakes". There was an offstage "audience" character who was "redundant"; and there was a knot in the novel's time line. Rushdie was persuaded to drop the character, and restructure the story chronologically.

On publication in the spring of 1981, the reviews were good, and the novel's reception generally enthusiastic. But then, once the book appeared in India, there came the first of the political controversies that have tormented Rushdie throughout his literary career: Mrs Gandhi sued him for a single defamatory sentence about her relationship with her younger son Sanjay. The case never came to court; and eventually the offending sentence was dropped. Now that Mrs Gandhi and her "Emergency" are history, the text becomes less topical, but more timeless. Rushdie himself says that "*Midnight's Children* is a product of its moment in history, touched and shaped by its time in ways which its author cannot wholly know."

In its own time, it has been an acclaimed prizewinner, winning both the Booker prize in 1981, and "the Booker of Bookers" in 1993 and again in 2008. Chosen for the BBCs "Big Read" in 2003, its status as a contemporary classic seems assured. Rushdie himself has written, with appropriate modesty, that "if it can pass the test of another generation or two, it may endure". Posterity awaits.

– 92 –
Housekeeping
by Marilynne Robinson (1981)

Ever since President Obama identified *Gilead* as one of his favourite contemporary books, Marilynne Robinson's reputation has been dominated by her trilogy (including *Home* and *Lila*) about the Ames family of Iowa. Yet, almost 25 years before, Robinson completed and published a first novel which prefigures the mood and preoccupations of almost all her later work.

For me, *Housekeeping* remains her masterpiece, an unforgettable declaration of imaginative and narrative intent. It is also, as many critics have pointed out, the work of an American writer, and Calvinist, intimately at home with the Bible and the great transcendentalists, Ralph Waldo Emerson, Henry David Thoreau and Herman Melville.

In the simple spirit of these masters, Robinson's prose, replete with metaphor and simile, is achingly quotable: "To crave and to have are as like as a thing and its shadow. For when does a berry break upon the tongue as sweetly as when one longs to taste it, and when is the taste refracted into so many hues and savours of ripeness and earth, and when do our senses know any thing so utterly as when we lack it? And here again is a foreshadowing – the world will be made whole. For to wish for a hand on one's hair is all but to feel it. So whatever we may lose, very craving gives it back to us again." There's no one else in America today writing with such natural inner music.

Housekeeping is the story of two orphans, Ruth and her sister Lucille Stone, living in remote Idaho by the lakeside town of Fingerbone. These abandoned girls are raised by a succession of relatives, and finally their aunt Sylvie, a strange drifter who becomes the novel's compelling central character. Sylvie commits to staying in Fingerbone to "keep house" for her nieces, though neither believes she will stay with them for long. Ruth says: "I was reassured by her sleeping on the lawn, and now and then in the car. It seemed to me that if she could remain transient here, she would not have to leave." Sylvie, who is like a "mermaid in a ship's cabin", wanders by the lake while the family house goes to pieces. Ruth, our narrator, is at home with her aunt's transient spirit, and comfortable with solitude: "Once alone," she says, "it is impossible to believe that one could ever have been otherwise. Loneliness is an absolute discovery."

By contrast, Lucille wants to escape Sylvie's spell. In an echo of Robinson's own divided nature, the Stone sisters, inseparable in childhood, begin to grow apart. Ruth, a natural rebel, goes deeper into her family's dark past; the more conventional Lucille moves away. Then the Fingerbone community steps in. Sylvie's guardianship is challenged with the threat that she and Ruth should be separated. Robinson believes in family. She writes: "Families will not be broken. Curse and expel them, send their children wandering, drown them in floods and fires, and old women will make songs of all these sorrows and sit on the porch and sing them on mild evenings."

So, rather than submit to yet another assault on their strange and transient association, Ruth and Sylvie burn down their house and escape together across the lake. The townspeople, who cannot understand the idea of self-sufficient "homeless" women, decide Ruth and Sylvie are insane and that they must have drowned in the lake.

In the words of an early *New York Times* review, this novel is "about people who have not managed to connect with a place, a purpose, a routine or another person. It's about the immensely resourceful sadness of a certain kind of American, someone who has fallen out of history and is trying to invent a life without assistance of any kind, without even recognising that there are precedents. It is about a woman who is so far from everyone else that it would be presumptuous to put a name to her frame of mind".

As a modern classic, *Housekeeping* can bear any weight of interpretation. Like Fingerbone's lake water, it has become a mirror in which generations of new readers can find themselves, as if for the first time.

A Note on the Text:

When I interviewed Marilynne Robinson at the Cambridge literary festival in November 2014, and asked her about the genesis of *Housekeeping*, her account was typically low-key and matter-of-fact, without any of the ostentation you might expect from the author of such an immense literary achievement. She had written the novel, in longhand, for her own pleasure, she said, without much thought about its afterlife, found it taken up by friends, then represented by the New York literary agent Ellen Levine, who sold it without delay to the American literary publishing house Farrar Straus and Giroux (which published it in the States in 1980), and in the UK to Faber.

In her *Paris Review* interview of 2008, she supplied a bit more detail, but not much: "When I went to college, I majored in American literature, which was unusual then. But it meant that I was broadly exposed to 19th century American literature. I became interested in the way that American writers used metaphoric language, starting with Emerson. When I entered the PhD programme, I started writing these metaphors down, just to get the feeling of writing in that voice. After I finished my dissertation, I read through the stack of metaphors and they cohered in a way that I hadn't expected. I could see that I had created something that implied much more. So I started writing *Housekeeping*, and the characters became important for me. I told a friend of mine, a writer named John Clayton, that I had been working on this thing, and he asked to see it. The next thing I knew, I got a letter from his agent saying that she would be happy to represent it."

What she, modestly, did not say to me was that, unknown as she was, an early rave review in the *New York Times* ensured that the book would be noticed. "Here's a first novel that sounds as if the author has been treasuring it up all her life, waiting for it to form itself," began the critic, Anatole Broyard. "It's as if, in writing it, she broke through the ordinary human condition with all its dissatisfactions, and achieved a kind of transfiguration. You can feel in the book a gathering voluptuous release of confidence, a delighted surprise at the unexpected capacities of language, a close, careful fondness for people that we thought only saints felt." Broyard's awed enthusiasm was soon echoed by many critics and readers.

From the first, the reviews of *Housekeeping* were united in their admiration for the luminous subtlety of her work, and her powerfully simple, almost Biblical, way with language. This passage, typical of Robinson's prose, introduces a new, timeless, and utterly distinctive voice into the magical polyphony of the American novel:

"Cain killed Abel, and the blood cried out from the ground – a story so sad that even God took notice of it. Maybe it was not the sadness of the story, since worse things have happened every minute since that day, but its novelty that He found striking. In the newness of the world God was a young man, and grew indignant over the slightest things. In the newness of the world God had perhaps not Himself realised the ramifications of certain of his laws, for example, that shock will spend itself in waves; that our images will mimic every gesture, and that shattered they will multiply and mimic every gesture ten, a hundred, or a thousand times. Cain, the image of God, gave the simple earth of the field a voice and a sorrow, and God himself heard the voice, and grieved for the sorrow, so Cain was a creator, in the image of his creator."

It's well known, possibly notorious, that Robinson's next work of fiction, *Gilead*, did not appear for almost 25 years. Again, when I interviewed her about *Gilead* for the *Observer* at her home in Iowa in 2005, her literary voice was undimmed, its concerns as deep-rooted, and the simple magic of her prose as potent as ever. Once again, she displayed an impressive detachment from the process of writing. It hadn't, after all, been a 25-year struggle; she could write quite quickly; her favourite writing clothes were loose trousers ("pants") and a sweatshirt – she "dressed like a bum"; the new book had come to her more or less fully formed, the fruit of an accidental vacation, and so on. Who knows how much of this is true? Robinson does not like to give much away. She mainly shuns the literary circuit. Perhaps this is why some American writers, especially, have fallen over themselves to pay tribute to her work.

Barbara Kingsolver writes: "I honestly believe reading [Robinson's] prose slows down my respiration and heart rate, bringing me to a state of keen meditative attention. This novel is a marvel of carefully measured revelation." More remarkable, perhaps, it Bret Easton Ellis's acknowledgement that "it's so beautifully written, the prose gives me the chills when I read it… it's very meditative and very – a very different experience from most contemporary novels."

In 2008, Barack Obama let slip that Robinson's fiction, especially *Gilead*, was among his favourite reading. She, in amused confirmation of this, has joked about getting Christmas cards from the White House.

At the moment, she is planning another volume in her Ames/Gilead sequence.

– 93 –
Money: A Suicide Note
by Martin Amis (1984)

Perhaps more than any other novelist in this series, Martin Amis, who is also an outstanding essayist and critic, has punctuated his career with stern and candid reflections about the fates of writers and the afterlives of books. The only measure of success a writer should worry about, says Amis, is whether you're still being read in 50 years. There is, he insists, "only one value judgment in literature: time".

Money, a neo-Rabelaisian comedy, joins *London Fields* as probably Amis's best bid for posterity, a zeitgeist book that remains one of the dominant novels of the 1980s. The hero of *Money*, according to its author, is "a semi-literate alcoholic", John Self, whose appetite for pornography, drugs and fast food marks him out as an Amis favourite. Self's self-loathing is compulsive: "My clothes are made of monosodium glutamate and hexachlorophene. My food is made of polyester, rayon and lurex. My rug lotions contain vitamins. Do my vitamins feature cleaning agents? I hope so. My brain is gimmicked by a microprocessor the size of a quark, and costing ten pee and running the whole deal. I am made of – junk, I'm just junk." At the same time, Self glories in his supremacy, especially at the table: "There have been rich meat and bloody wine. There have been brandies, and thick puddings. There has already been some dirty talk. Selina is in high spirits, and as for me, I'm a gurgling wizard of calorific excess."

Like many figures from the 80s, this ad-man narrator thinks he's running the show – his life, loves, career, sleazy hedonism and all – but, actually, he's a victim. Self, who is crisscrossing the Atlantic to make his first feature film, "Good Money" (later, "Bad Money"), becomes progressively mired in an accumulation of complex financial and sexual crises, linked to the corruptions of money, expressed through a series of hilarious set-pieces, which bring him to the edge of breakdown. Here, in a further provocation to English literary practice, the author steps into the narrative as "Martin Amis" and tries to prevent Self's self-destruction. Thereafter, *Money* spirals towards its teasing, postmodern conclusion.

It's probably wrong to interrogate Self's brilliant monologue for the satisfactions of traditional English fiction. The narrator is all: "I've got to get this stuff out of my system. No, more than that, much more. I've got to get my system out of my system. That's what I've got to do." *Money*, according to Amis, is a novel of voice, not plot. The meaning of the "suicide note" subtitle emerges as part of the denouement, in a narrative resolution that's more Nabokov than Dickens, to cite two of the influences presiding over the novel.

The thrill of *Money*, which is turbo-charged with savage humour from first to last page, is Amis's prodigal delight in contemporary Anglo-American vernacular. In this novel, and *London Fields*, and finally *The Information*, he developed a voice that mesmerised a generation. The loquacious monsters of his fiction remain vivid and indispensable voices in the raucous polyphony of a new age, an essential precursor to the breakthroughs of the imminent new century. These are voices that are never less than wonderfully quotable: "The future could go this way, that way. The future's futures have never looked so rocky. Don't put money on it. Take my advice and stick to the present. It's the real stuff, the only stuff, it's all there is, the present, the panting present." Amis has always been the novelist of the here and now.

A Note on the Text:
Amis has said that *Money* is "a novel of voice", and has described writing it, long-hand, in a notebook before translating that voice into typescript. In his *Paris Review* interview, he said: "The common conception of how novels get written seems to me to be an exact

description of writer's block. In the common view, the writer is at this stage so desperate that he's sitting around with a list of characters, a list of themes, and a framework for his plot, and ostensibly trying to mesh the three elements. In fact, it's never like that. What happens is what Nabokov described as a throb. A throb or a glimmer, an act of recognition on the writer's part. At this stage the writer thinks, here is something I can write a novel about. In the absence of that recognition I don't know what one would do. It may be that nothing about this idea – or glimmer, or throb – appeals to you other than the fact that it's your destiny, that it's your next book. You may even be secretly appalled or awed or turned off by the idea, but it goes beyond that. You're just reassured that there is another novel for you to write. The idea can be incredibly thin – a situation, a character in a certain place at a certain time. With *Money*, for example, I had an idea of a big fat guy in New York, trying to make a film. That was all."

In the same interview, Amis concedes that: "*Money* was a much more difficult book to write than *London Fields* because it is essentially a plotless novel. It is what I would call a voice novel. If the voice doesn't work you're screwed. *Money* was only one voice, whereas *London Fields* was four voices."

When *Money* was published, the reviews generally recognised a landmark novel, founded on, but engaged in, an argument with, the English literary canon partly prefigured in this series. The *New York Times* wrote: "The plot of *Money* is in a basic, grand tradition. A guy gets totalled. Maybe he survives in comedy but he's spectacularly brought down. What makes this book special and important is that it revitalises its tradition. Its transatlantic urban showbiz patter and smart literary patterns could have been just a jaded fast-lane bummer, a depleting ride in John Self's purple Fiasco – 'a vintage-style coupe with oodles of dash and heft and twang'. But instead the book's dash and heft and twang serve a deeper energy, a reimagined naivete that urgently asks a basic, grand question: what on earth are the rest of us supposed to make of the spectacle of a fellow human getting totalled?"

In Britain, the *Spectator*, not always an Amis fan, said of *Money* that it was "an epitaph to that decade (the 1980s) much more authentic and searching than *The Bonfire of the Vanities* or *Less Than Zero*."

– 94 –
An Artist of the Floating World
by Kazuo Ishiguro (1986)

Kazuo Ishiguro is probably best known for *The Remains of the Day*, his Booker prizewinner; *The Unconsoled*, a very long novel of hallucinatory strangeness; and *Never Let Me Go*, a contemporary favourite widely taught in schools. But the pitch-perfect novel that both expresses his Japanese inheritance and also captures the haunting beauty and delicacy of Ishiguro's English prose is his second work of fiction, *An Artist of the Floating World*.

This, as its title suggests, is a tour de force of unreliable narration, set in post-Second World War Japan, during the American occupation. Masuji Ono, a respected artist in the 30s and during the war but now retired, is garrulously recalling the past, from a highly subjective point of view.

Ono, who passes his time gardening and pottering, opens his narrative with a low-key sentence whose meaning will resonate throughout the story: "If on a sunny day you climb the steep path leading up from the little wooden bridge still referred to around here as 'the Bridge of Hesitation', you will not have to walk far before the roof of my house becomes visible between the tops of two ginkgo trees."

This kind of hesitation and uncertainty runs through everything that follows. Everything, for Ono, is provisional and troubling: art, family, life, posterity. *An Artist of the Floating World* presents, with the menace of an almost dream-like calm, the reminiscences of a retired painter in the aftermath of a national disaster.

Outside his home, there's the grim reckoning that has followed the horrors of Nagasaki and Hiroshima. The American occupation is crushing Japan's national pride. A new generation of young veterans wants to forget the imperial past. At the same time, in the tranquil seclusion of house and garden, Masuji Ono has time for some increasingly troubled reflections. He has lost his wife and son in the war, but lives on with two daughters, one of whom is married. But for a puzzling anxiety about his second daughter Noriko's marriage negotiations, Ono could slip into old age. Instead, he must take "certain precautionary steps" against the necessary inquiries of his prospective son-in-law.

It becomes clear that Ono's past conceals some guilty secrets which "the artist" must reluctantly address, secrets that illuminate the larger themes of guilt, ageing, solitude, and the baffling incomprehension between young and old. Slowly, in a sequence of perfectly choreographed revelations, we discover that Ono was trained as a decadent artist, an illustrator of the night-time "floating world" of the prewar geishas. During the "China crisis" in the 30s, however, he broke away from that ukiyo-e tradition to develop a more patriotic form of art. Now, as he tries to marry off his daughter, Ono's prestige as a former pro-government painter has come to haunt him.

While Ono grapples with the challenges of peacetime, and Noriko begins to negotiate her marriage, this crucial rite of passage forces Ono to reflect on his former role as a pro-government artist who advised the Committee on Unpatriotic Activities, and who (the reader discovers) once betrayed one of his protégés to the secret police for imprisonment and torture.

The tragedy implicit in the book is that Ono's long digressions into the past revert, inexorably, to the troubles of the present. His reminiscences are teasingly equivocal, for instance: "Of course, that is all a matter of many years ago now and I cannot vouch that those were my exact words that morning." However, the truth is ultimately laid bare. Ono is forced to revise his memories, with increasingly wretched personal recognition. "I am not one of those," he says towards the heartbreaking finale, "who are afraid to admit to the shortcomings of past achievements."

A Note on the Text

In an interview with the *Paris Review*, Ishiguro describes the genesis of his second novel by referring to his first: "There was a subplot in *A Pale View of Hills* about an old teacher who has to rethink the values on which he's built his life. I said to myself, I would like to write a full-blown novel about a man in this situation – in this case, an artist whose career becomes contaminated because he happens to live at a certain time."

Ishiguro's fiction has certainly mined the complexities involved in the unreliable, first-person narrator. *An Artist of the Floating World* is perhaps the supreme example of his art. It is, at face value, deeply Japanese, but many of its themes – secrecy, regret, discretion, hypocrisy and loss – are also to be found in the 20th century English novel. No surprise, perhaps, that his next work of fiction, *The Remains of the Day*, should be about a butler, inspired by PG Wodehouse's Jeeves. Kazuo Ishiguro may have been born in Nagasaki, but the discreet and subtle complexity of English (and Japanese) life is his subject.

– 95 –
The Beginning of Spring
by Penelope Fitzgerald (1988)

She published her first novel in 1977 and won the Booker prize with *Offshore* in 1979, aged 63. Not since Daniel Defoe has a writer, and self-styled outsider, enjoyed such a remarkable late flowering of imaginative creativity. Before she died, at 83, in 2000, Fitzgerald had published nine novels in about 20 years. In the US, *The Blue Flower* (1995) is her best-known book, but *The Beginning of Spring* is probably her masterpiece. Like many of the greatest novels in this series, its peculiar magic almost defies analysis. The closer you get to it, the more elusive its mystery and technique. It remains a brilliant miniature, spanning just a few weeks in 1913, a short book with a sly and gentle sensibility, that somehow comprehends a whole world, and many lives.

Frank Reid, from a Salford printing family, has grown up in czarist Russia in the dangerous decades before the revolution. When the novel opens (the first line is like a stage direction: "In 1913 the journey from Moscow to Charing Cross, changing at Warsaw, cost fourteen pounds, six shillings and threepence and took two and a half days"), Frank's English wife, Nellie, has inexplicably left her husband and gone back to England. This is the breakup that now dominates Frank's life, much as the impending revolution hangs over imperial Russia.

Frank, inveterately English, is stoic in his distress. The printing business must carry on; his young children must be cared for; he must await Nellie's return – and the end of winter. Fitzgerald is an instinctively humorous writer whose intuition of life's tragedies never oppresses her delight in the human comedy. When Lisa Ivanovna, with her "pale, broad, patient, dreaming Russian face", joins the Reid household to help out, Frank falls hopelessly in love. But then, a Russian enigma who is not what she seems, Lisa mysteriously disappears. With all of Frank's future suddenly up in the air again, spring has come. "A horse-and-cab pulled up outside," Fitzgerald concludes, with one final, tantalising revelation still up her sleeve.

The audacity of *The Beginning of Spring*, and its greatness, is its cheerful willingness to trespass on a literary terrain already made famous, and familiar, through the works of Turgenev, Chekhov and even late Tolstoy. With extraordinary and lyrical brevity, Fitzgerald creates a whole world, but from the inside out, so that all her English and Russian characters become united and universal in a shared humanity.

A Note on the Text:

According to Hermione Lee, whose *Penelope Fitzgerald: A Life* (London, 2013) is the indispensable guide, the author worked on the novel that was to have been called "The Greenhouse" throughout 1986 and 1987.

The idea, Fitzgerald later said, "first came to me from a friend of mine who was Swiss but had been brought up in Russia… they had a greenhouse and stayed in Moscow all through the first world war, the Bolshevik revolution, arrival of Lenin… and all this time [were] allowed fuel (coal, wood, birch bark, newspaper) because Russian officials have [a] passion for flowers". What appealed to Fitzgerald was "a sort of noble absurdity in carrying on in unlikely circumstances".

She was also very interested in the period 1912-13, just before the First World War. It was, she said, "a time of very great hope… of the coming of the 20th century, hopes of a New Life, a new world, the New Woman, a new relationship between the artist and the crafts-man". Needless to say, almost all this historical background is ruthlessly subordinated to the tale Fitzgerald eventually tells, a story that finds its course by indirections, comic asides and odd scenes like an interlude with a bear. Fitzgerald's Russia is both completely authentic, yet firmly located deep in her imagination.

In fact, Fitzgerald only made one trip to Russia (in 1975), but the experience stayed with her and she supplemented her memories with *Baedeker's Russia 1914* and the Russian supplements of the *Times*. She also researched railway stations, train timetables, merchants' houses, ministries, churches, birch trees, dachas and mushrooms, and came to know exactly what was involved in the running of a small printing house in pre-revolutionary Moscow.

When she had finished, Fitzgerald toyed with calling the novel "Nellie and Lisa", but was dissuaded by her editor Stuart Proffitt at Harper Collins in London, who offered "*The Coming of Spring*", a phrase that his author swiftly improved upon.

It was, she would say later, her favourite book, and she liked to tease by telling some admirers that she had never been to Russia in her life, and others by saying she'd often been there. Proffitt remembers the mischievous way in which Fitzgerald projected versions of herself on friends and acquaintances. Her work is similarly multifaceted, with a fascination for the world's flotsam and jetsam – the oddball, the outcast and the marginal.

The reviews for *The Beginning of Spring* were good: "marvellous, intelligent and beautifully crafted" (*Daily Telegraph*), "one of the outstanding novels of the year" (*Times Literary Supplement*); "a complete success" (*Guardian*); and "a tour de force" (*London Review of Books*). Jan Morris, writing in the *Independent*, captured the novel's essential magic: "How is it done?" wrote Morris. "How could she know so much about the minutiae of dacha housekeeping or the rituals of hand-printing craft, or the habits of Moscow nightwatchmen, or the nature of the entertainment at the Merchants' Club? The plot may be inexplicit, but it is told with a virtuoso storyteller's technique, is illuminated by classic moments of comedy and keeps one guessing from the first page to the very last line."

The Beginning of Spring was shortlisted for the Booker (she had already won with *Offshore*), but it lost out to *Oscar and Lucinda* by Peter Carey.

Penelope Fitzgerald died in 2000. An edition of her letters, *So I Have Thought of You*, edited by Terence Dooley (London, 2008), is the perfect complement to her nine novels.

– 96 –
Breathing Lessons
by Anne Tyler (1988)

Anne Tyler shares with Jane Austen, both a fascination with the domestic complexity of married life and an instinct, as a writer, to protect her privacy and keep her art to herself (Tyler rarely gives interviews).To her fans, she is the pitch-perfect author of *Dinner at the Homesick Restaurant* and *The Accidental Tourist*, but it's *Breathing Lessons*, her novel set on a single summer's day in the midlife of 50-ish Maggie Moran, that I've chosen to represent her deeply American and deeply classical qualities. As an American girl, she grew up in a Quaker community, and was raised on books such as *Little Women*, fiction based in the precise observation of family life that spoke to a passionate audience of women readers. As a mature writer, she also cites Eudora Welty as a lasting influence.

Breathing Lessons, for which Anne Tyler won a Pulitzer in 1989, displays her extraordinary gifts in supreme harmony: exquisite narrative clarity, faultless comic timing, and the Tyler trademark of happy-sad characters inspiring a mid-American domestic drama that somehow slips the surly bonds of the quotidian to become timeless and universal.

Maggie Moran and her husband, Ira, are driving from Baltimore to Deer Lick, Pennsylvania, for the funeral of Max, the late husband of Maggie's best friend, Serena. On the road, with many detours, her marriage is slowly laid bare.We unravel the story from, first, Maggie's, then Ira's and finally Maggie's point of view. By close of play, through a sequence of brilliantly executed digressions, we know all about the Moran household, its secrets, lies, frustrations and, ultimately, its resilience.Tyler, who diffuses a melancholy optimism through her fiction, seems to say that an enduring marriage can become as natural as breathing.

As well as the poignant and unanticipated crises of the funeral and its aftermath, which is not the focus of Tyler's attention, there is also high comedy. On the return journey, the middle chapters describing the Morans' encounter with Mr Otis and his loose wheel, are a tour de force of comic prose in which the spirit of Jane Austen (often invoked by Tyler's fans) is never far absent. Tyler is also sometimes compared to John Updike, and even John Cheever, but I think her longing for a vanished and vanishing America, combined with her faultless ear for American speech, puts her in a class of her own.

A Note on the Text:

Compared with most contemporary American novelists, we know very little about Anne Tyler, which is the way she likes it. In a recent *Observer* interview, her readers got a glimpse of her modus operandi, but almost no clues about her work. "She writes in longhand," Tim Teeman reported, "then types her words out, then records her words, listens to them, and then adds to and edits the words on a computer." Since she has never given a *Paris Review* "Writers at Work" interview, this is all we know about her methods, and there is virtually no further information on the record about the genesis of *Breathing Lessons*.

There is, however, a snapshot of Tyler's reaction to its success. According to the *Observer*, the morning after *Breathing Lessons* won the Pulitzer prize for fiction in 1989, "she politely dismissed an inquisitive reporter with the explanation that she was too busy writing to talk; they had interrupted her in the middle of a sentence. 'Allergic' to interviews, Tyler is a writer not a celebrity. Outside the New York loop of young, edgy literati and excluded from the Gentlemen's Club of elder literary statesmen, Tyler, now in her 60s, lives in quiet, productive seclusion in Baltimore, where nearly all her novels are set."

What else do we know? She prefers to write her first drafts in longhand, sitting on a sofa. Her favourite novel used to be *Dinner at the Homesick Restaurant*, now it's her latest, *A Spool of Blue Thread*. She told the *Observer* that "I start every book thinking 'This one will be different' and it's not. I have my limitations. I am fascinated by how families work, endurance, how do we get through life."

The same could be said of *Breathing Lessons*, which is fundamentally a portrait of a marriage. In the *New York Times*, the writer Edward Hoagland celebrated the novel as follows: "Anne Tyler, who is blessedly prolific and graced with an effortless-seeming talent at describing whole rafts of intricately individualised people, might be described as a domestic novelist, one of that great line descending from Jane Austen. She is interested not in divorce or infidelity, but in marriage – not very much in isolation, estrangement, alienation and other fashionable concerns, but in courtship, child-raising and filial responsibility. It's… a mark of her competence that in this fractioned era she can write so well about blood links and family funerals, old friendships or the dogged pull of thwarted love, of blunted love affairs or marital mismatches that neither mend nor end. Her eye is kindly, wise and versatile (an eye that you would want on your jury if you ever had to stand trial), and after going at each new set of characters with authorial eagerness and an exuberant tumble of details, she tends to arrive at a set of conclusions about them that is a sort of golden mean."

As well as winning the Pulitzer prize for fiction in 1989, *Breathing Lessons* was also *Time* magazine's book of the year.

– 97 –
Amongst Women
by John McGahern (1990)

John McGahern was a great Irish writer among a brilliant generation that included the playwright Brian Friel and the poets Michael Longley and Seamus Heaney. Equally gifted as a writer of short stories, his finest novels (a small oeuvre) include *The Dark* and *That They May Face the Rising Sun*. His influence lives on in the work of Colm Tóibín, who once described him as "the Irish novelist everyone should read".

He was sacked from teaching for writing about child abuse, and later worked on building sites in London before establishing himself as a novelist. His books, based on his country roots, describe a declining way of life.

Amongst Women, a title derived from the words of the Hail Mary in the Roman Catholic rosary, is McGahern's masterpiece, uniting all the dominant themes of his work in a single, deeply affecting family drama. Its characteristically limpid opening sentence – "As he weakened, Moran became afraid of his daughters" – encapsulates the main theme. This will be the story of an IRA veteran facing up to approaching death at home in the bosom of his family. His wife, Rose, and their three daughters who love and fear their father, now care for him as his health fails and the shadows draw on. As so often in Irish life, it is the drumbeat of the past that continues to torment his final days.

Moran, a fighter in the civil war of the 1920s, and a fierce former guerrilla commander, is presented as a typically obdurate kind of Irish father. *Amongst Women* explores the patriarchal faultlines of an Irish society that, since the novel was published, has almost vanished. In this lost world of terrorists and priests, the menfolk discover their true selves in bitter sectarian violence, but cannot sustain the intimacies of family life. As his wife says: "He's a different sort of person altogether behind the walls of his own house." This Ireland is a prison. As Moran says: "I'm afraid we might all die in Ireland if we don't get out." So Moran's own ultimate death becomes a strange moment of release for his family, especially his daughters, who are now free to become themselves.

At barely 190 pages, McGahern's study of Irish family life is a miracle of unaffected brevity and unconsciously an elegy for a lost world. It is also a hauntingly beautiful evocation of a world and a landscape that McGahern knew well, the liminal society of County Leitrim, caught between Eire and "the six counties" of the north.

A Note on the Text:

When it was first delivered to McGahern's London publishers, Faber & Faber, *Amongst Women* was called "Monaghan Day", after the Moran family's market day routine when the old man's former comrades would visit him at home in "Great Meadow" and relive forgotten battles from the civil war. The change of title was McGahern's idea and it reflected the constant process of revision through which he put all his work. I remember him telling me that, in one early draft, his novel had been several times its final length. It was always McGahern's practice to keep cutting and cutting his text until he had distilled his prose to its deeply potent essence.

McGahern was also a farmer, with a keen sense of country life. Whenever he earned money from his books, he would buy another field for his cows, whom he loved. In a typically witty inversion, he liked to joke that he was driven to write in order to keep the farm (and its cows) in business.

Amongst Women, caught the mood of the Irish reading public when it came out and became, locally, a bestseller, establishing McGahern as the pre-eminent writer of Irish prose. Hilary Mantel, writing in the *New Statesman,* declared him to be "one of the greatest writers of our era". The other reviews were generally good, and the novel was shortlisted for the Booker prize. When it lost to AS Byatt's *Possession*, McGahern, whom I knew well at that time, was privately disappointed not to have won, but still sparkled with ironic comments about the shenanigans surrounding the prize-giving.

When the novel won the Irish Times/Aer Lingus Literary Award in 1991, one of the judges, John Updike, wrote that "McGahern brings us that tonic gift of the best fiction, the sense of truth – the sense of transparency that permits us to see imaginary lives more clearly than we see our own".

In that gift lay McGahern's genius.

– 98 –
Underworld
by Don deLillo (1997)

As this series approaches the present, the process of making a final selection from great contemporary fiction becomes progressively more contentious. In the impossible choice between Thomas Pynchon, Richard Ford, Cormac McCarthy, Joan Didion, Don DeLillo, Michael Ondaatje, Robert Stone and Paul Auster, I have opted for DeLillo's 11th novel.

Underworld is the work of a writer wired into contemporary America from the ground up, spookily attuned to the weird vibrations of popular culture and the buzz of everyday, ordinary conversations on bus and subway. According to Joyce Carol Oates, he is "a man of frightening perception", an all-American writer who sees and hears his country like no other. This ambitious, massive (832pp) and visionary edifice certainly looks like a masterpiece; widely acclaimed by critics on first appearance, it is often chosen by lists like this.

From its first appearance in October 1997, a moment I remember well as the *Observer's* literary editor, *Underworld* was spoken of as a towering performance and hailed as that elusive literary hippogriff, the great American novel. In his review, the novelist William Boyd wrote, "In *Underworld,* we have a mature and hugely accomplished novelist firing on all cylinders... reading the book is a charged and thrilling aesthetic experience and one remembers gratefully that this is what the novel can do." The *Observer* also described it as "an epic to set alongside *Moby-Dick* and *Augie March*". Such ideas were possibly reinforced by DeLillo's quotable opening line: "He speaks in your voice, American, and there's a shine in his eye that's halfway hopeful."

Underworld opens on 3 October 1951 with one of the most famous baseball games ever played, the Brooklyn Dodgers versus the New York Giants, in which Bobby Thomson made the Shot Heard Round the World, hitting the ball deep into the crowd. This brilliant opening, juxtaposed with the first atomic detonation made by the Soviet Union on the far side of the world, launches a cold war narrative with the sub-theme of late-20th century American subconscious, a longstanding DeLillo preoccupation.

From this numinous date in US popular culture, DeLillo marches with growing confidence through the second half of the 20th century, loosely following the fate of the missing baseball. *Underworld's* narrative is not sequential and, after the 1951 prologue, tracks through some key moments of recent American history, notably Vietnam and the Cuban missile crisis, and also through the life of DeLillo's protagonist, Nick Shay, a waste-management officer, and his faithless wife Marian. Historical figures such as Lenny Bruce, J Edgar Hoover and Frank Sinatra make cameo appearances. As well as the elusive baseball, *Underworld's* recurrent theme, and narrative hook, is Nick's struggle with memories of a juvenile crime whose full story, with Oedipal overtones, is revealed towards the end of an epic journey through the American hinterland.

A Note on the Text:
DeLillo has devoted a life of writing to the shadow side of American life, painting a dysfunctional freaks' gallery of the wrecked (David Bell in *Americana*), the sick (Bill Gray in *Mao II*), the mad (Lee Harvey Oswald in *Libra*) and the suicidal (Eric Packer in *Cosmopolis*). In *White Noise,* the protagonist, Jack, who teaches Hitler studies, riffs hilariously on death and mass murder. It is said that DeLillo used to keep two files on his writing table, labelled "Art" and "Terror". Through his lifelong explorations of the American psyche, DeLillo has become credited with extraordinary powers of literary clairvoyance. The war on terror is said to be foreshadowed in *Mao II*. The planes that flew into the twin towers are possibly alluded to on the cover of *Underworld*. Parts of *White Noise* are echoed in the anthrax scare of 2001, and so on.

In his *Paris Review* interview with DeLillo, Adam Begley prefaces the conversation with a vivid note that conjures the experience of meeting DeLillo. Begley writes: "A man who's been called 'the chief shaman of the paranoid school of American fiction' can be expected to act a little nervous. I met Don DeLillo for the first time in an Irish restaurant in Manhattan, for a conversation he said would be 'deeply preliminary'. He is a slender man, grey-haired, with boxy brown glasses. His eyes, magnified by thick lenses, are restless without being shifty. He looks to the right, to the left; he turns his head to see what's behind him."

DeLillo says that *Underworld* was inspired by the front page of the *New York Times*, 4 October 1951. He also told the *Paris Review*: "Sometime in late 1991, I started writing something new and didn't know what it would be – a novel, a short story, a long story. It was simply a piece of writing, and it gave me more pleasure than any other writing I've done. It turned into a novella, *Pafko at the Wall*, and it appeared in *Harper's* about a year after I started it. At some point I decided I wasn't finished with the piece. I was sending signals into space and getting echoes back, like a dolphin or a bat. So the piece, slightly altered, is now the prologue to a novel-in-progress, which will have a different title. [This became the opening chapter of *Underworld*.] And the pleasure has long since faded into the slogging reality of the no man's land of the long novel. But I'm still hearing the echoes."

Elsewhere, he has spoken of the suggestive connections between Pluto, the god of the classical underworld, and the popular American unconscious. When I interviewed him for the *Observer* in 2010 about his novella *Point Omega*, he described his creative methods: "I'm always keeping random notes on scraps of paper. I always carry a pencil and a notebook. Coming on the train today I had an idea for a story I'm writing and jotted it down – on just a little scrap of paper. Then I clip these together. I'll look at them in, say, three weeks' time, and see what I've got. You know, I've never made an outline for any novel that I've written. Never."

This is an approach that possibly sponsors the teeming structure of a novel like *Underworld*, but the upshot can be stunning. From a variety of reviews, Martin Amis (in Esquire) hailed "the ascension of a great writer"; Malcolm Bradbury (in the *Times)* spoke of "something to take home for the millennium"; Blake Morrison (in the *Independent*) declared that "DeLillo ranks with the best of contemporary American novelists"; and Fintan O'Toole (in the *Irish Times*) acclaimed "one of the defining novels of the postwar period". Finally, that fearsome American critic, Harold Bloom, identified *Underworld* as "the culmination of what DeLillo can do", a novel that "touched what I would call the sublime"·

– 99 –
Disgrace
by JM Coetzee (1999)

Disgrace was a Booker prize winner in 1999, making JM Coetzee the first writer to win the trophy twice (first with *Life & Times of Michael K*). In 2003, he was also awarded the Nobel prize in literature. But beyond the awards, Coetzee is notable as a great South African writer who, together with Breyten Breytenbach and the late André Brink, grappled with the savage complexity of the apartheid and post-apartheid years. Coetzee also took the novel in English into new imaginative and moral territory. From his many outstanding works of fiction, *Disgrace* is unquestionably his masterpiece.

In an apt connection to the beginnings of the 100 Best Novels series nearly two years ago, *Disgrace* has been compared by some critics to the work of Daniel Defoe. David Lurie, on whom Coetzee visits a contemporary catalogue of humiliations, is a fairly average, twice-married, fiftysomething lecturer at a Capetown university who, accused of sexual misconduct with one of his students, chooses not to defend himself but rather to suffer his fate with a noble, slightly grumpy, stoicism. In his mind, Lurie has committed no offence; he prefers to get fired and suffer disgrace than endure a politically correct process of rehabilitation. He will not give his *bien pensant* academic tormentors the satisfaction they crave. "Pass sentence," he says, "and let us get on with our lives." He retires to the country to live with his daughter Lucy, and address the meaning of this self-inflicted injunction. It's here that *Disgrace,* moving up a gear, begins seriously to engage with the aftermath of apartheid.

At first, there is hope. Country life in the eastern Cape, and Lucy's company, seem to offer the prospect of sanity. But the conflicts of South Africa will never go away. The farm is attacked by a gang of black men, Lucy is raped, and Lurie beaten up. His daughter refuses to press charges, even though one of her assailants is a former "dog man" on the property. The novel ends on a note of utter bleakness. Lurie resolves to stay on the farm to protect his daughter, a domestic act of love by a broken man in search of redemption but almost too confused to know where to find it. Everyone, Coetzee seems to be saying, is a victim. Somewhere, the shade of Samuel Beckett must be smiling.

A Note on the Text:
Coetzee is a writer whose scholarly literary interests can be detected, and followed, quite openly in his work. It is, indeed, instructive to see his creative journey refracted through the Anglo-American literary tradition. His first book, *Dusklands* (1970), is partly about Vietnam, partly a study of an Afrikaner ancestor written in the spirit of Hawthorne's *The House of Seven Gables*. Later, he also studied Beckett, Ford Madox Ford and Jonathan Swift.

Braided into this austere tapestry of influence is Coetzee's political vision, his version of late 20th-century South Africa. Here, he is at pains to avoid the head-on political outrage of a writer such as Nadine Gordimer, a fellow Nobel laureate. Coetzee's approach is unflinching and subtly fierce, but always much more oblique, avoiding specifics of location and landscape. First, in *Waiting for the Barbarians* and then in *Life & Times of Michael K*, he created a world that is simultaneously African but also universal. Coetzee's vision made a sharp, original commentary on the South Africa of apartheid, but it also explored the human condition with a bleak, dispassionate sympathy that many readers have found unforgettable.

Disgrace, published on the eve of the millennium, is more apparently rooted in a southern African context of "truth and reconciliation". On closer examination, however, its focus is almost exclusively on Lurie and his crisis, addressing the urgency of his sexual needs in an opening sentence of quasi-documentary simplicity:"For a man of his age, fifty-two, divorced, he has, to his mind, solved the problem of sex rather well." For the next 218 pages (in the British edition) the reader never leaves Lurie's head, any more than we leave Robinson Crusoe's in Defoe's masterpiece.

But Coetzee is a writer of his time, too. Later in *Disgrace,* echoing Beckett, Lurie will insist on his identity as a man in a world where even language, the tool of his trade, can no longer be trusted. "Only the monosyllables can still be relied on," he declares at one point, "and not even all of them." What is remarkable about Coetzee's vision as a novelist is that it remains intensely human, rooted in common experience and replete with failure, doubt and frustration. As the critic Adam Mars-Jones wrote in his *Guardian* review of *Disgrace* on its publication in July 1999, "any novel set in post-apartheid South Africa is fated to be read as a political portrait, but the fascination of *Disgrace* is the way it both encourages and contests such a reading by holding extreme alternatives in tension. Salvation, ruin."

This highly perceptive and specific judgment was echoed, more loosely, by other reviews. For the *Times*, *Disgrace* was "a great novel by one of the finest authors writing in the English language today". For the *Independent,* "Coetzee's prose is chaste and lyrical – it is a relief to encounter writing as quietly stylish as this." The *Sunday Telegraph,* alluding to Conrad, declared rather loftily that "the journey to a heart of narrative darkness has become a safe literary destination, almost a cliché". However, the review went on, "*Disgrace* goes beyond this to explore the furthest reaches of what it means to be human; it is at the frontier of world literature."

When Coetzee became the first writer, later followed by Peter Carey (*True History of the Kelly Gang*) and Hilary Mantel (*Wolf Hall)*, to win the Booker prize twice, he declined to attend the presentation dinner. He is, thankfully, too serious about his work to be bothered by such distractions.

– 100 –
True Story of The Kelly Gang
by Peter Carey (2000)

Peter Carey arrived exuberantly on the international literary scene as the dominant Australian writer of his generation with his second novel *Illywhacker* in 1985. He went on to win the Booker Prize with *Oscar and Lucinda* (1988), but it was not until the publication of *True History of the Kelly Gang* in 2000 that his lifelong fascination with the antipodean predicament and his own impish love of narrative innovation met in the voice of the bushranger Ned Kelly, an archetypal Australian hero.

This tour-de-force of storytelling, Carey's great gift, is a postmodern historical novel, a quasi-autobiography, narrated in the Australian vernacular with primitive grammar and scant punctuation, a dazzling act of ventriloquism, in a style inspired by an extraordinary fragment of Kelly's prose known as "the Jerilderie Letter".

Kelly's life as an outlaw, after a childhood dominated by his family's run-ins with the law, culminated in his leadership of the Kelly Gang, who terrorised and also thrilled the inhabitants of NE Victoria, a moment of Australian folklore which reached a bloody climax in a shoot-out in the country town of Glenrowan. Kelly survived wearing a home-made suit of steel plate armour, but would die soon after on the gallows, a local hero.

This series began with the English dissenter, John Bunyan, in Bedford gaol, imagining the progress to redemption of a humble pilgrim. At the turn of the millennium, it ends with an expat Australian novelist exploring the nature of storytelling through the short, violent life of a colonial outlaw on a fierce, mad, doomed quest for freedom. From these, and countless other examples, I would argue that fiction flourishes in extremis.

A Note on the Text:

For Peter Carey, an expat novelist settled in New York City, *True History of the Kelly Gang*, which is set in North-East Victoria, in and around small towns like Mansfield, Benalla, Wangaratta and Bendigo, is both an exploration of his cultural heritage, and also a strange act of nostalgia.

As an adolescent, Carey was sent to Geelong Grammar, one of Australia's top boarding schools. For the son of a motor car salesman from Bacchus Marsh, this was a dislocating experience. In his Paris Review interview, he describes his parent's sacrifice to send him to a top school. "Why Geelong Grammar? Because it was the best. It cost six hundred pounds a year in 1954, which was an unbelievable amount of money—and they really weren't that well off—and they did it. I suppose it did solve a few child-care problems. I never felt I was being exiled or sent away, but I was only eleven years old. No one could have guessed that the experience would finally produce an endless string of orphan characters in my books. It took me ages to figure that out. I thought the orphans were there because it's just easier—you don't have to invent a complicated family history. But I think in retrospect that it's not a failure of imagination.... it's also the story of Australia, which is a country of orphans. I have the good fortune that my own personal trauma matches my country's great historical trauma. Our first fleet was cast out from 'home.' Nobody really wanted to be there. Convicts, soldiers were all going to starve or survive together. Later, the state created orphans among the aboriginal population through racial policies, stealing indigenous kids from their communities and trying to breed out their blackness. Then there were all these kids sent from England to Dr. Barnardo's Homes, which were institutions for homeless and destitute children, some of them run in the most abusive, horrible circumstances. There was one near us in Bacchus Marsh called Northcote Farm."

However, this elite education did contain one memorable year, much closer to ordinary Australian experience, when the 14-15 year old Geelong grammarians were sent to live upstate in the bush at an outward bound school near Mansfield, Victoria, in the foothills of Mount Buller, a place called Timbertop.

This is the landscape of Carey's novel, and Kelly's obsession with horses and the bush takes inspiration from his own teenage years.

Ned Kelly's voice, like so many in colonial Australia, is Irish. In his *Paris Review* interview, Carey addresses this explicitly: "When I got to *True History of the Kelly Gang*, I let myself do something that goes back to the beginning of my reading. I was nineteen and just discovering literature. I was reading Joyce, and at the same time I read the *Jerilderie Letter,* a letter written by Ned Kelly in a town where he was robbing a bank. It's a very Irish voice. I know it's not Joyce, but it does suggest even to a nineteen-year-old the possibility of creating a poetic voice that grows out of Australian soil, that is true to its place and hasn't existed before. I had that in my mind from very, very early. It was astonishing to me that I could finally do it."

The critics agreed. For the *Guardian* "Carey is without question the pre-eminent literary voice of post-colonial Australia. John Updike, writing in the *New Yorker*, declared that "the ingenuity, empathy, and poetic ear that Carey brings to his feat of imposture cannot be rated too high."

True History of the Kelly Gang won the Booker Prize in 2001, only the second time a writer has won it twice.

★★★

In conclusion, "100 Best Novels" has deliberately excluded all kinds of translation, but there is one writer, as great as any listed here, who died in 2001, whose work deserves to be remembered. W. G. ("Max") Sebald still towers over the global literary landscape with four inimitable titles: *The Emigrants, Vertigo, The Rings of Saturn, Austerlitz*. Sebald wrote in his native German, but his translated texts add up to a profound masterpiece of contemporary English. *Ave atque valem.*

A Bend in the River, VS Naipaul   220
A Single Man, Christopher Isherwood   205
Adventures of Augie March, The, Saul Bellow   179
Adventures of Huckleberry Finn, The, Mark Twain   69
Age of Innocence, The, Edith Wharton   117
Alice's Adventures in Wonderland, Lewis Carroll   58
All the King's Men, Robert Penn Warren   162
Amongst Women, John McGahern   240
An Artist of the Floating World, Kazuo Ishiguro   233
As I Lay Dying, William Faulkner   136
At Swim-Two-Birds, Flann O'Brien   155

Babbitt, Sinclair Lewis   121
Beginning of Spring, The, Penelope Fitzgerald   235
Bell Jar, The, Sylvia Plath   210
Big Sleep, The, Raymond Chandler   150
Brave New World, Aldous Huxley   138
Breathing Lessons, Anne Tyler   238

Call of the Wild, The, Jack London   95
Catcher in the Rye, The, JD Salinger   177
Catch-22, Joseph Heller   197
Clarissa, Samuel Richardson   25
Clockwork Orange, A, Anthony Burgess   202
Cold Comfort Farm, Stella Gibbons   140

David Copperfield, Charles Dickens   50
Disgrace, JM Coetzee   245
Dracula, Bram Stoker   87

Emma, Jane Austen   31
End of the Affair, The, Graham Greene   175

Frankenstein, Mary Shelley   33

Gentlemen Prefer Blondes, Anita Loos   125
Good Soldier, The, Ford Madox Ford   107
Golden Bowl, The, Henry James   97
Golden Notebook, The, Doris Lessing   200

Grapes of Wrath, The, John Steinbeck   157
Great Gatsby, The, F Scott Fitzgerald   129
Gulliver's Travels by Jonathan Swift   23

Hadrian the Seventh, Frederick Rolfe   99
Heart of Darkness, Joseph Conrad   89
Heat of the Day, The, Elizabeth Bowen   167
History of Mr Polly, The, HG Wells   103
Housekeeping, Marilynne Robinson   226

In Cold Blood, Truman Capote   207

Jane Eyre, Charlotte Brontë   44
Joy in the Morning, PG Wodehouse   160
Jude the Obscure, Thomas Hardy   83

Kidnapped, Robert Louis Stevenson   71
Kim, Rudyard Kipling   94

Little Women, Louisa May Alcott   62
Lolita, Vladimir Nabokov   184
Lolly Willowes, Sylvia Townsend Warner   131
Lord of the Flies, William Golding   182

Maltese Falcon, The, Dashiell Hammett   134
Middlemarch, George Eliot   64
Midnight's Children, Salman Rushdie   224
Moby-Dick, Herman Melville   54
Money, A Suicide Note, Martin Amis   230
Moonstone, The, Wilkie Collins   60
Mrs Dalloway, Virginia Woolf   128
Mrs Palfrey at the Claremont, Elizabeth Taylor   216
Murphy, Samuel Beckett   148

Narrative of Arthur Gordon Pym of Nantucket, The,
     Edgar Allan Poe   39
New Grub Street, George Gissing   81
Nineteen Eighty-Four, George Orwell   169
Nineteen Nineteen, John Dos Passos   142

Nightmare Abbey, Thomas Love Peacock   36

Of Human Bondage, W Somerset Maugham   115
On the Road, Jack Kerouac   187

Party Going, Henry Green   153
Passage to India, A, EM Forster   123
Picture of Dorian Gray, The, Oscar Wilde   78
Pilgrim's Progress, The, John Bunyan   19
Portnoy's Complaint, Philip Roth   213
Prime of Miss Jean Brodie, The, Muriel Spark   195

Rabbit Redux, John Updike   218
Rainbow, The, DH Lawrence   110
Red Badge of Courage, The, Stephen Crane   85
Robinson Crusoe, Daniel Defoe   21

Scarlet Letter, The, Nathaniel Hawthorne   52
Scoop, Evelyn Waugh   146
Sign of Four, The, Arthur Conan Doyle   76
Sister Carrie, Theodore Dreiser   91
Song of Solomon, Toni Morrison   220
Sybil, Benjamin Disraeli   42

The Sun Also Rises, Ernest Hemingway   133
The Way We Live Now, Anthony Trollope   66
Thirty-Nine Steps, The, John Buchan   109
Three Men in a Boat, Jerome K Jerome   73
To Kill a Mockingbird, Harper Lee   192
Tom Jones, Henry Fielding   27
Tristram Shandy, Gentleman, The Life and Opinions of,
    Laurence Sterne   29
Tropic of Cancer, Henry Miller   144
True Story of the Kelly Gang, Peter Carey   100

Ulysses, James Joyce   118
Under the Volcano, Malcolm Lowry   165
Underworld, Don DeLillo   242

Vanity Fair, William Thackeray   48
Voss, Patrick White   190

Wind in the Willows, The, Kenneth Grahame   101
Wuthering Heights, Emily Brontë   46

Zuleika Dobson, Max Beerbohm   105